THE
CHANGE
MAKERS

————— T H E —————

CHANGE

MAKERS

From Carnegie to Gates, How the Great

Entrepreneurs Transformed Ideas into Industries

MAURY KLEIN

TIMES BOOKS

Henry Holt and Company | New York

Times Books
Henry Holt and Company, LLC
Publishers since 1866
115 West 18th Street
New York, New York 10011

Henry Holt® is a registered trademark of
Henry Holt and Company, LLC.

Distributed in Canada by H. B. Fenn and Company Ltd.

Library of Congress Cataloging-in-Publication Data
Klein, Maury, 1939–
   The change makers : from Carnegie to Gates : how the great entrepreneurs
transformed ideas into industries / Maury Klein.— 1st ed.
     p. cm.
   Includes bibliographical references and index.
   ISBN 0-8050-6914-3
   1. Entrepreneurship—United States. 2. New business enterprises—United States.
3. Creative ability in business—United States. 4. Businesspeople—United States—
Biography. 5. Industrialists—United States—Biography. 6. Carnegie, Andrew,
1835–1919. 7. Gates, Bill, 1955– I. Title.
   HB615 .K6137 2003
   338'.04'0973—dc21   2002032439

First Edition 2003

Designed by Paula Russell Szafranski

Printed in the United States of America

1   3   5   7   9   10   8   6   4   2

For Judith Swift, who has been waiting . . .

and Rod Davis, truly a gentleman and a scholar

| Contents |

| Introduction |

This book explores a subject that has fascinated people for gen-
erations, yet has scarcely been discussed: what is it that separates
the great entrepreneurs from merely good businessmen? A vast
outpouring of literature has tried to explain what an entrepreneur
is or what is required to become a successful one. Even more works
have celebrated the role of the entrepreneur in the building of the
American economy and the American way of life or damned them
for their depredations by denouncing them as the infamous Robber Barons. Scholars and writers have probed and dissected the
lives of great entrepreneurs for clues to their characters and personalities as well as their talents. A few have assembled brief portraits
of them into galleries and sought to compare their traits or isolate
their distinguishing characteristics. None have managed to define
what qualities elevate the great entrepreneur above his peers.

One obstacle to this quest has been the American obsession
with money. Nothing fascinates Americans more than wealth, and

nothing baffles them more than what it means to acquire great wealth. Most of the great entrepreneurs (and a good many others) amassed huge fortunes in the course of their work, and such is the role of wealth in American life that popular attention has always focused more on the money they made than on what they accomplished. The blinders of wealth have done much to distort our ability to understand these men or grasp the fact that they created vastly more wealth for others—and for society—than they gained for themselves.

This focus on wealth is misleading for two reasons. First, the vast majority of American fortunes belong to people who did little if anything creative to acquire them. There is no automatic or necessary connection between wealth and achievement. Secondly, money was for most of the great entrepreneurs a by-product of their real interest, important as both a personal reward and a way of keeping score but not the driving passion behind their work. None of the great entrepreneurs made the piling up of a great fortune his prime directive (although some started with that goal in mind), and several of them made busy second careers out of giving away most of the money they made. George Bernard Shaw once said that "You cannot combine the pursuit of money with the pursuit of art."[1] Whatever the truth of that point, he did not consider the related questions of whether the pursuit of money might be an art in itself or whether money might result from activities that flowed from deeper needs such as the urge to create something.

One perspective on the great entrepreneurs and their achievements has been entirely neglected. No one has looked at their work as a form of creativity. Yet enterprise on a large scale can be viewed as an act of both creativity and expression, much like a work of art or a theory of nature or the envisioning of a political system. Seen in this context, the entrepreneur occupies a place on a broad spectrum of creativity that includes artists, scientists, political figures, and mathematicians, among others. Creative people in different fields have far more in common than has been realized. They work in an incredible variety of mediums and the products of their labors come in many forms and guises, some more tangible or enduring than others. What they all have in common is that they do what they do for reasons that go far beyond financial gain, and riches alone seldom if ever fulfill the inner need that drives them.

Given the vast role played by creativity in human affairs, as well as our fascination with its rainbow of products, it is surprising how little has been written directly on the subject. One need not get bogged down in a prolix debate over theories of art and aesthetics or prolonged discussion of what an artist is. The crucial point here concerns the nature of creativity itself and what forms it takes. To say that artists have a monopoly on creativity is as absurd as claiming that only scientists understand nature.

One great paradox of our times is that we live in a world dominated by huge organizations and yet we forget that every one of these behemoths owes its origins to the genius and determination of some individual. In this sense the great entrepreneurs literally created the means of their own destruction. They were the crucial catalysts in the most profound transformation of civilization, the bridge between "one world dying, another struggling to be born." The first generation of them erected mighty organizations that towered like skyscrapers on the darkling plain of an emerging industrial society. Their successors, born into a world cluttered with such skyscrapers, have succeeded in creating even grander structures, sometimes at the cost of sending rival edifices crashing into rubble. Amid the shadows cast by this vertical landscape of giant organizations, the very nature of the individual and individualism has been recast and redefined, with enormous consequences for everything from the tenor of society to the most trivial details of everyday life.

The great entrepreneurs created this imprint not only by forging huge organizations but also by introducing technology into every realm of life. Except in a few instances, they did not invent the new instruments of modernity; rather they invented the means to spread them throughout the fabric of society until they became both indispensable and inseparable. Technology is what separates modern from premodern society with an unbridgeable chasm, and with it came the most unsettling, disruptive force in modern times: change as a norm—indeed a way of life—rather than as a novelty. Most of the strife and tension in modern times can be traced in one form or another to these roots of change. The broad clash in cultural values so aptly characterized by Benjamin R. Barber in *Jihad vs. McWorld* offers one striking example of this separation.

The role of the great entrepreneurs is important for another compelling reason. Warren G. Harding and Calvin Coolidge were right: the business of America is business and has been for at least one hundred fifty years. Business lies at the heart of American culture and has long been the driving force in American history. To ignore or downplay its role in American life is to leave Hamlet out of the play and pretend that the other characters matter more. Rosenkranz and Gildenstern may be amusing and intriguing, but they are merely byplay to the main event. The watershed event in American history is not the Civil War but the industrial and managerial revolutions of the late nineteenth century, which created a society and way of life forever separated from almost everything that had gone before. The forms and styles of business have varied widely over the centuries, but the drive that lay behind the formation of enterprises has remained a constant. Not by accident did Americans erect the largest and most formidable material civilization in history.

So profound has the influence of business been on modern life and culture that it has in the past half century succeeded in transforming every area of human experience first into a business and then into a larger business. This process began on a modest scale around the 1880s and gained momentum steadily through the twentieth century so that American life has now reached a point at which the operative principle is that the more things change, the more they become big business. If you wish to challenge this assumption, try to identify one area of American life that has not been organized into some kind of business. What other culture has transformed nature into a playground, plain work shirts and pants into designer clothes, every basic human emotion into service industries, and reality into a commodity?

This book examines the creators of this newfound material civilization by exploring several basic questions: Who were they? What did they do? How did they do it? What did they have in common? What special gifts or talents did they possess? What separates them from ordinary, albeit successful, entrepreneurs? What factors or conditions account for their achievements?

In seeking answers to these questions I have explored the lives of twenty-six entrepreneurs whose careers cover a broad range of both time and activities. Those readers seeking a guidebook for how to become a great entrepreneur will be disappointed at the findings. Although I had hoped to find clear patterns that might suggest some formula that explains the great entrepreneurs or at least ties them together, the evidence suggests something quite different. Nor is there an easy way to grasp what they achieved. In many respects they resemble a random sample, but they do possess some qualities in common that help explain, if not categorize, their success. The mix includes some whose careers included spectacular failures as well as achievements—men, for example, who created a great company but could not organize or manage it. The list also contains some of the usual suspects like Carnegie and Rockefeller along with others whose name or accomplishments may not be familiar to you but whose companies you will certainly recognize.

The book also seeks to leave the impression that the gift of creativity unites rather than separates people in different fields of endeavor. These men and their work are as interesting in their way as the careers and personalities of artists, composers, scientists, writers, athletes, and other creative people. They bear a relationship to their creation that is strikingly similar to that of other creative people. Their similarities outweigh the differences in what they do or where their talent lies. But, like creativity itself, they cannot fit comfortably into any pigeonhole. What they do have in common is the extent to which their stories are compelling and their achievements monumental.

| Prologue |

Say Good-bye to the Robber Barons

The present is the past biting into the future.

—EDWIN LAND[1]

The title is, of course, wishful thinking. For seventy-five years historians like myself have struggled to banish this label applied with such force and ease by Matthew Josephson in his 1934 book of the same title. Like so many glib phrases, it misleads far more than it informs, but it has proven so handy to historians, journalists, writers, and general readers that it remains a staple slogan to describe businessmen of the nineteenth century. As a result, any book dealing with the great entrepreneurs of American history must begin by removing or at least qualifying this warning label.

One reason why the term *robber barons* has remained the default cliché for this group is that Americans simply have never known quite what to do with the great entrepreneurs. In politics, war, and most other fields they have eagerly sought out individual heroes as emblems of greater themes and in their embrace have usually been willing to overlook the hero's personal or moral shortcomings. In business, however, attitudes have been not only mixed but

1

frequently hostile. No great entrepreneur occupies a position in the national pantheon anywhere near that of George Washington or even John J. Pershing. Historians such as Jonathan R. T. Hughes attribute this unease to the Puritan heritage; others broaden the explanation to a persistent tension between the spiritual and the material in American history, a tension reflected in the often contradictory American attitude toward wealth and those who possess it.[2]

Although no group of people has done more to shape and change every aspect of American life since 1850 than the great entrepreneurs, no group is less understood or more defined by clichés. Much has been written about what the great entrepreneurs did, how they did it, and why, but rarely has the discussion transcended the old bookend labels of *robber barons* or *industrial statesmen.* As a result, much of what we think we know about them is misconceived or just plain wrong. For more than a century the perspectives on the great entrepreneurs have been shockingly narrow. Except for a handful of scholars and writers who have taken the trouble to observe the entrepreneurs and their accomplishments closely, most accounts range from unabashed admiration to moral outrage and fulmination against the evils of the accumulation of wealth or power, or worst of all, both. One classic example of this attitude is Gustavus Myers's *History of Great American Fortunes* (1910), a compendium of righteous indignation glazed with errors of fact and misinterpretation. Bill Gates put the matter bluntly when he said, "I don't think the rich get much credit for anything."[3]

After the Civil War, businessmen seized center stage from the politicians in American life and thereby made themselves targets of those who, among other things, resented the sweeping changes brought about by their innovations. The rise of big business in the late nineteenth century drew fire from the writers known as muckrakers, whose point of view deeply influenced later generations of progressive and liberal historians. Mark Twain and Charles Dudley

Warner crowned the late nineteenth century as the "Gilded Age," the excesses and iniquities of which outraged the muckrakers and their successors, the debunkers. Unable to put the larger experience into perspective, tormented by its contradictions and paradoxes, they seized upon its dominant business personalities as sufficient explanation for its aberrations.

These writers were hardly the first to cope with a revolution by personalizing the vast forces that impelled it, and certainly their targets were inviting and flamboyant. As Justin Kaplan observed, their stereotypes turned this into the "age of the glittering phrase. During a Tragic Era (Claude Bowers) and Age of Negation (Charles Beard), the American people, lulled into a Pragmatic Acquiescence (William James) and betrayed by a bloodless Genteel Tradition (George Santayana), created a Chromo Civilization (E. L. Godkin) and watched complacently as the Robber Barons and the Politicos (both Matthew Josephson), working hand in till, pillaged and plundered the country in a Great Barbecue (Vernon Parrington)."[4]

The legacy of the muckrakers and debunkers was as unfortunate as it was imposing. For much of the twentieth century the writing of business history bogged down in an increasingly sterile debate between the "robber baron" school and defenders of the entrepreneurs, who hailed them as industrial statesmen. The futility of this impasse prompted Alfred D. Chandler, Jr., to move business history to new ground with his pioneering works *The Visible Hand* in 1977 and *Scale and Scope* in 1990. Other historians turned to quantitative studies, social history ("from the bottom up"), gender, race, and class studies, and other approaches that all shared one common dilemma with the Chandlerian school: They downplayed or ignored the role of the individual in business history at the expense of broader institutional or cultural themes, prompting one historian to complain that "business history has, in recent years, acted much like a neutron bomb, wiping out the people while leaving the buildings intact."[5]

Perhaps the worst fault of the "robber baron" concept is that it simply gets in the way of understanding who these men were and what they accomplished. As Michael Novak observed, "They left behind great institutions that have been socially productive for generations after their deaths. These men did more than make money. . . . They were hugely ambitious, creative, sometimes vain, tough, and even ruthless . . . and certainly not saints. . . . The attempt to understand them under the heading 'greed' reveals both historical amnesia and ideological distortion." Historian Joseph Frazier Wall, in his definitive biography of Andrew Carnegie, stressed that "whatever else Carnegie and Rockefeller may have been—ruthless, selfish, and wasteful of men and resources—they were . . . empire builders, not extortionists, and it is that drive for imperium that distinguishes them from their partners."[6]

The description of great entrepreneurs as empire builders is both accurate and apt. It is one characteristic that separates them from those figures who qualify as history's real robber barons—the smaller, rapacious businessmen (and politicians) who took advantage of a wide-open system merely to reap profits rather than attempt to impose order on it. They create nothing and care nothing for the companies they exploit. Warren Buffett took their measure accurately: "Boone Pickens and Jimmy Goldsmith and the crew . . . aren't creating value; they are transferring it from society to shareholders. That may be a good or bad thing but it isn't creating value—it's not like Henry Ford developing the car or Ray Kroc figuring out how to deliver hamburgers better than anyone else."[7]

There is a striking parallel between the rise of the great corporations and the process of political consolidation into nation-states. Both took place at roughly the same time in history; one sought to bring order out of economic chaos, the other out of political chaos. Both fused small, fiercely competing entities into larger, more stable ones that did not eliminate competition so much as move it to a higher level. In both cases, successful leadership required a degree of vision and purpose lacking in petty chieftains. Put another way, the great entrepreneur is to a robber baron or businessman what a statesman is to a politician. Their greatness lies not only in what they do but in what they conceive.

Nevertheless, the beguiling robber-baron cliché, ever vivid and simplistic, lingers on as the enduring popular shorthand for the great entrepreneurs. A few scholars and writers, myself included, have tried to counter it through biographies of major entrepreneurs and other work. This effort has gained some momentum with the appearance of Ron Chernow's biography of John D. Rockefeller, Jean Strouse's account of J. P. Morgan, and my own of Jay Gould and E. H. Harriman. Enough studies have now emerged to attempt a group portrait from a perspective that neither attacks nor defends the entrepreneurs but, like the better biographies, tries to understand who they were and what they did. I propose to view them as fiercely driven men with a creative bent who share a number of qualities with those people we commonly think of as artists, and who expressed that creativity through the genre of building great enterprises and business empires.

No less than robber baron, the word *entrepreneur* has been reduced to an empty cliché. For a culture that prides itself in mangling and mauling its language, it should come as no surprise that the term has been stretched and tortured beyond all meaning. George Gilder, kneeling reverently at the altar, ordained entrepreneurs as those "who know the rules of the world and the laws of God. Thus they sustain the world. . . . They are the heroes of economic life." Cheerleader Robert L. Shook, in putting together a gallery of entrepreneurs, burbled that "with an estimated twelve million entrepreneurs in the United States and Canada, I had a vast selection to choose from." Some readers may find it difficult to imagine a universe in which so many people were privy to the inside dope of both the planet and the Almighty.[8]

Peter Drucker, the management guru, described entrepreneurs more sensibly as people who "create something new, something different; they change or transmute values." Historian Gerald Gunderson saw their primary activity as "the creation of additional human opportunities." Richard Tedlow of the Harvard Business School characterized them as "people of enormous, innate optimism" who "travel light" and "leave others behind. . . . They believe that honest, intelligent effort will be greeted by appropriate reward." He agreed with Drucker that it was their "ability to be oriented toward a future beyond imagining to others—to think anew and act anew—which defines these men as genuine visionaries." To Professor Rosabeth Kanter they are people who "always operate at the edge of their competence."[9]

A special issue of *Newsweek* devoted to "e life" opened with an article on the "cult of the entrepreneur." Few writers have done more to cultivate or exploit that cult than A. David Silver, whom Gilder called "perhaps the leading student of the psychology of entrepreneurs." Actually, Silver is a venture capitalist who claimed to "have worked closely with and been an investor in over 100 entrepreneurial companies since 1966." His study of entrepreneurs is an intriguing blend of shrewd insights, simplistic generalizations, helpful advice, and contradictions cheerfully ignored. While admitting that "we know very little about entrepreneurs and the entrepreneurial process," Silver did not hesitate to list and describe ten "significant characteristics" of entrepreneurs and a six-step "entrepreneurial process."[10]

Entrepreneurs, according to Silver, belong to a group of people who are "loving, caring and sensitive, and who have one goal: to do some one thing extremely well." They are not interested in power, prestige, high visibility, or wealth per se. Driven primarily by guilt, they have a gift for making complex things simple and a unique talent for formulating problems, are extraordinarily self-reliant, and cannot conceive of failure. They possess "uncommon courage" and bring to their work "an uncanny will to win." Completely absorbed in their quest, they have no time for outside interests or activities, and are "happy virtually all of the time" in their commitment to work despite its grueling nature and the toll it takes on the rest of their lives. "Entrepreneurs behave in special ways," Silver emphasized. "They are born, not made."[11]

At the same time, Silver depicted the entrepreneurial process as "a series of defined steps" that others could learn. "Non-entrepreneurs," he insisted, "can learn the entrepreneurial process . . . to create mini-revolutions in their organizations." At the time of his writing (1983) more than two hundred business schools and numerous seminar companies were striving to teach just that—although not very well, in his opinion. Silver sought to regularize and systematize a process that had always been the province of unique individuals, "to give ordinary people more scope for becoming their own masters." The bundle of contradictions inherent in this notion was blithely ignored; nor was any explanation offered as to how ordinary citizens could become someone who was "born, not made" merely by aping the latter's techniques.[12]

Modern users, led by Peter Drucker, have extended the term beyond the individual to institutions. "The 'new technology,'" observed Drucker, "is entrepreneurial management. . . . Management is the new technology . . . that is making the American economy into an entrepreneurial *society.*" In depicting what he called a "profound shift from a 'managerial' to an 'entrepreneurial' economy," Drucker laid out the guidelines for transforming innovation and entrepreneurship into "a practice and a discipline." What the modern economy required, he concluded, was "an entrepreneurial society in which innovation and entrepreneurship are normal, steady, and continuous." At the heart of this argument lies

Drucker's conviction that "entrepreneurship is neither a science nor an art. It is a practice." More than that, it is "behavior rather than personality trait. And its foundation lies in concept and theory rather than in intuition."[13]

If entrepreneurship can be reduced to a mere practice codified by theory and performed by organizations, where does that leave the role of individuals and of creativity? Kanter conceded that "in the past entrepreneurs and the entrepreneurial spirit have for the most part been seen as existing outside of and apart from the corporation. . . . It is still an open question whether large organizations can accommodate, let alone take advantage of, individuals with an entrepreneurial spirit." Predictably, a new term has emerged to describe the behavior of entrepreneurs within organizations. "Intrapreneurs" have been defined as "managers who keep their entrepreneurial edge and act as though they were steering dynamic, upstart companies—all within the walls of giant corporations." Historian Thomas C. Cochran concluded that "students of entrepreneurship generally have come to agree that while it is a definable function, entrepreneur is a term denoting an ideal type rather than a term continuously applicable to a real person."[14]

Before venturing too deeply into the morass of things that entrepreneurs are supposed to be and do, it is worth looking at the origins of the term. The word means "beginner" or "undertaker" and appeared early in the French language in a very different context. In the sixteenth century it was applied to men who led military expeditions and then extended to other types of adventurers. After 1700 it was used to describe contractors who built bridges, roads, harbors, and fortifications, and later it was even applied to architects. This usage prompted a French writer to define an entrepreneur as one who bought labor and materials at uncertain prices and sold the resulting product at a fixed or contracted price. Another Frenchman, Richard Cantillon, in a 1755 essay, gave the term a more modern and technical meaning by declaring that the essence of the entrepreneurial function was to bear uncertainty.[15]

By 1800, different writers had given the word different meanings based on what sector of the economy they studied. In 1815 Jean Baptiste Say (1767–1832), "an aristocratic industrialist who had had unpleasant practical experience," gave the term its classic definition, which survived until the twentieth century. Say defined an entrepreneur as one who brought the factors of production together and found "in the value of the products . . . the re-establishment of the entire capital he employs, and the value of the wages, the interest, and the rent which he pays, as well as the profits belonging to himself." But Say said nothing about the entrepreneur's role in regard to innovation or capital formation. Other writers viewed his function merely as "one who receives profit," and often made no distinction between an entrepreneur and a capitalist.

For a century the concept remained in the shadows of emerging economic theory, which concentrated on measurable aspects of economic activity and could find no place for a human element. However important the role of individuals, as well as social and cultural factors, might be deemed, they were not measurable and therefore not usable in general economic theory. Moreover, most businesses tended to be small, family-held firms, which obscured to outside eyes any distinctive entrepreneurial role. After 1870, however, the dramatic growth of large corporations in the United States led several American economists to consider that role as something apart from either ownership or the supply of capital. Francis A. Walker distinguished between entrepreneurs and capitalists, calling the former the primary agents of production. Frederick B. Hawley in 1882 identified risk-taking as the distinctive role of the entrepreneur, and John R. Commons elaborated on that role in terms that foreshadowed some of the later arguments of Joseph A. Schumpeter.

Schumpeter, the man responsible for calling history's attention to the seminal role of entrepreneurs, was an economist who departed sharply from the tradition of his brethren by stressing the primal role of individual initiative over abstract forces in economic development. Prior to Schumpeter, few practitioners of his trade paid much attention to the behavior of actual human beings except as inputs to some theoretical construct. Schumpeter not only moved people to center stage but also emphasized the critical role played by social relationships in economic life. In so doing he became, as historian John E. Sawyer observed, "himself the innovator, the entrepreneur of entrepreneurial theory."[16]

Schumpeter first spelled out his argument in *The Theory of Economic Development,* which appeared in German in 1911 and went out of print by 1916. Ten years later Schumpeter grudgingly agreed to a second edition, for which he dropped one chapter, rewrote two others (including the one that discusses entrepreneurship), and made some other revisions. A third German edition merely reprinted the revised 1926 version and became the basis for an English translation published in 1934. In this and later works Schumpeter gave the entrepreneur a much larger role that stressed innovation as his stock in trade. He characterized one basic element of the economic process in deceptively simple terms: "The carrying out of new combinations we call 'enterprise'; the individuals whose function it is to carry them out we call 'entrepreneurs.'"[17]

Conceding that the entrepreneurial function "must always appear mixed up with other kinds of activity," Schumpeter took pains to clarify its essence by insisting that only one salient function distinguished entrepreneurial activity from other types. "Everyone is an entrepreneur," he emphasized, "only when he actually 'carries out new combinations,' and loses that character as soon as he has built up his business, when he settles down to running it as other people run their business." Later he characterized entrepreneurial function as "simply the doing of new things or the doing of things that are already being done in a new way (innovation)." The new thing need not be grand or of historic importance: "It need not be Bessemer steel. . . . It can be the Deerfoot sausage." Entrepreneurship was therefore not a profession or even a lasting condition, and entrepreneurs did not form any kind of social class as did capitalists or landowners—although successful entrepreneurs could raise themselves to such an elevated status. Unlike these ranks, however, the entrepreneurial function could not be inherited or passed on.[18]

In a later article Schumpeter clarified these distinctions. An entrepreneur was not a manager; the former set up a new enterprise while the latter ran it, although the two functions might shade off into each other. Neither was the entrepreneur a capitalist. The ownership of means of production, while helpful to the entrepreneur, was not essential to his function. Schumpeter also carefully separated leadership, or innovation, from invention. While an entrepreneur might be an inventor or vice versa, the two functions were radically different. "As long as they are not carried into practice," he wrote, "inventions are economically irrelevant. And to carry any improvement into effect is a task entirely different from the inventing of it, and a task, moreover, requiring entirely different kinds of aptitudes." Put another way, the inventor produced ideas and the entrepreneur got things done, but those things might or might not embody new ideas of the sort spawned by inventors. An inventor became an entrepreneur only when he had the ability to produce or market or make a business out of what he created.[19]

The "carrying out of new combinations," as Schumpeter defined it, involved five kinds of activity: 1) the introduction of some new type or quality of goods; 2) the introduction of some new method of production: 3) the opening of a new market; 4) the acquisition of some new source of supply of raw materials or partly finished manufactured products; and 5) the imposing of some new organization on an industry. Such innovations in the economic system, he observed, "did not take place in such a way that first new wants arise spontaneously in consumers and then the productive apparatus swings round through their pressure. . . . It is . . . the producer who as a rule initiates economic change, and consumers are educated by him if necessary . . . [and] taught to want new things." Some agent was required to set this process in motion, which defined in simple terms what the entrepreneur was and what he did. In broad terms he introduced change into the economy.[20]

In economic life, as elsewhere, habit and tradition became traps that blinded people from seeing beyond their possibilities or grasping their limitations. Schumpeter described this trap in one of his most memorable passages: "Past economic periods govern the activity of the individual. . . . All the preceding periods have . . . entangled him in a net of social and economic connections which he cannot easily shake off. They have bequeathed him definite means and methods of production. All these hold him in iron fetters fast in his tracks." For precisely that reason, argued Schumpeter, "the carrying out of new combinations is a special function, and the privilege of a type of people who are much less numerous than all those who have the 'objective' possibility of doing it. Therefore . . . entrepreneurs are a special type, and their behavior a special problem." What separated them from ordinary people was this ability to overstep the boundaries of routine, both in vision and action.[21]

Surprisingly, even those later writers who acknowledge Schumpeter as the pioneer in describing the entrepreneurial function seldom quoted his work directly. It is remarkable how prescient his observations were and how fully they anticipated so many subsequent studies that echoed his ideas while ignoring him completely. He understood the overwhelming urge toward routine, which was the enemy of original thinking or insight: "Everything we think, feel, or do often becomes automatic and our conscious life is unburdened of it." The familiar was not only comfortable but safe, shielding one from contradiction and criticism. Routine did not require new thought or energy, whereas going beyond it put one in a place without clear rules or data for making decisions. "Carrying out a new plan and acting according to a customary one," asserted Schumpeter, "are things as different as making a road and walking along it."[22]

Schumpeter was hardly alone in emphasizing the role played by the dead weight of past thinking, habits, and values. It had become part of the intellectual and emotional baggage of the fin de siècle generation. The great playwright Henrik Ibsen returned to the theme in several plays. In *Ghosts*, for example, Mrs. Alving says, "I'm inclined to think that we're all ghosts. . . . It's not only the things that we've inherited from our fathers and mothers that live on in us, but all sorts of dead ideas and old dead beliefs, and things of that sort. They're not actually alive in us, but they're rooted there all the same, and we can't rid ourselves of them."[23]

Going beyond the routine was a bold act that required not only new action or original thought but also the courage to pursue it in the face of uncertainty. "Action must be taken without working out all the details of what is to be done," Schumpeter observed. "Here the success of everything depends upon intuition, the capacity of seeing things in a way which afterwards proves to be true, even though it cannot be established at the moment, and of grasping the essential fact . . . even though one can give no account of the principles by which this is done." Schumpeter characterized this element of boldness as leadership, the willingness not only to find a new path but to show it to others as well. The entrepreneur, he added, "also leads in the sense that he draws other producers in his branch after him."

Having detached himself so strikingly from the traditional bounds of economics, Schumpeter wandered even more freely into the then young and fertile field of psychology. He saw the entrepreneur, like other types of leaders before him, as driven by the urge "to found a private kingdom, usually, though not necessarily, also a dynasty." The entrepreneur lusted after both power and independence, and often possessed "the will to conquer: the impulse to fight, to prove oneself superior to others, to succeed for the sake, not of the fruits of success, but of success itself." Schumpeter also found in the entrepreneur "the joy of creating, of getting things done, or simply of exercising one's energy and ingenuity. . . . Our type seeks out difficulties, changes in order to change, delights in ventures." These activities required a different and not always pleasing type of personality. The entrepreneur, he conceded, "may indeed be called the most rational and the most egotistical of all. . . . [He is] more self-centered than other types, because he relies less than they do on tradition and connection and because his characteristic task . . . consists precisely in breaking up old, and creating new, tradition."

In stressing the role of intuition, Schumpeter differed from later writers, like Drucker, who aspired to turn entrepreneurship into a practice. He made a clear distinction between what he called an "adaptive response" and a "creative response." The former responded to change within the bounds of familiar or traditional channels, while the latter resorted to actions outside these bounds. Schumpeter identified three characteristics of creative responses. They could not be "predicted by applying the ordinary rules of inference from the pre-existing facts." Second, they shaped the course of subsequent events and their long-term outcome. Finally, they had something to do with the "quality of personnel available in a society," the relative quality of personnel in a given field, and with "individual decisions, actions, and patterns of behavior."[24]

At the same time Schumpeter offered insights that in some ways anticipated the views of Drucker and other later writers. "In the large-scale corporation of today," he observed in 1947, "the question that is never quite absent arises with a vengeance, namely, who should be considered an entrepreneur." Much of his later work focused on the question of whether the rise of large organizations meant a decline in the importance of the entrepreneurial function. The innovator became less important because "modern milieus may offer less resistance to new methods and new goods than used to be the case. So far as this is so, the element of personal intuition and force would be less essential than it was." It would give way to "the teamwork of specialists" and change would become "more and more automatic . . . the economy would progressively bureaucratize itself." Thus would emerge the world in which Drucker and others sought to inject the entrepreneurial function as a routine component.[25]

Taken together, these remarkable observations form a composite profile of the entrepreneur, this instigator of new combinations. He (for in those days they were all men) was one who initiated change even when it upset the existing order of things, and thereby forced a kind of enlightenment on both consumers and his business rivals. To perform this function required a special kind of person with the ability to transcend the fetters of daily habit and routine and view things in a different light. This effort required not only vision but the talent and energy to realize it through vigorous action. It required courage to endure the uncertainty that accompanied this departure from the known, to sustain the intuitive leap that had prompted it, and to absorb the criticism and hostility it usually aroused in those who resented change. In doing this, the entrepreneur, willingly or not, had to exert leadership. He was at heart an empire builder with a lust for power, a craving for independence, and a fierce, even joyous urge to compete. These traits often produced an abrasive, unpleasing personality.

This composite portrait will seem familiar to readers who have delved into more recent studies of entrepreneurs and their function. Schumpeter's insights have been echoed repeatedly by other writers, and—as will be seen throughout this book—by our corps d'entrepreneurs, none of whom likely ever read Schumpeter or his descendants. The alert reader will also notice something else about

Schumpeter's composite profile. One of the most striking things about his description of the entrepreneur and his function is how well they fit the artist and the act of creation. Although Schumpeter never expressed it in exactly these terms, in many respects he portrayed the entrepreneur as an artist and his essential function as a creative act.

The entrepreneurs who occupy center stage in this study consist of twenty-six men whose lives and careers span the period from the mid–nineteenth century to the present. Their ranks include some of the usual suspects, like Andrew Carnegie and John D. Rockefeller, along with the some less obvious choices such as Robert Noyce, John H. Patterson, J. C. Penney, and Theodore N. Vail. The selection of these figures is rooted more in intuition than in scientific method, although they were chosen to fit certain broad criteria. Their work covers the entire post–Civil War era of industrialization and reflects the important shifts in its character—the transitions from capital goods to consumer goods to service sectors—as well as a variety of talents and skills. They are astonishingly diverse yet have a surprising number of similarities and connections to one another. Above all, they share one characteristic that singles them out as great entrepreneurs and serves as their membership card for this study: They all displayed in their work a gift for striking originality of insight and the ability to pursue it to fruition.

Obviously it is not practical to present biographical sketches of all twenty-six men. However, their stories will emerge as the narrative progresses. Readers interested in pursuing the life of any one of them can find sources for doing so in the notes and bibliography. As in a play, some will take larger roles than others. It is no accident that only two of the subjects are living at the time of this writing. To be effective, this study required entrepreneurs who had completed the full trajectory of their careers and could be viewed with some perspective. This need eliminated many living figures who might seem prime material for this survey, but whose story and stature might change radically in the coming years. The two living subjects included here, Warren Buffett and Bill Gates, were selected because they filled certain gaps in the criteria mentioned earlier. Buffett's career is far enough advanced to warrant inclusion. While Gates is young enough for his future to include some unpredictable twists and turns, the nature and scale of his accomplishments to this point justify his presence even before the final chapters of his career are enacted.

The twenty-six entrepreneurs are listed below.

Name	Born	Died	Birthplace	Company
Warren E. Buffett	1930		Omaha, Nebraska	Berkshire Hathaway
Andrew Carnegie	1835	1919	Dunfermline, Scotland	Carnegie Steel Company
Pierre Samuel du Pont	1870	1954	Wilmington, Delaware	Du Pont Company
James Buchanan Duke	1856	1925	rural North Carolina	American Tobacco Company and British-American Tobacco Company
William Crapo Durant	1861	1947	Boston, Massachusetts	General Motors
George Eastman	1854	1932	Waterville, New York	Eastman Kodak Company
Thomas Alva Edison	1847	1931	Milan, Ohio	Thomas A. Edison Incorporated
Henry Ford III	1863	1947	Dearborn, Michigan	Ford Motor Company
William Henry Gates	1955		Seattle, Washington	Microsoft Corporation
Jay Gould	1836	1892	Roxbury, New York	Missouri Pacific Railroad and Western Union Telegraph Co.
Edward Henry Harriman	1848	1909	Hempstead, New York	Union Pacific Railroad
Samuel Insull	1859	1938	London, England	interlinked regional utility companies
Ray A. Kroc	1902	1984	Oak Park, Illinois	McDonald's
Edwin Herbert Land	1909	1991	Bridgeport, Connecticut	Polaroid Corporation
Cyrus McCormick	1809	1884	Rockbridge County, Virginia	International Harvester
Robert Noyce	1927	1990	Burlington, Iowa	Intel
John Henry Patterson	1844	1922	near Dayton, Ohio	National Cash Register Company
James Cash Penney	1875	1971	near Hamilton, Missouri	J. C. Penney
John Davison Rockefeller	1839	1937	Tioga County, New York	Standard Oil Company
Theodore Newton Vail	1845	1920	near Minerva, Ohio	Anerican Telephone & Telegraph (AT&T)
Cornelius Vanderbilt	1794	1877	Staten Island, New York	New York Central Railroad
Samuel Moore Walton	1918	1992	Kingfisher, Oklahoma	Wal-Mart
John Wanamaker	1838	1922	Near Philadelphia, Pennsylvania	John Wanamaker and Company
Thomas John Watson	1874	1956	East Campbell, New York	International Business Machines Corporation (IBM)
George Westinghouse	1846	1914	Central Bridge, New York	Westinghouse companies
Frank Winfield Woolworth	1852	1919	Rodman, New York	F. W. Woolworth Company

| 1 |

The Enigma of Creativity

To Ernestine, who understands the likeness of all creative
people.   —JOHN CHAMBERLAIN[1]

Nothing that human beings do is more important or exciting
or produces more momentous results than creativity. It is in many
ways the essence of our being, the very wellspring of what defines
our uniqueness as creatures, yet it remains a tantalizing mystery to
us. Surprisingly little has been written on the subject, even in this
age of academic overkill when the most trivial of questions in the
forest of knowledge have been chopped and chainsawed into mean-
ingless splinters. The reasons are not hard to find. Every aspect of
creativity is an elusive subject, intangible and enigmatic, defying
the hammer blows of pedantry, the cage of statistics, and the tortuous vivisection of deconstruction. Moreover, it is a subject that
resists the pigeonholes of specialization. Who owns the intellectual property rights to creativity? Philosophers? Psychologists?
Sociologists? Artists? Scientists? Delegates from all of these fields
have taken a whack at the subject.

Historically, creativity has always been associated with the arts and is usually contrasted to science. The one is portrayed as intuitive and subjective, the other as objective, empirical, and grounded in reasoning. Both of these stereotypes are misleading if not entirely wrong. The creative impulse, however it is defined, finds expression in every area of human endeavor. "The act of creation itself," insisted Arthur Koestler in his seminal book on creativity, "is based on essentially the same underlying pattern in all ranges of the continuous rainbow spectrum." Psychiatrist Albert Rothenberg, who has also probed the subject deeply, agrees that "creativity is manifest in many and diverse types of human endeavor, including all varieties of art, religion, philosophy, engineering, business activities . . . and in commonplace activities such as cooking, sports, and interpersonal interaction."[2]

Clearly, creativity is not limited to artists. The scientist displays it in connecting ideas or observations and transforming them into insights or actions; so do inventors, philosophers, mathematicians, businessmen, and athletes. "The equation of science with logic and reason, or art with intuition and emotion, is a blatant popular fallacy," asserted Koestler. "No discovery has ever been made by logical deduction; no work of art produced without calculating craftsmanship." Rothenberg emphasized that "so-called intuitive thinking and other types of leaps of thought analogous to what are commonly designated as artistic intuition and inspiration have played a definite role in scientific discovery." Scientists themselves have traced some of their most important discoveries back to just such experiences. Jules-Henri Poincaré, the great mathematician, recalled that the insight leading to one of his more important discoveries came as he was about to step into a carriage to go for a drive. Albert Einstein described the flash of discovery that revealed how Newton's theory of gravitation could fit into a broader theory of relativity as "the happiest thought of my life."[3]

What, then, is creativity? Opinions vary widely on both its essence and its elements. Rothenberg defined it as "the state or the production of something *both new and valuable*," and admitted that his approach excluded "everything but the achievements of genius."[4] Robert Grudin agreed that "studies of creativity usually recount the actions of genius," but creativity is hardly limited to geniuses and that term is no less ambiguous and elusive. Psychological explanations have followed two basic approaches. One places emphasis on rationality, the other on "classical association-ism," which views thinking as a chain of ideas. Psychiatrists have tended to associate creativity with various types of personality dis-orders. Alfred Adler posited a "compensatory theory of creativity," which viewed people as producing art, science, and other creations to "compensate for their own inadequacies." Other psychoanalytic theories subordinate creativity to some other process and regard it as an expression of neurotic behavior. After surveying a half cen-tury of psychological studies pertaining to creativity, Rollo May admitted to being struck by "the general paucity of the material and the inadequacy of the work." Nevertheless, he conceded, "it is still true that creativity is a stepchild of psychology."[5]

But at bottom psychologists are as baffled as anyone else about the nature of creativity. The mystery also fascinates most creative people themselves, including entrepreneurs, who struggle to explain exactly how they do what they do. For most of them it is an intuitive process. Edwin Land, the founder of Polaroid, once said that "every creative act is a sudden cessation of stupidity." Andrew Carnegie doted on the notion of "genius" and was firmly convinced that he could recognize it in anyone, but he was helpless to explain what it was or how it was created. "A man who is liable to rapid thinking very often arrives at conclusions without being able to tell the process," observed Jay Gould, the great railroad and telegraph entrepreneur, "and yet he is satisfied the conclusions are correct. . . . If you undertake to give the evidences by which they are reached you could not tell how it was done." As noted earlier, Schumpeter had almost exactly this same notion.[6]

E. H. Harriman, another major railroad entrepreneur, was renowned for the speed and originality of his thinking, which left mere mortals scrambling to keep up with him. Robert S. Lovett, a close friend and associate, marveled that "his mental processes were unlike any that I have ever seen. He never arrived at conclusions by reason, or argument, or any deliberate process that I could observe. His judgments seemed to be formed intuitively. The proposition was presented to him and he saw it. It was much like turning a flashlight on a subject. If interested, he saw it, and did not care and probably did not know how it was revealed. And his vision and measure of it was almost unfailingly clear and correct."

Lovett was not alone in his fascination with Harriman's gift. The great banker James Stillman, another close ally, once said that his friend's brain was "a thing to marvel at. And yet it was that kind of brain which, if you could take it apart as you would a clock, and put it on a shelf to look at, would be distinguished by the incredible simplicity of its mechanism, and its ability to make the most complex problems solvable." The man himself had no explanation. Asked by a reporter how he did it, Harriman puzzled over the question for a while, then replied, "I think that the mind is like these—what d'ye call 'em on this desk?—these pigeon holes. A man comes to me. I listen and decide on what to do; and then—it goes into a pigeon hole."

"And it's always there?" asked the reporter. "No trouble in finding it again at any time?"

"It's always there," Harriman replied. He thought about it some more, then could only reiterate, "It's always there. Whenever I need it again I find it there."

"And you don't know how you do it?"

"I don't know how I do it."[7]

Inventors who became entrepreneurs as well were no less curious about the process of discovery. The greatest of them all, Thomas A. Edison, agreed that "the first step is an intuition, and comes with a burst. . . . It has been just so in all of my inventions." Land was fascinated by what he called the "hunting process," which he described this way:

> There may be many abortive first approaches at the verbal levels
> to fields which are then rejected as being either not significant
> enough or not feasible—and then, quite suddenly a field will
> emerge conceptually so full blown in the creator's mind that the
> words can scarcely come from his mouth fast enough to describe
> the new field in its full implication and elaborateness.

This arrival at sudden insights extends to many fields. "I have the result," the celebrated German mathematician Carl Friedrich Gauss once exclaimed, "but I do not yet know how to get it." The gap (often chasm) between understanding and explanation plagues creative people of all stripes. "As artists are not necessarily the best interpreters of their own work," noted Michael Novak, "so practitioners in many fields do not need to know the theory of what they are doing and, if asked, state it badly—maybe even in the wrong key."[8]

This notion of intuition—the flash of insight that unravels the mystery—lies at the core of much writing on creativity. It remains elusive precisely because it is rooted in the unconscious and therefore arrives without warning at unexpected times. Artists and scientists alike have stressed its pivotal role in the creative process. In art the notion that discovery consists of revelations from the unconscious has influenced such movements as expressionism, dadaism, and surrealism. Arthur Koestler alluded to the "poet's or the mathematician's trancelike condition while he concentrates on a problem" as one in which he was "exploring the inner environment, and ignoring the input from the senses." However, Eugene K. von Fange, cautioned that "the sudden 'flash' is more often incomplete or inaccurate than it is correct."[9]

As a leader of courses in creative engineering at General Electric, which instituted its Creative Engineering Program in 1937, Fange viewed a creation as something "useful . . . of benefit to mankind," but added that *all thinking is mentally directed creativeness. We think only when we wish to achieve a conclusion that, by implication, did not exist before.*" One factor common to all creations, he argued, was a *"new association of existing elements, as far as the creator himself is concerned."* But that breakthrough did not come easily or quickly. "It is not far wrong," Fange observed, "to say that creative work is the successive isolation of 'what is not.'" In the professions, the entire process of discovery and development often did not belong to one person alone. Who then was the source of creativity, he asked: "the one who conceived the initial idea, the one who first made a model function properly, or the one who actually designed it for production?"[10]

One obvious answer might well be all of the above.

Jacob W. Getzels and Mihaly Csikszentmihalyi described artistic creativity as a process that begins when a person "experiences a conflict in perception, emotion, or thought." The artist then formulates a problem that articulates the hitherto unarticulated conflict, finds a way to express the problem in visual form, manages to resolve the conflict through symbolic means, and thus achieves a new "emotional and cognitive balance." Rothenberg concluded that creativity in any field did not consist of an isolated or single act but resulted from "a long series of circumstances, sometimes occurring in an unbroken chain or sequence but often interrupted, reconstructed, and repeated over a period of time." During that process it moved from "disguise and disorder to illumination and order . . . from personal preoccupation to generic and universal concerns."[11]

Did this process involve mystical or magical elements unique to genius? D. N. Perkins thought not. He dismissed the standard notion of creativity as "one of those 'high mysteries' . . . stubbornly inscrutable, essentially ineffable," and argued instead that "the processes underlying creation are commonplace." Rejecting the idea that "the business of creation is the business of the unconscious mind," Perkins suggested instead that "creating occurs when ordinary mental processes in an able person are marshaled by creative . . . intentions." What seemed to be intuition or insight could be explained in terms of "recognizing, realizing, and reasoning to a considerable extent." He found no evidence that creativity derived chiefly from "specifically creative abilities," and argued that it probably depended more on "traits other than abilities." Creative people were not blessed with unique abilities but rather did more—often much more—with ordinary ones. For Perkins these "connections between the marvelous and the mundane" did much to explain the mystery of creation. [12]

Even insight fell into this category. Perkins described it as "doing more with less . . . the person's own mind provides what in more ordinary circumstances would be supplied from without." But this involved no special processes. Where Koestler, Rothenberg, and others viewed insight as something beyond reasoning, Perkins argued that "very often insight can come about just exactly through reasoning." The same held true for the creative capacity to transcend existing frames of reference. "Reasoning, remembering," he insisted, ". . . often break boundaries." Invention, too, could be explained apart from the usual resort to the mystical or ineffable. "The essence of invention isn't process but purpose," Perkins wrote. "Purpose is what organizes the diverse means of the mind to creative ends." Moreover, invention often occurred "not because a person tries to be original, but because the person attempts to do something difficult."[13]

Perkins's argument is intriguing but unconvincing. It contains some internal contradictions and inconsistencies, and fails to account for the ultimate source of inspiration. Having stressed the primary role of ordinary processes carried to extraordinary lengths, he conceded that "the great creators tend to have talent. They reveal a natural knack for thinking and doing in their specialties . . . those gifts support their creative endeavors. . . . A talent is an extraordinary and inborn ability for doing something—remembering music, say. A specifically creative ability, inborn or not, would be an ability that in itself made a person more creative." But this amounts to a circular argument and does not get at whatever the ingredients are that translate such a talent into creativity. What separates an ordinary composer with a gift for remembering music from a Mozart or Beethoven? Is this distance between talent and genius merely one of degree?[14]

No one has examined the mystery of creativity more thoroughly and deeply than Arthur Koestler, a writer best known for his political works—most notably *Darkness at Noon*. His thick book *The Act of Creation* (1964), the second work in a monumental trilogy dealing with the mind, remains the most erudite, painstaking, and provocative study of the subject. Koestler found that "verbal thinking, and conscious thinking in general, plays only a subordinate part in the decisive phase of the creative act." As noted earlier, Schumpeter shared the view that intuition lay at the heart of creative action, but Koestler carried the point to its farthest shore by stressing the dichotomy between language and creativity. Language served as the strongest, most complex, and most flexible form of human communication, yet it could also become "a screen between the thinker and reality. This is the reason why true creativity often starts where language ends."[15]

Perhaps that explains why, when a revelation hits home, a typical response is to say, "I *see* it now." Koestler found evidence that some people possess the faculty of "so-called eidetic imagery—that is, of really *seeing* mental images with dream-like hallucinatory vivid-ness." This gift turned out to be common in children but rare in adults. In this way, creative people are visionaries in the most literal sense, able to grasp visually what they often cannot convey in lan-guage. However, this does not address the main issue, which is the source of the image. What elements are involved in the process of seeing things in new and unexpected ways?[16]

The key function in the creative process seems to be an ability to connect seemingly unrelated ideas and derive hitherto unsuspected meaning or significance from that connection. The occurrence of such insights is never predictable. "The history of discovery," noted Koestler, "is full of such arrivals at unexpected destinations, and arrivals at the right destination by the wrong boat." But it is nei-ther a random nor an accidental event in the sense that it might happen to anyone. As Louis Pasteur observed, "Chance favors the prepared mind." Koestler called this ability the process of "bisocia-tion," as opposed to "association," the most common form of think-ing, which he characterized as merely "the exercise of a habit." Learning, by contrast, he defined as "the acquisition of a new skill" and bisociation the "combination, re-shuffling and re-structuring of skills."[17]

Rothenberg gave this notion another twist by describing what he called "janusian thinking," which involved *actively conceiving two or more opposite or antithetical ideas, images, or concepts simultaneously. Opposites or antitheses are conceived as existing side by side or as equally operative and equally true.* This ability was for Rothenberg "a particular characteristic of the creative process and therefore is a function of the psychological structure of creative persons." Not everyone possessed this ability, which meant that it did "not arise from a general force present in everyone." Janusian thinking differed from dialectical progression in that it did not involve a synthesis or a sequence of reasoning but rather held two antitheses at the same time. One classic example was James D. Watson's conception of a double helix in which *"the chains were identical and opposite at the same time."* From that insight emerged the discovery of the structure of DNA. So too did Einstein's grasp of the relativity of gravity reflect janusian thinking. Polaroid's Edwin Land believed in what he called "orthogonal thinking," by which he meant going to the opposite extreme when one approach failed.[18]

To this notion Rothenberg added what he called "homospatial thinking," which he described as "a rapid, fleeting, and changing mental impression or conception that soon leads to separating out of various components." This differed from analogic thinking, which Rothenberg considered a crucial part of creative thinking but not the determining aspect of it. Analogic thinking involved comparing two or more different things through a procession of reasoned steps. By contrast, homospatial thinking consisted of *"actively conceiving two or more discrete entities occupying the same space, a conception leading to the articulation of new identities."* In effect, it superimposed or fused whole entities rather than considering their aspects side by side. It served to integrate janusian thoughts, most obviously by producing metaphors that helped explain or clarify problems.[19]

Conceptualizing in this way requires the ability to transcend the iron fetters of tradition. As people grow up and gain experience, they acquire habits and routines that govern both their thinking and their behavior. "All coherent thinking," Koestler declared, "is equivalent to playing a game according to a set of rules . . . a *'code'* of fixed rules." These rules and routines make life easier and more convenient by putting much of what we do on automatic pilot, but they also place boundaries and inhibitors on thinking. So do values, beliefs, and convictions, which forge channels that confine the way we think. The crucial first step toward creativity is developing the ability to relax these controls, escape the rules of verbal logic, and ignore the dogmas and taboos imposed by common sense.[20]

Escaping the clutches of habit involves a curious paradox. It requires a freeing of the mind from the usual way of looking at things. "Present habits will slowly but surely enclose us in a prison of complacency," said Fange in words reminiscent of Schumpeter. "They will build a thick wall of pride about the way we are now doing things." Koestler observed that "the prerequisite of originality is the art of forgetting, at the proper moment, what we know." Charles F. Kettering, the great engineer at General Motors, described an inventor as "a fellow who doesn't take his education too seriously." The biggest job in training a new recruit, he noted, was teaching him that everything was not in the books. "No matter what we are doing," he added, "if it is new we can always find a book that will tell us it can't be done." Edwin Land was adamant that experts were an obstacle who could only explain why something couldn't work. Ignoring them required "the art of the fresh, clean look at the old, old knowledge."[21]

Yet even Land readily conceded that the old knowledge provided a crucial base for moving beyond it. Rothenberg noted that the creative person began with a "high degree of knowledge of his field." Fange, too, conceded that a solid base of knowledge was needed to spur the mind toward new discoveries but argued that "it is growth in judgment, more than growth in knowledge or technique, that leads to advancement." Edison for one had an insatiable appetite for information. Although the popular image of him is one of countless hours spent toiling over his experiments, he also devoured every book or scientific journal he could find that offered promising clues to his work. So did Bill Gates, who immersed himself in business as well as technical literature. "At Harvard," noted his biographers, "Gates read business books like other male students read *Playboy*." The trick is to use knowledge as a spur rather than as a comfort pillow for settled channels of thinking.[22]

Such automatic routines of thought and behavior were precisely what Schumpeter had much earlier described in explaining the unique leap made by entrepreneurs. Koestler, too, emphasized that "when life presents us with a problem it will be attacked in accordance with the code of rules which enabled us to deal with similar problems in the past." When these traditional approaches failed to solve the problem, "thought runs around in circles . . . like rats in a cage." He outlined two avenues of escape from this impasse. One involved the plunge into a dreamlike state beyond the fetters of rational thinking; the other was a "spontaneous flash of insight which shows a familiar situation or event in a new light, and elicits a new response to it."[23]

Thus arose a paradox of creativity noted by many observers: "The more original a discovery the more obvious it seemed afterward. . . . The more familiar the parts, the more striking the new whole." Land, too, was struck by this aspect of creativity. "It is a curious property of research," he said in 1937, ". . . that after the problem has been solved the solution usually seems obvious." Moreover, a fresh insight was seldom something entirely new. "While creations in art, science, and other fields invariably appear to be new and unfamiliar," declared Rothenberg, "they cannot ever be completely so." The creative scientist, for example, "dips into the unknown with firm footing in the known." Robert Grudin described innovation as "the art of discovering what is old." For Koestler this meant "the uncovering of something which has always been there but was hidden from the eye by the blinkers of habit." The discovery seems so obvious afterward because its elements or components are familiar; only the combined or integrated form is new.[24]

Such flashes of insight seem intuitive because the mind functions on several levels at once, each one independent of the others. The essence of the creative act for Koestler is bringing them together. What makes this difficult is the paradoxical quality of awareness itself, which Koestler described as an experience that gradually decreases and fades away "with our increasing mastery of a skill exercised under monotonous conditions." Slowly but surely habit dulls the blade of awareness, undercutting the value of experience. For this reason inexperience, coupled with an inquiring mind, could be an asset. The novice, uninhibited by knowledge of the way things are supposed to be, could ask questions others considered stupid or never thought to ask, and could see problems and connections that others missed. Land once observed that "a premature attempt to explain something that thrills you will destroy your perceptivity rather than increase it, because your tendency will be to explain away rather than to seek out."[25]

If the ability to make connections is the key to creative thinking, the ability to ask new questions spurs the creative process. "Too often thinking is equated with rationality," observed Getzels and Csikszentmihalyi. "Yet we know that creative thinking, in art as well as science, does not seem to follow that route. Instead of accepting the premises of a structured problem, it fashions a new problematic configuration. . . . The crucial task of the creative person is precisely that of transforming potential into actual problems." Put another way, every creative act amounts to the solution of a newly envisaged problem. The formulation of that problem becomes the central issue, and one that could not be assumed at the outset. Max Wertheimer agreed, noting, "Often in great discovery the most important thing is that a certain question is found. Envisaging, putting the productive question, is often more important than the solution of a set question."[26]

Einstein, too, found this to be the case. "The formulation of a problem is often more essential than its solution, which may be merely a matter of mathematical or experimental skill," he wrote. "To raise new questions, new problems, to regard old problems from a new angle, requires creative imagination and marks a real advance in science." Creativity depends on the ability to step outside the boundaries of a given problem and, by viewing it in a different light, reconfiguring it along hitherto unexamined lines.

This amounts to redefining the problem and looking elsewhere for the solution.[27]

Grudin called creative achievement "the boldest initiative of mind" because it took one "simultaneously to the rim of knowledge and the limits of propriety." It was, above all, a solo act and could not be done by committee. As Land observed, "There is no such thing as group originality or group creativity or group perspicacity. . . . Profundity and originality are attributes of single, if not singular minds." Warren Buffett agrees. "My idea of a group decision," he said wryly, "is to look in the mirror." Robert Noyce once observed that "no businessman . . . would have developed the telephone. It's got to be a maverick—some guy who's been working with the deaf and gets the crazy idea that you could actually send the human voice over a wire. . . . A businessman would have been out taking a market survey, and since it was a nonexistent product he would have proven conclusively that the market for a telephone was zero." Land, who disdained market research, observed that "intelligent men in groups are as a rule rather stupid . . . helpless to do anything decent in the group."[28]

In the arts, creativity has always been regarded as a form of individual self-expression and the artist as the supreme form of individualist. But these same qualities apply no less to scientists, engineers, or creative people in other fields, including business. Testimony on this point comes from some unlikely sources, among them Earl Corder Sams, the closest associate of and successor to James Cash Penney. "It is a mistaken belief that assumes only those in the arts have the desire for self-expression," Sams declared. "All persons, whatever their occupations, have the natural desire to express themselves. . . . We try to encourage that desire." Ray Kroc said that "finding locations for McDonald's is the most creatively fulfilling thing I can imagine. . . . Out of that bare piece of ground comes a store that does, say, a million dollars a year in business."[29]

Here, too, creativity involves a paradox, this one of ego: the creation of some entity greater than the self yet reflecting the self in all its glory. In business and science as in art, some of the most creative people have found it difficult to separate the self from the creation. They have sought to build monuments to themselves as well as for the world. Nearly all of our entrepreneurs built great companies; one of them, Frank Woolworth, literally built a monument to himself in the form of the Woolworth Building.

Creativity and originality are not to be confused with technique or competence. "Technical virtuosity is one thing, creative originality another," Koestler underscored. "Original discoveries are as rare in art as in science. They consist in finding new ways of bisociating motif and medium." Originality for Koestler constituted the true mark of genius—the ability to open new frontiers for others to inhabit. Not surprisingly, many of the world's most original minds—Albert Einstein being a classic example—fared poorly in school, even in the very subject they later revolutionized. Their minds simply refused to stay in the prescribed channels of thought and habit but insisted on forging their own paths outside the muck of conventional wisdom.[30]

For scientists, this digging of original channels of thought involves the accumulation of new data and/or the reordering of old data into new patterns or theoretical frameworks. At its highest level the result is a new paradigm as described by Thomas Kuhn in his classic work. The outcome is seldom predictable and relentlessly individualistic. Koestler likened the process of collecting data to that of picking flowers and arranging them into a bouquet that reflected personal taste. He also compared data to the mound of tiles used to compose a mosaic, which could be arranged in any number of ways according to different patterns, broken up, then rearranged again. The final composition always had to overcome the stubborn resistance of habit. "Of all forms of mental activity," wrote historian of science Herbert Butterfield, "the most difficult to induce even in the minds of the young . . . is the art of handling the same bundle of data as before, but placing them in a new system of relations with one another by giving them a different framework."[31]

Discoveries can occur in a variety of ways. Grudin categorized most of them around two types, analogy and anomaly. Analogies, in turn, could be divided into two classes: "interdisciplinary analogies, which link apparently disparate fields of experience, and intradisciplinary analogies, which establish new connections between elements within a single field of experience." In both cases, the essential ingredient was the presence of some form of coincidence that prompted recognition of a relationship. For Koestler, analogy was a classic example of bisociation. "The real achievement in discoveries of the type mentioned," he stressed, "is 'seeing an analogy where no one saw one before.' . . . The essence of discovery is that unlikely marriage of . . . previously unrelated frames of reference."[32]

Anomalies provoke discovery through some disturbance or disorganization serious enough to challenge existing views. Kuhn described their characteristic feature as "their stubborn refusal to be assimilated to existing paradigms." Grudin outlined three types of anomaly: the uninvited guest, the empty chair, and rearrangement. The first involves the presence of some unexpected factor that requires explanation. In the second type, an attempt at explanation is thwarted by the absence of some necessary factor, which then has to be supplied theoretically. The third type contains all the necessary factors but in a disordered form of organization that requires rearrangement. What all three types have in common is the need to account for or deal with some element that disrupts the pattern of expectation.[33]

Peter Drucker defined systematic innovation as *"the purposeful and organized search for changes, and . . . the systematic analysis of the opportunities such changes might offer for economic or social innovation."* But this involves discovery of a different kind. While some forms of innovation lead to major changes, most successful innovations in business exploit change. In effect, the entrepreneur searches for sources of change and, discovering one, exploits it. In laying out the process, however, Drucker included some familiar categories of discoveries with new labels: "The unexpected . . . The incongruity . . . Changes in industry structure or market structure that catch everyone unawares." The creative entrepreneur is one who not only recognizes an anomaly but discovers a way to capitalize on it.[34]

This may sound more like analysis than discovery, and in a peculiar sense it is. The problem lies in the misconception that analysis is something opposite to inspiration or discovery because it is a rational, objective process of reasoning. Grudin argued that true analysis is entirely the antithesis of its dictionary definitions. It is personal rather than objective, and involves not the breaking down of a given subject or problem but the re-creation of it in a new form. "The relation between analysis and invention," he adds, "is nowhere more apparent than in one of the most effective analytic techniques: hypothesis. The hypothetical method is of a markedly creative character." Coming up with a hypothesis amounts to formulating a question to be asked, which has already been shown to be a crucial step in the creative process.[35]

Whatever form discovery takes, it usually marks only the beginning of a long and difficult process toward realizing the insight. The essence of creativity—and of entrepreneurship—requires not only conception but action as well. "Creativity," said Rollo May, "can be seen only in the act." The long and winding road to realization requires not only hard work but dedication and sacrifice, as well as the omnipresent risk of failure. It is by nature a road that often leads to a dead end. "Results? Why man, I've gotten a lot of results," exclaimed Thomas A. Edison. "I know several thousand things that won't work." It was Edison who coined the famous dictum that "genius is one percent inspiration and ninety-nine percent perspiration," and who also admitted that "I was always afraid of things that worked the first time."[36]

Few people better understood the pain and plodding involved in the hard work beyond the first flash of discovery. "Nothing that's good works by itself, just to please you," Edison once growled. "You've got to *make* the damn thing work." As the first inventor-entrepreneur, he won an international reputation for devices that astounded the world. Ever the showman, he made the end product seem easier and simpler than it was to an adoring public. But every one of them was born of long hours devoted to patient, often exasperating toil. In one instance, he plodded through 10,296 experiments to solve a problem in the storage battery he invented. He described the process this way:

> It has been just so in all my inventions. The first step is an intuition—and comes with a burst, *then* difficulties arise. This thing gives out and then that . . . little faults and difficulties . . . show themselves and months of anxious watching, study and labor are requisite before commercial success—or failure—is certainly reached.[37]

This pattern was hardly unique to Edison. No one captured its peculiar mixture of joy and agony better than Edwin Land:

> If you dream of something worth doing and then simply go to work on it and don't think anything of personalities, or emotional conflicts, or of money, or of family distractions; if you just think of, detail by detail, what you have to do next, it is a wonderful dream even though the end is a long way off, for there are about five thousand steps to be taken before we realize it; and [when you] start taking the first ten, and . . . twenty after, it is amazing how quickly you get through the

four thousand [nine hundred] and ninety. The last ten steps
you never seem to work out. But you keep on coming nearer to
giving the world something.[38]

In this remarkable statement Land touched on most of the elements involved in the creative act—joy, sorrow, frustration, sacrifice, dedication, painstaking work, setbacks, and failures, all
harnessed toward the goal of "giving the world something." Surprisingly few writers take note of the joy involved in discovery.
One of the exceptions, Michael Novak, noted that "many critics
seem never to have imagined the sheer fun and creative pleasure in
bringing a new business to birth. Such creativity has the stamp of a
distinctive personality all over it. In the pleasure it affords its creator, it rivals, in its way, artistic creativity." George Gilder viewed
entrepreneurs as "limited only by the compass of their own imaginations. . . . They stand before a canvas as empty as any painter's; a
page as blank as any poet's. Like creative artists, they bring
entirely new things into the world." Gilder also embraced a broad
definition of entrepreneurs: "Some are scientists, some are artists,
some are craftsmen; most are in business."[39]

A. David Silver argued that artists and entrepreneurs had many
things in common. Both were problem solvers and tended to be
"individualists, unconventional, sensitive, imaginative, intense,
complex, driven, and creative." Where the artist tried to solve
"many of life's problems" on a canvas, the entrepreneur focused
relentlessly on some one problem until he was "ready to pull out
one huge canvas and begin painting." Both had the intense urge to
do some one thing extremely well. Bill Gates described software as
"a great combination between artistry and engineering. . . . If you
ever talk to a great programmer, you'll find he knows his tools like
an artist knows his paintbrushes." Warren Buffett took a similar
view of his work: "I have a blank canvas and a lot of paint, and I get

to do what I want." Land put it another way. An artist, he noted, "teaches the painting. The painting teaches him. That's why you give up everything to be an artist."[40]

Artists and entrepreneurs are hardly alone in these qualities; the ecumenical nature of creativity reveals itself in many other fields of endeavor. Few creative people understand their work better than Tom Seaver, one of baseball's great pitchers. "Pitching is a beautiful thing," he once observed. "It's an art . . . a work of art when it's done right. It's like a ballet or the theatre. And, like any work of art, you have to have it in your head first—the idea of it, a vision of what it should be. And then you have to *perform.*"[41]

One element common to artists, entrepreneurs, athletes, and other creative people is a rage for order, the desire to impose form on something perceived to be formless. For artists it has long been acknowledged as the prime directive, but the principle applies with no less force to those in other fields of endeavor. "There's only nothingness and chaos out there," said Land, "until the human mind organizes it." Koestler made the intriguing observation that "every scientific discovery gives rise . . . to the experience of beauty, because the solution of the problem creates harmony out of dissonance." It also gives rise to a peculiar kind of insistence that the discovery take a particular cast. "When this breakthrough of a creative insight into consciousness occurs," wrote Rollo May, "we have the subjective conviction that the form should be this way and no other way." Peter Drucker echoed this point. "Entrepreneurs *know* what their innovation is meant to do," he wrote. "And if some other use for it appears, they tend to resent it." For artists, scientists, and entrepreneurs alike, this sense of certainty can lead to fabulous results or, as we shall later see, catastrophic failures.[42]

The process of discovery, whether in art, science, business, or any other field, must always swim against the powerful tide of conventional wisdom. Creativity works as both a blessing and a curse, not only on the creator but even more so on the world around him.

As Grudin noted, "No show of benevolence or proof of genius will ever wholly defuse the shock of a new thought." The very habits of thought on which people rely to function in life, and which serve as a barrier to creativity, also generate suspicion and hostility toward anything that threatens to disrupt the routine of things. The paradox of creativity is that in one stroke it spawns dueling forces of hope and fear. Edgar Degas once remarked that "a painter paints a picture with the same feeling as that with which a criminal commits a crime." Both threaten the status quo to which most people cling fervently as their anchor in life.[43]

This threat is a very real one. Picasso observed that "every act of creation is first of all an act of destruction." Discovery cannot help but rip the veil of convention that orders our vision of the world. The sense of loss begins with the discoverer. "The unconscious seems to take delight . . . in breaking through—and breaking up exactly what we cling to most rigidly in our conscious thinking," wrote Rollo May. "What occurs in this breakthrough is not simply growth; it is much more dynamic. . . . The guilt that is present when this breakthrough occurs has its source in the fact that the insight must destroy something." May saw this sense of guilt as being present in all genuinely creative work. "The creativity of the spirit," he added, "*does* and *must* threaten the structure and presuppositions of our rational, orderly society and way of life." Koestler found the same force at work, noting that "the re-structuring of mental organization effected by the new discovery implies that the creative act has a revolutionary or *destructive* side."[44]

If discovery disrupts, its execution destroys. Whether in art, science, business, or other fields, the new concept acts as a death ray seeking to destroy all obstacles in its path, indifferent to anything that is incompatible with it. Sometimes it encounters powerful resistance and may take years or even decades to prevail; on other occasions it may simply demolish everything in its path with astonishing swiftness. There can be no damage control because the damage caused is as unpredictable and unintentional as it is unavoidable. Of course, a new idea may die at birth or soon after if it is not nurtured and given a vigorous shove out of the cradle, but if it survives it cannot help but inflict casualties. Its struggle to survive and prevail has a distinctly Darwinian flavor about it. Indeed, Darwin's own great insight followed precisely this same ruthless pattern in rising to prominence.

Schumpeter understood this process very well and coined a term for it. He defined the essence of capitalism as an "evolutionary process" that "incessantly revolutionizes the economic structure *from within,* incessantly destroying the old one, incessantly creating a new one. This process of Creative Destruction is the essential fact about capitalism." Examples of creative destruction abound in business history. Power looms rendered the hand weaver obsolete. The building of bridges wiped out the livelihoods of transfer ferries, inns, and eateries. The automobile doomed the buggy, harness, and other industries revolving around the horse and carriage. The decline in the need for horses, in turn, opened thousands of acres of pasture for planting, which led to increased crop production. The emergence of giant agricorporations pushed smaller farmers toward oblivion. Computers sent typewriters into retirement, as they had earlier done with ledger books. Motion pictures rendered vaudeville extinct, as calculators did slide rules.[45]

In virtually every field of endeavor or production, innovation brought with it obsolescence of some kind. Every monument to material progress rose above a graveyard of its predecessors. To those graveyards went not merely a way of doing things but also a lifestyle built around it. The creation of centralized stockyards and refrigerator cars, frozen and fast foods, and the microwave oven transformed not only the way Americans eat but also the role of food and eating in the culture. The theory of relativity went far beyond the realm of physics in its implications and influence, as did Darwin's theory and numerous other scientific insights. The automobile brought in its wake a mutated landscape of roads, highways, malls, and suburbs. The jet plane changed not only the travel habits of Americans but also their sense of time and space.

Unlike other economists, Schumpeter looked past the unfolding of creative destruction to its agents, the entrepreneurs whose originality and energy unleashed the forces of change. Historian Fritz Redlich characterized them as "daimonic figures," because in their work "the destructive power is essentially connected with [the] creative power." In some cases this creative-destructive or daimonic element turns self-destructive as well, as happened with some of our entrepreneurs. This transformation may be considered the dark side of the creative process, occurring when the same characteristics that produce new creations become distorted and lead to negative results. Many of the entrepreneurs who came to unhappy ends were in effect victims of an inability to harness or restrain their own talents.[46]

It should be clear by now that artists have no monopoly on creativity, and that creative people of all stripes have a number of characteristics in common. Traditionally artists have been defined as those who practice one of the fine arts as opposed to artisans or craftsmen. The dictionary also defines an artist as "one who exhibits exceptional skill in his work" or who is "expert at trickery or deceit." But there is another, simpler way to approach the matter. For our purposes, an artist can be defined by the proposition that all creation embodies two basic functions: conception and execution. Everything else is essentially logistics. The great entrepreneur—indeed, all creative people who achieve greatness—is one who can not only conceive original things but execute the concept as well. This is why May stressed that *"creativity occurs in an act of encounter and is to be understood with this encounter as its center. . . .* Out of encounter is born the work of art."[47]

Artists also possess some mysterious driving force that takes the form of an urge to create something greater than the self, whether tangible or intangible, immediate or distant in its realization. When this drive connects or interacts with some vision (and who knows where that vision comes from), the result is a creative spark that produces work of originality in whatever form or medium it emerges. In this sense, too, the urge to create in business is in its way no less a form of originality or self-expression than is creativity in other fields. The great artist creates something that is an expression both of himself and of something larger and more enduring; so does the great entrepreneur. It is this creative impulse, along with a unique level of talent, that separates the great entrepreneurs from ordinary businessmen, just as it separates great artists from ordinary practitioners or pretenders.

Any consideration of creative people must divorce personality from achievement. A person's level of talent and creativity has little to do with moral judgments or evaluations of individual behavior. Neither artists, entrepreneurs, nor any other creative persons have to be high-minded or likeable people to accomplish what they do. In every field creative genius comes in many forms and guises. One need not like Jay Gould or John D. Rockefeller, who vied for the title of "the most hated man in America," to appreciate and admire what they achieved any more than one has to like Richard Wagner to understand or enjoy his music. Virtually every writer on the subject of creativity emphasizes the presence of damaged personalities or backgrounds in the most talented of people. Clichés abound on the subject, beginning with those of the mad artist, mad scientist, and guilt-driven entrepreneur. None of these factors detract from the worth of their accomplishments.

In the select world of creativity, entrepreneurs do have some important differences from artists. While the product of their genius may or may not be as enduring as a work of art, it usually has far more direct and profound effects on daily life. Whatever its nature, it is not passive but active, something not to be studied or admired or cherished but used to accomplish things on a grand scale. If artists change the minds and hearts of people, entrepreneurs change the texture of their everyday lives, often in profound ways. The work of any artist, however great, can be embraced or ignored; the presence of the telephone or electricity or the computer or automobile or the giant corporation cannot be ignored. The artist usually works alone or with a few others, while the entrepreneur has to work with people and organize endeavors on a grand scale. Perhaps most important, the entrepreneur produces fewer works, has less room for failure, and cannot simply discard failed efforts. For him or her, the consequences of failure can be as decisive as those of success.

| 2 |

Portrait of the Entrepreneur as a Young Man

Trust the younger men. Give them a fair chance.

— JOHN WANAMAKER[1]

Genius, like wealth, separates its possessors from the herd, but unlike wealth it cannot be inherited. The sources of creativity remain as great an enigma as its nature. What is the wellspring of creativity, and how is it tapped? To what degree is it innate or acquired? If innate, how is it developed? If acquired, what is the process or triggering mechanism? In Shakespeare's *Twelfth Night,* Malvolio offers the famous observation that some men are born great, some achieve greatness, and some have greatness thrust upon them. Is this distinction true or do great achievers have some common pattern in their lives that accounts for their rise to greatness?

These questions inevitably lead to an inquiry into the early development of creative individuals. Surprisingly few writers have searched for common threads of experience or development in the early years of the great entrepreneurs.[2] A. David Silver was intrigued enough with the problem to ask two psychiatrist friends for help in designing a questionnaire to investigate "the behavioral characteristics of successful entrepreneurs." The questions ranged over personality attributes, personal and professional life histories, and the subject's own views on his motivations to succeed. Silver then sent the questionnaire to one hundred entrepreneurs who had made at least $20 million from their enterprise. He got fifty-four responses, from which he formulated his own profile.[3]

Silver found that his entrepreneurs rarely came from the bottom of the economic ladder but were born to mostly extroverted middle-class parents who encouraged their children to succeed, gain recognition, and attain leadership roles in their communities. Those who struggled upward from the bottom, he concluded, were "too frequently full of bitterness and resentment to make a long-running success of their business." At the same time, the typical entrepreneur did not have a pampered childhood. His father either died early or was absent much of the time, leaving a "devoted, attentive mother" to hold the family together and spur the children onward. The young entrepreneur also bore a heavy burden of guilt and endured some form of deprivation as an adolescent, the most common being small size, physical illness, less wealth than his peers, poor educational development, or skin problems.[4]

From these roots emerged a pattern of development. The young entrepreneur-to-be left home, went to work, married, started a family, and then matured in a way that led him at some point to reject childhood values abruptly and violently. Cast adrift, he developed a new set of values and with them a new sense of purpose that drove him down the entrepreneurial path to do some one thing well. He let nothing stand in his way of realizing this quest. The suddenness of this shift, and the financial sacrifices required to carry it out, often threatened or destroyed his marriage, creating yet another source of guilt that spurred him onward. This was one reason why Silver thought that bachelors made poor entrepreneurs. Having never committed to a family, they had "much lighter guilt baggage to carry around. Less guilt transfers into less drive. The biggest strike against the bachelor is that he has not made and may not be able to make commitments."[5]

This profile pertains only to modern entrepreneurs and probably does not include among its ranks any who might qualify as one of the great entrepreneurs. Nevertheless, it offers a starting point for comparison with our pool of talent, who themselves are separated out by history. If one looks at their careers rather than birth or death dates, the twenty-six entrepreneurs embrace three distinct periods of American economic development: the nineteenth century, the "bridge period" (defined here as 1890–1914), and the twentieth century. To give them labels, they are the eras of enterprise, organization, and technology. By this definition, six of the entrepreneurs belong to the nineteenth century (Andrew Carnegie, Thomas A. Edison, Jay Gould, Cyrus McCormick, John D. Rockefeller, and Cornelius Vanderbilt), ten to the bridge period (James Duke, George Eastman, E. H. Harriman, Samuel Insull, John Patterson, James Penney, Theodore Vail, John Wanamaker, George Westinghouse, and Frank Woolworth), and ten to the twentieth century (Warren Buffett, Pierre du Pont, William Durant, Henry Ford, Bill Gates, Ray Kroc, Edwin Land, Robert Noyce, Sam Walton, and Thomas Watson).

This distribution makes sense in that the bridge period includes the years when the industrial economy underwent startling growth and consolidation and the consumer economy first emerged—what I have called the "Third America" in a book that characterized the entire period from 1860 to 1920 as the "Making of an Organizational Society." For this study I have divided that era into two parts; the second of these, the bridge period, is in many respects the pivotal era, linking the capital-goods economy of the nineteenth century with the consumer-goods economy of the twentieth century. As the organizational revolution transformed every aspect of American economic and social life during these years, it laid the structural foundation for the profound changes that were to reshape American life after World War I. In this sense the great entrepreneurs of that period were present at the creation, building on the accomplishments of their predecessors and laying the groundwork for their successors.[6]

Obviously this distribution also differentiates the early years and upbringing of our entrepreneurs. Seventeen of them were born before or during the Civil War, and only six during the twentieth century. The group contains only two immigrants (Carnegie and Insull) and one figure born into considerable wealth (du Pont). A dozen spent all or part of their childhood on farms, from which every one of them longed to escape. Twelve grew up in fairly comfortable middle-class homes, but a few of their number lived near the poverty line or underwent a sudden change of circumstances. Buffett's father lost his job and savings during the depression but managed to rebuild a secure financial base for his family. Duke's father was ruined by the Civil War but restored the family farm and processed tobacco. Durant's father abandoned the family when William was eleven, but his mother moved to Flint, Michigan, and lived comfortably with help from her father, a prominent Bostonian.

Carnegie's father was a weaver in Scotland who had lost his trade to mechanization before the family migrated to America. They arrived here virtually penniless. The death of George Eastman's father when George was fourteen plunged his family into genteel poverty, forcing his mother to move and then take in boarders. Edison's childhood was a financial roller coaster because his father was an unreliable provider. Gould's father always struggled to get by, first with a farm and then with a tin shop. Watson grew up with his four older sisters in a "cramped four-room cabin with no running water" near Painted Post, New York. His father did fairly well as a farmer until he became too ill to work. "I was absolutely sure that I was a smarter man than my father," Watson admitted.

"I was positive of that. I felt that I could prove it, if I were called upon to prove it." Vanderbilt's parents were hardworking farm people but never well off. Although Harriman's father was a minister, his attempts at earning a living were ineffectual and unrealistic. Penney's father was a good farmer and minister but always had to struggle for money. Woolworth's father was a farmer cursed with a streak of impracticality. "We had enough to eat," said Frank's brother Charles, "but the struggle to make ends meet was never absent."[7]

By far the strangest and most difficult childhood belonged to Rockefeller, whose father was a charismatic charmer and con man, as likable as he was untrustworthy. Big Bill Rockefeller was absent from home for long stretches, peddling snake oil or wooing local beauties. Often he returned with a thick wad of bills for his efforts, but the family endured constant swings between comfort and insecurity and moved several times before finally settling in Cleveland. At that point in his life, however, Big Bill, having earlier fathered two illegitimate children with another woman, secretly married a young Ontario girl, using the name Dr. William Levingston, and started another family. During the late 1850s he moved his new family to Philadelphia and managed to maintain this bigamous deception for the rest of his long life. This bizarre arrangement, and its effect on the family, plagued John D. Rockefeller for most of his days.[8]

Some of the entrepreneurs had financially comfortable childhoods. Buffett's father did well after recovering from his losses. Du Pont never wanted for anything material; neither did Gates, whose father was a well-connected attorney, or Vail, whose father managed an ironworks, or Wanamaker, whose father made bricks, or Land, whose father owned a prosperous salvage and scrap metal business. Insull's father had a streak of impracticality but ran a small dairy and then got a government post in Oxford that made the family comfortable for a time as well as providing a good education for his sons. Noyce's father was a minister in Iowa who moved around the state but kept the family stable. Walton's father, hardworking, careful with money, and a good trader, kept his family secure. Ford, McCormick, Patterson, and Westinghouse all grew up in the perpetual rural borderland between comfort and want.

For several of the entrepreneurs, however, financial security proved no buffer against emotional insecurity. Du Pont found himself the man of the family at fourteen when his father died in a plant explosion. Carnegie, Durant, and Eastman all lost their fathers at young ages, and in a sense so did Rockefeller even though Big Bill was very much alive. Duke's mother died when he was two, and Ford was devastated by the death of his mother when he was thirteen. Gould suffered the loss of his mother and two stepmothers by the age of nine. Buffett endured the private hell of a normally sweet and caring mother who fell into uncontrollable rages at the children, the more terrifying for being unpredictable. There was no escape from her savage verbal assaults. One effect on a young, cowering Warren was to impel him to shy away from conflict of any kind. Walton's parents were quarrelsome and never got along.[9]

Silver's notion of the "devoted, attentive mother" fits only a few of the great entrepreneurs. Carnegie was so devoted to his mother that he courted few women and put off marriage until the age of fifty-one, after his mother's death. Vanderbilt and Watson were always devoted to their mothers; Eastman, too, remained close to his mother all her life and never married. He had many women friends, but all were safely married. Edison and Rockefeller were both deeply influenced by pious, straitlaced mothers given to instilling stern values in their sons. Edison was twenty-four when his mother died; three weeks later his father took up with a local teenager by whom he had three more children. Harriman's mother provided the strong will, determination, backbone, and deep sense of family lacking in his father. Although Gates always got on well with his father, the driving force in his family was his mother. "In many ways," his biographers have observed, "Bill is something of a mamma's boy." Du Pont and Durant grew up close to their mothers but neither seem to have been unduly influenced or shaped by them. For Buffett, Duke, Gould, McCormick, Westinghouse, and probably Vail, the dominant influence came from their fathers. Of his dad, Buffett said, "I have never known a better human being."[10]

Neither does religion offer a cohesive insight into the great entrepreneurs. Many had parents who were deeply religious; three were the sons of ministers. Yet among this group only McCormick, Rockefeller, Wanamaker, and Penney were deeply inspired by religion and ordered their lives around it. The first three embraced their faiths at an early age, while Penney underwent a profound "miracle" of conversion in his fifties that changed his life. Others, notably Harriman and Watson, believed strongly in going to church but religion did not noticeably influence their business careers. Vail thought early of becoming a minister but soon lost the urge. So did Wanamaker, who said, "I would have become a minister, but the idea clung to my mind that I could accomplish more in the same domain if I became a merchant and acquired means and influence with my fellow merchants." Carnegie shed the Swenborgian beliefs of his father in favor of a humanist universalism. Land was bar mitzvahed but took little interest in religion or Jewish causes. Insull came from a family of dissenters and was indifferent to religion but tolerant of all creeds. Edison was an agnostic who dismissed God as an abstraction. Gates, too, became an agnostic, "loyal to no church other than a binary one."[11]

Education offers little that explains their success except perhaps in a negative role. Half of the entrepreneurs got as far as high school, but only five—Buffett, du Pont, Noyce, Patterson, and Walton—graduated from college as well. Of that group only Noyce and Buffett went on to graduate studies; Noyce earned a

Ph.D. in physics from the Massachusetts Institute of Technology, Buffett a master of science in economics from Columbia. However, Buffett has always been scornful of academic theorists. Four of the five college graduates belong to the twentieth century; the fifth, Patterson, got little from college and distrusted educated men all his life. "What I learned mostly," he said later, "was what not to do."[12]

Westinghouse enlisted in the Union army and tried college after being mustered out in 1865, but after three months he hurried back to the family shop. Gates started at Harvard but dropped out after his junior year. Later he told a friend that he went hoping to learn from people smarter than he was but left disappointed. Land entered Harvard at seventeen after graduating from Norwich Academy only to leave after one year to concentrate on his own research; he returned two years later but left again to go into business before receiving his degree. Durant and Rockefeller both dropped out of high school in the spring of their senior year to go to work. Rockefeller, Watson, and Woolworth all managed to take courses at commercial colleges.[13]

A few of the entrepreneurs valued education even though they got precious little of it. Gould was a voracious reader all his life. Insull received a solid education at schools in Oxford and maintained a life of the mind. Penney, whose father was a college graduate, believed strongly in the value of education, as did Wanamaker, who said, "Whatever education I have received has been picked up as I went along—just as a locomotive scoops up water without stopping." Gates conceded that he "got a pretty good education [at Harvard] even though I didn't stay long enough to get my degree," and thought that in the modern, complex world, "a college education [is] as critical today as a high school education was at one time." Few of the other entrepreneurs shared this belief. Duke, Kroc, Vanderbilt, and Westinghouse all hated school, and Vail had no use for it, saying that "schools teach too much science and unpractical things. Young men grow up to think the world owes them a living." Buffett quipped that "it seems like a waste to go to school and get a Ph.D. in economics. It's a little like spending eight years in divinity school and having someone tell you the ten commandments are all that matter."[14]

Penney believed that "the finest education for the young man or woman is that education which springs from the demands of the job itself." Although Kroc later gained renown for founding Hamburger University as the McDonald's training center, he never lost his dim view of higher education. He flatly refused to give money to any college that did not have a trade school, explaining that "our colleges are crowded with young people who are learning a lot about the liberal arts and little about earning a living." Yet many of the entrepreneurs donated huge sums to colleges and universities. Rockefeller founded the University of Chicago from scratch, while Duke and Vanderbilt upgraded tiny schools into major institutions bearing their names.[15]

For many of the entrepreneurs, education was only a brief interlude to be savored or endured before going to work. It is no surprise to find that most of the nineteenth-century boys headed off to work at early ages. A host of them were put to work on the family farm as soon as they could manage chores, then went on to other jobs. Edison started hawking newspapers and sundries on trains at twelve, the same age at which Vanderbilt started hauling produce from Staten Island to New York City in his father's boat. Carnegie found work as a bobbin boy in a textile mill at thirteen. At fourteen, Eastman found a post as an office boy in an insurance firm, Harriman became a pad shover on Wall Street, Wanamaker got a job as an errand boy for a Philadelphia publisher, and Westinghouse began working in his father's machine shop for fifty cents a day. Insull was fifteen when he started as an office boy for an auction firm. Gould left home at sixteen and made himself into a surveyor, while Ford went to Detroit at the same age to seek a job as a mechanic. At sixteen, Rockefeller dropped out of high school to find a job in the office of a commission merchant.

Duke, McCormick, and Westinghouse all worked with their fathers in a family business. Durant's first job consisted of stacking lumber in a family-owned lumberyard. Penney and Woolworth followed a common path, toiling first on the family farm and then finding jobs as clerks in the stores of local merchants—Penney at twenty and Woolworth at twenty-one. After a year of business college, Watson took a job as a bookkeeper but soon left it for one selling organs and pianos on the road. Vail, the least ambitious of our group, worked in a drugstore while in high school, then drifted to New York at nineteen to seek work in a telegraph office. His father was fond of saying that he expected to support his son in the years to come.[16] Patterson returned from college at twenty-three and could find no better post than that of toll collector on a local canal. Unable to support himself this way, he developed a wood and coal business on the side. Du Pont was spared the trouble of working as a boy by his family's wealth.

Necessity compelled most of the nineteenth-century entrepreneurs to seek work at an early age. Yet their later counterparts, though raised in more comfortable circumstances, followed a similar work pattern without leaving home. Buffett had paper routes at a very early age and turned them into a profitable business. While still in high school, he and a friend bought a used pinball machine for twenty-five dollars, installed it in a barber shop, and soon netted fifty dollars a week from it. Fascinated by stocks, he began charting their prices and bought his first shares of stock at eleven; at fourteen he used $1,200 of his paper-route profits to buy forty acres of Nebraska farmland. Walton, too, created thriving paper routes and sold magazines when he was only eight. He worked steadily at these and other jobs through high school and college. Using subcontractors during his college years, he earned nearly $5,000 from his paper routes during a depression year.[17]

Noyce worked at odd jobs to earn spending money as a kid and tinkered in his father's basement workshop. "I was drifting from flower to flower," he recalled, "trying to understand how the universe worked. . . . I think a small town has some significant advantages, particularly in that you can see a one-to-one relationship between work and success." During his senior year at Grinnell College, he was expelled for a prank and went to New York to work in the actuarial department of Equitable Life. The stay exposed him to Broadway shows and other delights. It also taught him something about statistics and their misuse. Although he passed all of his actuarial examinations, he decided that the insurance business was not for him. "I went into it with the idea that this was a secure and comfortable place to be," he recalled. "I came out of it with the feeling that it was a terribly boring place to be." Instead he returned to finish his degree at Grinnell and went on to MIT for his doctorate. In choosing his first job, he passed over the large established research laboratories in favor of Philco, a smaller company where he would not be stuffed into a pigeonhole but could do many different jobs and pick up a variety of skills.[18]

Although Gates did not need to work, he joined with some friends to create a payroll program for a company in exchange for free time on one of the early computers. "To look back now and think—geez, how did I get addicted to something like that?" he marveled. "It's hard to understand." Kroc found a job behind the soda counter of his uncle's drugstore when he was a freshman in high school. Land apparently did not work as a youngster, but his interest in science absorbed him at an early age. He devoured both novels and the physics textbooks of his mother, who had studied the subject at Norwich Free Academy—the same school that Land attended. Unlike their earlier counterparts, none of these four men had to work as boys to help their families. From this brief survey emerges one clear and unsurprising pattern: Whether from necessity or desire, nearly all of the entrepreneurs jumped early into work of some kind and developed a work ethic that served them well in later years.[19]

For some, the lesson came straight from their parents. Penney's father taught him "to magnify every job . . . make everything . . . count for something. . . . No work is menial." To ram the point of self-reliance home, he took the boy aside one evening after supper and said, "Jim, I just want you to understand. From now on you'll be buying your own clothes." Penney was eight years old at the time. "But Paw," protested Penney, "my shoes have holes, both of 'em. Could you get me a new pair, then let me start in?" His father shook his head. "No. You'll have to figure something out." In one respect at least, Big Bill Rockefeller proved a devoted father. He talked constantly about money and instructed young John in all the rules for its handling—one of which was to steadfastly keep sentiment from influencing business decisions. It was he who taught John to keep meticulous accounts, and he may also have inspired the boy's passion for religion by offering him five dollars if he read the Bible from cover to cover. The boy learned his lessons well; at fifteen he was already lending small sums to his father, charging whatever interest the traffic would bear.[20]

As young men, only a few of the entrepreneurs had a fascination for money and aspired to be rich. All of them longed for a better life and recognized that it required wealth. Buffett, Gates, Gould, Harriman, Penney, Rockefeller, and Woolworth had a special passion for becoming rich someday. Buffett, deeply impressed by his father's experience during the depression, talked about it as early as age five. "I'm going to be rich," young Jay Gould told a friend. "I've seen enough to realize what can be accomplished by means of riches, and I tell you I'm going to be rich. . . . I have no immediate plan. . . . I only see the goal. Plans must be formed along the way." Rockefeller echoed this sentiment, telling a friend, "Someday, sometime, when I am a man, I want to be worth a hundred-thousand dollars. And I'm going to be, too—someday." Gates told a friend in eleventh grade that he would be worth a million dollars by the age of thirty; before heading off to Harvard he told another friend, "I'm going to make my first million by the time I'm twenty-five." Few others put the matter so frankly. Penney expressed a more typical response when he recalled that "all through those [early] years, our minds were exclusively taken up with business and making money."[21]

Even Vail reached a point where he exclaimed in exasperation, "I have had all of the dam' farm I want. I am going where I can make some money." Watson understood the importance of money much as Gould did. "They say money isn't everything," he observed. "It isn't everything, but [it] is a great big something when you are trying to get started in the world and haven't anything. I speak feelingly." All of the entrepreneurs burned with ambition and recognized that money was both an instrument for realizing their goals and the scorecard for measuring their success. None cared to be without money, yet the subject raised ambivalent feelings in some of them. "I was in business to make money," Carnegie admitted freely, and at twenty-eight rejoiced, "I'm rich; I'm rich." Five years later, in a memo to himself, he wrote that "the amassing of wealth is one of the worse species of idolatry. No idol more debasing than the worship of money." Rockefeller also tried to keep his distance from its corrupting influence. "The impression was gaining ground with me," he recalled, "that it was a good thing to let the money be my slave and not make myself a slave to money."[22]

However much money might have been an end in itself, it cannot alone explain the incredible drive shown by all the entrepreneurs. Nor can it account for the vision or competitiveness most of them possessed at an early age. Even Pierre du Pont, who might have cruised comfortably through life, revealed a strong determination to succeed at everything he took up. Edison, called by one historian a "compulsive achiever," thrived on competition.

"I don't care so much about making my fortune," he said, ". . . as I do for getting ahead of the other fellow." Buck Duke recalled, "I resolved from the time I was a mere boy to do a big business. . . . I loved business better than anything else." Harriman too was driven by an overpowering desire to succeed, which made him an unrelenting competitor in everything he did. "Business is a good game," said Bill Gates. "Lots of competition and a minimum of rules. You keep score with money." No one competed more ferociously than he did. Sam Walton admitted that "I have always pursued everything I was interested in with a true passion—some would say obsession—to win." Rockefeller summed it up for all the entrepreneurs when he said simply, "I was after something big."[23]

The quest for something big required ambition, a competitive streak, vision, a strong will to succeed, endless energy, and a powerful work ethic—all of which can be found in our entrepreneurs. Did this blend of qualities require a certain type of personality or particular set of physical traits? Evidently not, if the sample used here is any indication. These twenty-six men represent a wide variety of sizes, shapes, and characteristics. Carnegie, Durant, Harriman, Kroc, Noyce, Vail, Walton, and Wanamaker were ebullient and outgoing, while du Pont, Eastman, Gould, Land, and Westinghouse were shy and protective of their privacy. Several were strong, strapping men; others were small and somewhat frail. Duke, Ford, Gates, and Vanderbilt were as crude and gruff as du Pont, Insull, Noyce, and Vail were polished and mannered. Where Duke, Gates, Harriman, McCormick, Patterson, Vanderbilt, and Watson could be forceful or intimidating, Buffett, du Pont, Eastman, Gould, and Walton came across as aloof or self-effacing.

Some relished sports—Kroc bought a baseball team and both Vail and Harriman played the game—as much as others disdained them. A surprising number had a passion for flowers, most notably Duke, du Pont, Eastman, Gould, and McCormick. Gould owned what was at the time the largest private greenhouse in the nation; du Pont created one of the great botanical collections in the world at his Longwood estate. Where Carnegie, Eastman, Ford, Gould, Harriman, Insull, Noyce, and Vail developed a variety of outside interests, Durant, Edison, Patterson, Penney, Vanderbilt, Westinghouse, and Woolworth had practically none at all. Duke, Gould, Harriman, McCormick, Vail, and Vanderbilt loved horses, especially trotters; Edison despised the animal. Buffett loved playing bridge. "I've always said," he once observed, "I wouldn't mind going to jail if I had three cell mates who played bridge." Gates became absorbed by the Japanese game of Go and majored in poker at Harvard. Kroc enjoyed playing the piano and did it for a living in his youth. As a young man, Noyce sang in choruses, acted in plays and on radio, played the oboe, and was a diver on the Grinnell College championship swim team. Walton's true passion, which he called "my one self-indulgent activity," was bird hunting.[24]

As might be expected of men with unusual drive and energy, most of the entrepreneurs enjoyed robust health in their youth, but there are exceptions. Gould suffered a near-fatal illness at eighteen that required months of recovery. Penney fell ill at twenty-two, quit his job, and moved to Colorado because he was thought to be consumptive. Both Wanamaker and Woolworth were frail children. Wanamaker contracted tuberculosis at nineteen and, like Penney, went west to seek a cure. Woolworth's health broke down when he was twenty-three, forcing him back to the family farm for months of recuperation. Although a big, strapping farm boy, Duke suffered from a pigeon-toe condition so severe that it bordered on deformity. Despite these setbacks, every one of these men not only recovered but afterward plunged into their work with phenomenal vigor.

The marital pattern of the entrepreneurs bears only a superficial resemblance to Silver's profile. Fifteen of them married in their twenties, three in their thirties, and five in their forties. Vanderbilt wed at nineteen, Carnegie at fifty-one, and Eastman remained a bachelor. Of the twenty-five who married, fifteen remained so until one of the partners died. Gates also remains married. Three others lost their wives and remarried (Penney did so twice); only Patterson remained alone after his wife died. Four of the men—Duke, Durant, Kroc (twice), and Noyce—divorced and remarried. At last report Buffett remains separated from but close to his wife. Several of the marriages, most notably those of Insull, Vanderbilt, and Watson, endured despite severe inner tensions; many more, including Carnegie, Gould, Harriman, Land, Rockefeller, Vail, Walton, Westinghouse, and Wanamaker seemed to be good matches and partnerships. If, as Silver asserts, these entrepreneurs were driven by guilt, it did not in most cases stem from their marriages.

If one tries to discover who inspired or shaped the entrepreneurs as young men, the results are both mixed and surprising. In four cases both names are on the list. Edison became a dominant influence on the careers of both Ford and Insull, Patterson was the mentor for Watson, and Walton borrowed heavily from Penney's philosophy. Buffett, Duke, and McCormick were all deeply influenced by their fathers; Buffett also owed much to one of his professors at Columbia, Benjamin Graham. Seven men drew upon other mentors for their education or inspiration. For Carnegie that influential figure was Tom Scott of the Pennsylvania Railroad, for du Pont it was businessman Tom Johnson, and for Land the nineteenth-century physicist Michael Faraday. Penney drew the basic idea for his approach to retailing from his first employers, Guy Johnson and Michael Callahan; Woolworth regarded his early employer W. H. Moore as his mentor. Noyce owed much to his college physics teacher, Grant O. Gale, and to Nobel Prize–winning physicist William Bradford Shockley. However, half the men on the list reveal no clear-cut dominant influence or inspiration on their careers.

It should be obvious by now that a portrait of the entrepreneur as a young man is more a gallery of portraits in which no one size fits all. These twenty-six men were as distinctive as individuals as they were at business, and no formula comes even close to encapsulating their personalities or characteristics. Their group portrait offers the wanna-be entrepreneur no clear profile of background, behavior, or beliefs. If they had all filled out Silver's questionnaire, the results would doubtless have befuddled social scientists eager to find patterns. There is, in short, no "typical" great entrepreneur and never has been. If the sample were doubled or tripled, it is highly likely that the results would magnify their differences more than their similarities.

What, then, do the great entrepreneurs have in common besides success on a grand scale? The answer lies in a set of traits that are neither surprising nor new. They all possessed ambition, which eventually took the form of some compelling vision that drove them to realize it at whatever cost. In that quest they all had unflagging energy fueling a work ethic that did not always follow the usual rules but did produce results. They all showed an overpowering desire to succeed and the strength of will to let no obstacle stand in their way. And they were strongly motivated by whatever elements in their lives combined to spur them onward. More than that, they tended to be fiercely competitive, driven to win at whatever they took up. Although few of them ever mentioned or would even admit such a thing, they were probably driven by the greatest goad of all: the fear of failure.

| 3 |

The Entrepreneurs and
Their Visions

Microsoft won't be immortal. All companies fail. It's just a
question of when. My goal is to keep my company vital as
long as possible.   —BILL GATES[1]

Artists are regarded as agents of change. So are entrepreneurs,
and the great entrepreneurs, like great artists, serve as instruments
of change. The two types share some important characteristics.
They possess streaks of originality in their work and an ability to
conceive new approaches to it. This gift for seeing past the conventional wisdom and viewing things with fresh eyes leads them to
insights that galvanize their work. The great entrepreneurs also
possess a wide variety of talents and developed styles of their own
that maximized their abilities. They often come to the source of
their greatest achievements through a painful process of trial and
error marked by failures. Many were more criticized than appreciated or honored for their accomplishments in their lifetime. Their
talents spawn imitation as well as resentment.

  Like other creative people, the great entrepreneurs usually
began with some flash of insight, a vision of what could be done
and how, followed by an obsessive quest to realize it. Twenty-six

men, twenty-six visions, each of them filled with commonplace, even obvious, elements put together in a unique way and fueled by a voracious determination to bring them to fruition. Like all great artists, they worked within different mediums dictated by their interests and by the times in which they lived. For our purposes, the twenty-six entrepreneurs can be divided into five broad mediums, or "schools": the producers, the organizers, the merchandisers, the technologists, and the investors.

> PRODUCERS: Andrew Carnegie, James Duke, George
> Eastman, Henry Ford, Cyrus McCormick, John Patterson,
> John D. Rockefeller
> ORGANIZERS: Pierre du Pont, William Durant, Jay Gould,
> E. H. Harriman, Samuel Insull, Theodore Vail, Cornelius
> Vanderbilt
> MERCHANDISERS: Ray Kroc, James Penney, Samuel Walton,
> John Wanamaker, Frank Woolworth
> TECHNOLOGISTS: Thomas Edison, Bill Gates, Edwin Land,
> Robert Noyce, Thomas Watson, George Westinghouse
> INVESTORS: Warren Buffett

Obviously this division is somewhat arbitrary. The talents of many individuals extended to more than one medium. Rockefeller was also a supreme organizer, Eastman a splendid technologist. McCormick might also qualify as an organizer or a technologist. Artists often work in more than one medium, and their work in one can be examined without damage to that in others. Nor were all the entrepreneurs ultimately successful in their medium. Durant conceived and founded a great organization but proved utterly incapable of managing it. Gould was superb at development, less so at management. Many of the entrepreneurs possessed a great talent in a medium not included: salesmanship.

The Producers

Among the producers, Carnegie and Rockefeller stand alone in developing giant industries around basic resources. The other five men created products that, once introduced, became an indispensable part of American life. Four of those products were machines or new technologies; the fifth relied on a new machine to make mass production of it possible. All seven men succeeded in redefining their industry and elevating it to unprecedented scales of production. Each one had a vision that drove him to this highest level of achievement.

Carnegie envisioned a virtually limitless market for iron and steel—first from rails, bridges, and other products for railroads, and then with the beams required for the multistoried buildings that were transforming the hearts of cities. He saw that iron and steel held the key to industrialization and believed they could be produced in huge quantities by maximizing efficiency of operation. For him this meant, above all, an unremitting effort to lower costs and introduce new techniques and technologies as quickly as possible. If a better method or technology appeared, he did not hesitate to tear down even a new facility to install it. He introduced accounting and strict costing into his shops, and brought the Siemens gas furnace into his works because the numbers told him it would raise profits by cutting unit costs—a basic truth that did not dawn on his competitors for many years. In a field ruled by the practical lore of iron masters, he introduced principles of chemistry into the operation of blast furnaces.[2]

Where other iron makers shut down in hard times, Carnegie kept his furnaces operating. He believed in expanding during depression years when costs were low. This approach gave him a decisive competitive advantage when prosperity returned. As Jonathan Hughes put it, "He bought in depressions, rebuilt in depressions, restaffed in depressions, then undercut his competitors when business was good." The results were astonishing. When Carnegie started out, the British ruled the iron and steel world. Carnegie's ruthless efficiency drove the price of steel rails down from $160 a ton in 1875 to $17 a ton in 1898, and the lower price still fetched record profits for him. By 1901, Carnegie's plants turned out 80 percent as much steel as all the works in Great Britain combined. Even Alfred Krupp's steelworks in Germany, with its renowned "Prussian discipline," could not approach Carnegie's productivity. The four thousand workers at Carnegie's Homestead plant turned out three times as much steel as did the fifteen thousand men in Krupp's works.[3]

What Carnegie did for iron and steel, Rockefeller did for oil in an age when the industry was still very new, the overall supply of oil unknown, and its chief use remained illumination. He saw that the oil industry was destined for great growth if rigid efficiency and coordination could be imposed on its chaotic state. Like Carnegie, he monitored costs closely and drove them steadily downward. Like Carnegie, too, he believed that the way to eliminate competitors was to *eliminate* them—either by crushing them or by buying them out. By 1877 he had rationalized the oil refining business and controlled 90 percent of the oil refined in the United States. He then expanded rapidly into transportation and production until he dominated 25 percent of all American crude production, humbled the railroads into giving him rebates on not only his own oil but also on that of his competitors, and then created a pipeline empire to replace the railroads.[4]

Rockefeller forged this gigantic empire by creating new forms of organization that became the model for big business in America. First came the trust in 1882 and then the holding company in 1889, which enabled Standard Oil to perfect its brilliant committee-based organization, governed by a group of executives among whom Rockefeller functioned not as dictator but as first among equals.

The result was a colossus that oversaw 20,000 wells producing oil that traveled through 4,000 miles of pipelines and 5,000 tank cars to giant refineries in key locations. Standard Oil employed 100,000 people and exported 50,000 barrels of oil to Europe daily. "That he created one of the first multinational corporations," wrote Ron Chernow, "selling kerosene around the world and setting a business pattern for the next century, was arguably his greatest feat."[5]

James "Buck" Duke also created a multinational corporation, British-American Tobacco (BAT), called by his biographer "the nearest approach to a world trust ever organized in any industry." Duke saw that a new technology, the Bonsack machine, could bring the efficiency and profits of mass production to the moribund cigarette industry. He also believed that relentless marketing and advertising could turn the lowly cigarette into a national habit. By staking his business future on a balky, unproven machine that no other manufacturer wanted, and by pouring unprecedented sums into promoting his brands, Duke vaulted from nowhere to dominance of what would become a giant industry. As Robert Sobel observed, "Duke operated in a less vital field than did Carnegie or Morgan, but he controlled it more completely than either man." By 1901 his companies produced nearly 93 percent of all cigarettes, 80 percent of the snuff, 62 percent of the plug tobacco, and 59 percent of the smoking tobacco made in the United States.[6]

When it was perfected in 1884, the Bonsack machine produced 12,000 cigarettes its first day compared to 2,500 rolled by an exceptional workman. Improvements raised that figure, and Duke secured a virtual monopoly on the machines, which enabled him to churn out 250,000 cigarettes each day at a cost well below that of his competitors. His aggressive and imaginative marketing also induced rival firms to join him. Like Rockefeller, Duke forged a gigantic firm to dominate his industry through both horizontal and vertical integration. Created in 1890, American Tobacco Company proved an astounding cash cow; for eighteen years it netted annually 33 percent on its tangible assets and had 40 percent profit margins on the sale of its cigarettes. By 1898 it was exporting 1.2 billion cigarettes, a third of its output. Duke's invasion of the British market led to an agreement in 1902 with Imperial Tobacco to form BAT as a vehicle for American and Imperial to conquer the rest of the world market.[7]

George Eastman shared Duke's vision of a worldwide market for his product, but for a very different purpose. In an age when photography was still a young and technically complex art limited to professionals and diligent amateurs, Eastman saw an unlimited market among ordinary people eager to record their past and present if a much cheaper and simpler camera, film, and development process could be created. He proceeded to do this so effectively that by 1897 the camera had become a permanent fixture in American culture. "By separating the two main functions of photography— the picture taking and the processing—Eastman revolutionized the industry," noted his biographer. Even more important, he developed "a whole system that included the machinery and the standardized parts to deliver it. The last major gap between everyman and photography was filled in." In doing this he pioneered in mass production "while Henry Ford was still learning to be a machinist," and changed his model lines "long before the idea of planned obsolescence hit the automotive industry."[8]

When Eastman bought his first camera in 1877, he paid $49.58 plus another $5 for lessons on how to use it. Developing the film was also expensive and required special skills. Eleven years later he offered the public his new Kodak camera for $25 and provided a printing and enlarging service as well. In marketing his new device, Eastman coined its original name, wrote much of the advertising, and came up with what has long been deemed one of the best slogans ever: "You press the button, we do the rest." In 1901 he completed the revolution with another new camera, the Brownie, which sold for one dollar plus another fifteen cents for the film. Eastman understood that the camera was really a device to sell film. He did far more than merely democratize photography; he institutionalized the preservation of memories and shoved American culture down the path of substituting visual for verbal communication.[9]

What Eastman did for memory, Henry Ford did for mobility. As Jonathan Hughes put it, "Ford liberated the common man on a greater scale than any hero in history. . . . After the Model T, no American had to work or live or *be* in any place that did not appeal to him." Ford's single, unrelenting vision was to produce a simple, reliable, durable automobile that anyone could afford. He succeeded beyond his wildest dreams and in the process transformed not only American culture but the face of the nation as well. In the process he gave the new century—the age of consumerism—an advanced version of its most important principle, mass production, which allowed high volume at low cost. "I will build a motor car for the great multitude," Ford declared in 1907, "constructed of the best materials by the best men . . . after the simplest designs that modern engineering can devise . . . so low in price that no man making a good salary will be unable to own one—and enjoy with his family the blessings of hours of pleasure in God's great open space."[10]

One year later he delivered on his promise. The Model T infatuated Americans as no machine had before and no car ever would again. As Peter Drucker observed, he designed a car "that could be totally mass-produced, largely by semi-skilled labor, and . . . driven by the owner and repaired by him." The first Model T in 1908 cost $850, much cheaper than nearly anything else on the market; by 1927, the model's final year, the price had dropped to $263. Ford's plant at Highland Park, north of Detroit, became the prototype for innovation in mass production with its moving assembly line, interchangeable parts, and unprecedented wage of five dollars a day. It was soon dwarfed by the gigantic River Rouge plant, which employed nearly a hundred thousand workers. From these temples of production a new Model T poured forth every forty-five seconds. By 1926 Ford had sold more than half the cars made in the nation and more than doubled the output of his nearest rival, General Motors.[11]

Cyrus McCormick liberated the farmer and his helpers from the toil of harvesting grain by hand, which had been their lot since the dawn of agriculture. His first reaper, developed in 1831, could clear ten acres a day using eight men and a horse or two, a figure that required five men with scythes and ten helpers to match. Although not the only such machine invented, his reaper was the first and only one to contain all seven parts that remained essential to later versions into the next century. McCormick's vision lay not only in his invention but in his sense that a huge market for it could be realized only if he could produce in quantity, maintain strict quality control, and create a network of agents to sell the machines and provide service for them afterward. He invented not only a device that revolutionized agriculture but also a business system that became a model for the automobile industry, among others.[12]

Sensing where his future markets lay, McCormick moved to Chicago in 1848 and erected a factory there to build as many reapers as he could sell. Other machines, such as the harvester and automatic binder, soon followed. Selling a seasonal product enabled him to improve each year's model and organize an efficient factory system. It also allowed McCormick to concentrate on promotion and sales, which were crucial to a new product that customers had to be taught how to use. The system of agents he developed served to promote and service his machines as well as sell them. McCormick prepared descriptive pamphlets that advertised the machine and instructed in its use and care. He even provided credit to buyers. Like Rockefeller and Duke, he invaded overseas markets and made the reaper a worldwide product.[13]

Unlike McCormick, John H. Patterson did not invent his machine or have a market waiting eagerly for it. His vision lay in a simple syllogism: "Every merchant must account for cash. The cash register accounts for cash. Therefore, every merchant needs a cash register." Formerly a successful coal dealer, Patterson bought control of a failing company at age forty. With no manufacturing experience whatever, he renamed it the National Cash Register Company (NCR) and transformed it into a wildly successful business. After making significant improvements to the machine, he created a unique approach to selling and advertising a device that no one wanted. Business owners were dubious; their clerks, many of whose fingers had long been in the till, were fearful and hostile. The cash register was considered "a challenge to honesty."[14]

To overcome these prejudices, Patterson constantly improved his machines. More important, he changed salesmanship from a haphazard vocation into a serious profession using scientific methods. He put his agents on commission and gave them exclusive territories—both new ideas at the time—and in 1894 opened the nation's first training school for salesmen. Like McCormick, he devised instructional advertising that was simple to grasp, but Patterson flooded potential customers with it. In one case he sent five thousand merchants a mailing for eighteen straight days. He rejected the notion that a market could be saturated and in 1900 instituted the quota system for his agents. Sending his first representative abroad in 1885, he persevered until he developed a large foreign business. As one writer said of him, "Patterson made the world his market and his cash register an indispensable aid to business."[15]

The Organizers

All seven of these men created organizations where none had existed before. Some inherited companies and remade them into something else; others created them from scratch. Vanderbilt,

Gould, and Harriman left their imprint on the first big business in America, the railroads; Gould also played a key role in the telegraph industry. Durant, Insull, and Vail pioneered in organizing three industries rooted in new technologies: the automobile, electric power, and the telephone. Du Pont took a very old family firm and transformed it into a very modern corporation; later he stepped into Durant's poorly managed company and converted it into an efficient and dominant organization. As individuals and businessmen, the organizers stand out as the most diverse of our five groups. They could hardly be more different in personality.

The exploits of Cornelius Vanderbilt, the earliest of our entrepreneurs, might seem modest in comparison with the others, yet they were no less important. For more than forty years Vanderbilt loomed as the most imposing figure in both key forms of early transportation, steamships and railroads. From the New York river trade and later coastal shipping, Vanderbilt earned a fortune exceeding $20 million by the eve of the Civil War. Then, at the advanced age of sixty-six, he transferred his interest to railroads and put together one of the two strongest systems in the young nation, the New York Central. He saw that a group of local, ramshackle roads could become enormously profitable if welded together in a strong organization and given efficient management. Near the end of his life, amid the worst depression the country had yet known, he boldly spent $40 million to transform his main line into the world's first continuous four-track railroad at a time when most American railroads had yet to be double-tracked. The gamble paid handsome profits.[16]

On both land and sea Vanderbilt employed the same methods. He was a ruthless competitor who asked no quarter and gave none. Ever willing to risk large sums on an enterprise, he took on properties formerly ruled by corrupt owners and gave them sound, honest management along with heavily watered stock that his policies soon squeezed dry. "If you have been running a road and you spend nine or ten millions to run it," he declared, "if I cannot do it for eight, and do it as well, I am ready to go from the road . . . that has been my principle with steamships." He was the first to see that three feuding and floundering railroads would be infinitely more valuable if unified into one efficient line. On the water, Vanderbilt, a peerless seaman, ground rivals into submission through dogged effort and rigorous efficiency. To the railroads he brought not only efficiency and a bruising competitive spirit but organization as well. For another generation the New York Central remained the rarest of breeds: a family-owned railroad system—and a prosperous, dividend-paying one at that.[17]

Few of the entrepreneurs rival Jay Gould in intelligence, ability, or sheer creativity. Rockefeller considered him the greatest businessman in America; others deemed him the smartest man in the nation. In the brief span of a quarter century, Gould reconfigured the railroad map of the country, both by what he did and by what he forced others to do. He saw earlier than anyone else that the future of the rail industry lay in the creation of large systems and the development of new territory. As head of the Erie Railroad, he compelled both Vanderbilt's New York Central and the mighty Pennsylvania Railroad to reverse longstanding policies and expand westward to meet his threat. He took charge of the moribund Union Pacific Railroad, expanded it rapidly, and made it into one of the dominant transcontinental lines. After leaving that road, he bought the Missouri Pacific, a small road running from St. Louis to Kansas City, and transformed it into a mighty seven-thousand-mile system. His expansion thrusts forced every major system in the nation to rethink its strategy and policies.[18]

Had Gould's legacy been confined to the railroads—then the country's largest industry by far—it would still be an imposing one. But he also came to dominate the telegraph industry as well as the elevated rail lines of New York City. He built telegraph companies, sold them to the industry giant, Western Union, and then in 1881 acquired that company. Under his rule Western Union more than doubled its miles of wire. Gould understood thoroughly the symbiotic relationship between the railroads and the telegraph, and used it to the advantage of both industries. At its peak his rail empire totaled nearly 8,500 miles of track. No entrepreneur took greater risks or invested more of his fortune in the work of expansion and development in new territory. Nor did any man pioneer more financial techniques or display a greater mastery of them.[19]

While E. H. Harriman's résumé was considerably shorter than Gould's, it was no less decisive in its influence. Harriman came late to railroads; at the age of fifty he was a successful Wall Street banker with only brief experience in the managing of railroads. Yet in 1898 he took hold of the Union Pacific, just emerging from a long and debilitating bankruptcy, and transformed it into not only a powerful rail system but a thoroughly modernized one as well. Like Gould, Harriman understood that the rail industry had entered a new era in which the old rules no longer applied. The future belonged to giant, efficient systems capable of hauling huge volumes of freight over long distances at low rates. Harriman astounded the industry by spending $160 million to upgrade all parts of the Union Pacific system. He modernized not only the physical plant but its operations, organization, business practices, financing, and safety records.[20]

To the amazement of skeptics, his management policy turned the system into one of the great cash cows in American business. In 1901 he acquired the Southern Pacific, a combination of railroads and steamships that was the largest transportation system in the world. Within a few years he poured $247 million into making it the equal of the Union Pacific, then concocted an entirely original scheme of railroad management to carry out his policy of integrating the two systems. He applied the same principles to other roads under his control with similar results in most cases. In one decade he rose from obscurity to become the man who led the rail industry into the twentieth century. He also conceived a bold plan for a combined rail-water transportation system that would circle the globe and was hard at work on it when he died.[21]

William Crapo Durant, or Billy, as everyone called him, was a man whose reach forever exceeded his grasp. His vision of the infant automobile industry's potential far outstripped that of Henry Ford, whose company he almost acquired on two separate occasions. Durant saw not only that the future belonged to the motorcar but that the future of the industry lay in the creation of a firm capable of integrating the production and supply of different cars to different segments of a market that as yet scarcely existed. In 1904 he took charge of the floundering Buick Motor Company and turned it into a winner. Seven years later he joined Louis Chevrolet in forming the Chevrolet Motor Company and by 1915 had given it a national organization of plants, wholesale offices, and dealers. But Durant's major contribution came in 1908—the same year Ford introduced his Model T—when he created a new company called General Motors.[22]

What Durant had in mind was a combination that would do for the automobile industry what United States Steel—the giant corporation that included Carnegie's company along with others— had done for that field. As Peter Drucker observed, Durant viewed "the change in the market structure as an opportunity to put together a professionally managed large automobile company that would satisfy all segments of what he foresaw would be a huge 'universal' market." General Motors would include a diverse line of cars, a wide array of parts-manufacturing firms to supply the assembly plants, and a variety of other businesses, such as trucks, refrigerators, and home lighting. In 1918 Durant was asked to help finance an electric icebox made by an obscure inventor. He did so, gave it the snappy name of Frigidaire, and folded it into General Motors.[23]

Durant's fatal flaw was his inability to manage the behemoth he had created. Although he drew into the company a dazzling corps of the industry's elite—including Walter Chrysler, Charles Nash, Alfred P. Sloan, Charles F. Kettering, and Charles Stewart Mott— Durant relished one-man rule and lacked the patience to organize and systematize his constant stream of acquisitions. Crisis was his mother's milk; as a friend noted, "W.C. is never happy unless he is hanging to a window sill by his finger tips." In 1910 his expansion policy produced a fiscal crisis that cost him control of the company. Undaunted, he regained control six years later thanks to financial support from Pierre du Pont, who soon discovered that he had joined forces with a whirlwind. In short order Durant repeated his pattern of reckless expansion and loose management, got caught in the sharp economic downturn of 1920 (which forced GM to write off nearly $85 million in inventory as dead loss), and again lost control of General Motors. Although he went on to found Durant Motors, he never repeated his earlier success.[24]

Unlike Durant, Pierre du Pont proved to be the quintessential organization man, an ironic turn for a man born and bred in one of the nation's oldest family firms. Founded in 1802, the Du Pont powder works became an insular enclave for the family and its workers alike. Taking hold of the company with two cousins in 1902, Pierre gradually emerged as the dominant influence. Chipping away at the crust of tradition and resistance to new ideas, they turned Du Pont into a modern corporation in two years. By 1919 Pierre had transformed it into a chemical as well as explosives giant, and made it one of the most profitable manufacturing companies in the world. He did this by overlaying traditional family control with modern organizational structures and managerial techniques.[25]

Many, if not most, of the great family firms foundered or fell when the well of heirs and/or talent ran dry. They were then sold or incorporated and separated from the family's control. Pierre managed the astonishing feat of modernizing Du Pont while keeping it in the family's hands. His vision was that these two goals could be made compatible by changing the family's relationship to the company. As his biographers observed, "Pierre never doubted that if the company was to be a successful profit-making enterprise, the impersonal test of return on investment must be the criterion of performance. Family loyalties and idiosyncrasies must give way to efficiency and system. . . . The firm no longer had the obligation to provide the family with jobs. Instead it should assure them of larger dividends."[26]

The creation of one of the world's great chemical companies would be monument enough, but Pierre did something else equally impressive: He took hold of General Motors in its darkest hours and imposed on it modern techniques of planning, management, and organization. Pierre and the Du Pont company gained control of GM from Durant in 1920. He threw his influence behind Alfred Sloan's elaborate plan of organization, helped find good executives to bring it to life, and introduced new managerial planning tools, such as monthly forecasts. Within a remarkably short time the floundering automobile giant emerged as an efficient, well-run organization that dominated the industry for decades. Thus did Pierre play a crucial role in the organization of two of the largest and most powerful modern American corporations.[27]

Samuel Insull did for the electric power industry what Gould and Harriman had done for the railroads. His ruling vision was that an enormous market existed for power and light if ways could be found to produce and distribute it cheaply and efficiently. Working out of Chicago, Insull pioneered in solving most of the major problems in creating an electric power system. He mastered the unique economics of central station supply, learned new ways to cost and price the delivery of electricity, developed or acquired new technologies for those purposes, and organized a large-scale enterprise on principles that would, in his biographer's words,

"establish the pattern for rate-making throughout the world."
During the 1890s, when depression racked the nation, Insull
enlarged his company to ten times its original size. By 1905 his
annual production of electricity had doubled for the seventh time
in thirteen years; within another five years it quintupled to an output that exceeded New York Edison, Brooklyn Edison, and Boston
Edison combined. By 1907 Insull had grown his two companies,
Chicago Edison and Commonwealth Electric, to sixty times their
original size.[28]

The key to Insull's success lay in a host of innovative policies.
He prodded General Electric to build ever larger turbines; relentlessly drove costs and rates down; devised a system to electrify
rural areas profitably; pioneered new financing techniques, such as
the open-end mortgage and the retailing of corporate bonds; and
initiated a successful movement for, not against, government regulation of utilities. Every one of these developments stunned and
often appalled rival operators. More than any other man, he made
available to the American people a cheap and abundant supply of
electric power—the key to nearly every major technology of the
twentieth century. As his biographer noted, "Systemization and
rural and small-town electrification were advanced almost a generation through the efforts of Insull." The two countries that created the most admired government-owned systems, Canada and
England, came to Insull for lessons on how to do it.[29]

Theodore Vail's vision of telephone service paralleled that of
Insull's for electric power. While others puzzled over the potential
use and value of this new contraption, Vail foresaw a national network providing integrated connections within a framework that
amounted to a quasi-monopoly. Years later, in 1908, he embedded
this vision in a slogan: "One policy, one system, universal service."
No man did more to realize this goal. During the early 1880s Vail
helped build the Bell system; in 1885 he became president of a
new subsidiary, American Telephone & Telegraph (AT&T), which

was formed to develop long-distance service. His fondest dream was to create a national telephone system, but when he could not secure sufficient capital from the owners, he left AT&T in 1887 and did not return until 1907. During his absence AT&T became the parent Bell company and the system continued to expand. But the original Bell patents expired in 1894, and by 1902 no less than 295 independent companies competed with Bell across the nation.[30]

Although most of the independents had inferior equipment and little capital, they could become formidable if combined and improved by some aggressive investor. Vail met this threat with a policy of friendly mergers, absorbing rival companies on generous terms and upgrading their service. He reorganized Western Electric, a subsidiary he had created in 1881, into a primary supplier of telephones and a first-rate research facility. By improving service, favoring public service commissions, keeping rates low, and showing the public the benefits of a unified telephone system, Vail fended off critics and charges of monopoly. In 1909 he acquired control of Western Union but agreed to relinquish it in 1913 as part of an agreement to avoid an antitrust suit. As Robert Sobel observed, "He formulated a theory of utility monopoly under private control . . . and convinced political leaders of its soundness." Vail also created a genuinely national system; the first transcontinental conversation took place in January 1915. When Vail left the company in 1919, AT&T had assets of $1.5 billion, second only to United States Steel and twice those of Standard Oil.[31]

The Merchandisers

The merchandisers were the harbingers of the emerging consumer economy in which the desire for and possession of things—and still more things—extended steadily downward from people of wealth to those of modest means. In many characteristics, and in personality, they were as much alike as the organizers were different from one another. Wanamaker erected palaces of consumption to make shopping a pleasurable experience in itself for the well-to-do and middle class. Woolworth, Penney, and Walton built temples of thrift that allowed poorer people to stretch their dollars and thus participate more freely in the growing national ritual of consumption. Kroc rationalized and revolutionized the food service industry, which prior to his coming was almost as disorganized and chaotic as the oil industry before Rockefeller.

John Wanamaker was neither the first great merchandiser—A. T. Stewart, among others, preceded him—nor the creator of the principles that made him famous. He was, however, the first to combine several disparate elements into one operation that made his "New Kind of Store" the largest and most successful in the nation. Wanamaker's vision was deceptively simple: A great business could be founded and run according to the Golden Rule. Everything he did drew from the premise that the public must be satisfied. "We cannot—indeed, should not—survive without the public's trust," he insisted. To that end he published in 1874 the four principles that became his hallmark: satisfaction guaranteed, money back if not satisfied, one set price for every item, and cash payment only. In addition to these principles, he had earlier instituted a "free entrance" policy, meaning that, unlike other stores, customers could roam freely without a salesman at their elbow.[32]

Wanamaker opened his first clothing store, Oak Hall, in Philadelphia in 1861. Within eight years it became the largest and best-known store in the nation. His secret lay not only in his policies but in his lavish use of advertising, most of it written by himself and deployed in a variety of formats ranging from print to billboards to balloons. Unlike many merchants, his ads were truthful; he practiced what he preached. The point, he stressed was "not to sell, but to help people buy." In 1875 he bought an abandoned Pennsylvania Railroad depot and two years later turned it into his "Composite Store," featuring dry goods. In less than a decade it evolved into one of the first—and certainly the largest— department stores in the country. The advertisement for the opening in 1877 listed sixteen separate departments of merchandise. Over the years the store expanded to include more kinds of goods, including even a Ford automobile agency in 1903. In 1902 he broke ground for a giant new Wanamaker store, which became a landmark emporium in Philadelphia.[33]

Wanamaker did not stop there. Early in the 1870s he opened stores in several other cities, laying the foundation for a chain as well as an extended manufacturing operation. But he soon disposed of them because he feared the loss of quality and service in stores he could not personally oversee. Gradually, however, he began producing various goods for his store, and in 1896 acquired A. T. Stewart's old store in New York. He not only revived that business but built an opulent new store across the street and connected the two via a double-deck "Bridge of Progress." He also bought wholesale companies to supply his stores. All this work, including the new stores in Philadelphia and New York, was self-financed. These emporiums inaugurated the consumer era of shopping as spectacle, with their fabulous decors, giant auditoriums with huge organs and free daily concerts, and a host of other amenities that pampered shoppers. In these and other ways Wanamaker ushered merchandising into a new era, one in which the consumer was king—or often queen.[34]

So did Frank W. Woolworth, but in a very different market. Where Wanamaker embellished the shopping experience, Woolworth kept everything lean. Where Wanamaker catered to the growing upper and middle classes of the big cities, Woolworth envisioned an equally lucrative market in the less affluent people of smaller cities and towns if the goods could be made cheap enough. Starting with a small store in Lancaster, Pennsylvania, in 1879, he forged a retailing empire numbering a thousand stores established on principles that remained in place for decades after his death in 1919. Woolworth did not invent his basic concept; the five-cent counter had become a fad in small stores when he began his career as a clerk. He was but one of many young men who aimed to open a five-cent store of his own, which he did in 1879. When this effort fizzled, he realized that the range of merchandise available to sell at that price was limited and changed the premise to five-and-ten-cent merchandise. This was a new idea, and it proved an immediate success. He stocked the Lancaster store with $410 in goods and sold 30 percent of them the first day.[35]

The key to Woolworth's success lay in his genius at buying. A tough, shrewd bargainer, he showed a gift for picking only goods that moved. Expansion appealed to him because he saw that buying on a larger scale would enable him to acquire a wider variety of better merchandise. To expand without going into debt, he introduced the partnership principle in which the partner shared the startup costs and managed the store in return for half its profits. As his chain grew, he began to bypass jobbers (no small feat in his day) and buy directly from the manufacturers, enabling him to cut prices even more. He watched expenses like a miser, paid low wages, and crusaded against waste of any kind. "We must have cheap help," he explained, "or we cannot sell cheap goods." Having erected an empire of nearly two hundred stores by 1909, he stunned everyone by opening his first store in England. Eventually his growing chain of stores there proved even more profitable than its American cousin. No one did more to establish the viability of making large profits from low-price merchandise.[36]

What Woolworth did for novelties, James Cash Penney did for soft goods. In creating his own chain-store empire, Penney followed in Woolworth's footsteps without knowing it. His inspiration came from the two partners who gave Penney his first chance to manage a store. From that tiny 1902 store in Kemmerer, Wyoming, grew a gigantic chain operation that by 1941 included

1,605 stores with sales exceeding $377 million. He called it the "Golden Rule" store and gained from it the insight that small towns offered a bonanza market for cheap but quality goods if prices were kept low, standards high, and all transactions were in cash. From his employers he borrowed the concept of the partnership: Hire a good man to manage a new store, sell him a one-third interest in it, and let him repeat the process by opening other stores on the same basis. This principle left Penney as senior partner and major investor in almost every store, overseeing a corps of manager-owners dedicated to their work.[37]

Penney's insights went well beyond the partnership principle. He was relentless at keeping costs low and standards high. Although he admitted being "hard on help," driving them almost as hard as he drove himself, he called his workers "associates" rather than clerks because he viewed them as potential partners. In 1913 he incorporated as the J. C. Penney Stores Company; the next year he formalized his business rules into the six Penney Principles. He ran a lean, almost anorexic operation, opened a central office in New York, worked out a decentralized buying structure, and always looked to expand. In 1917 Penney became chairman of the board and devoted himself to recruiting, training, inspecting stores, and spreading his business philosophy with its religious roots. He always pounded away at the theme of keeping prices low, moving goods, keeping stores clean, and putting customer satisfaction above profits. In 1941 Penney's stores were the only major department-store chain still selling only soft goods and not offering credit. By 1950 they had become the world's largest retail outlet for blankets, sheets, textiles, work clothes, men's shirts, and other items.[38]

No one learned Penney's lessons better than Sam Walton, who admitted cheerfully that "most everything I've done I've copied from somebody else." Walton took from Penney an appreciation of the value of small-town markets, putting customer satisfaction

above all else, keeping prices low, running a tight, no-frills operation, making managers partners, and calling workers "associates"
while giving them incentives to identify their own prosperity with
that of the company. He even came up with six basic principles
and ten rules for running a business. But Walton gave all these
ideas his own original twist and elevated their scale to new
heights. From his first Ben Franklin store in Bentonville,
Arkansas, Walton made himself the largest independent variety-
store operator in the country with eighteen stores. Then, in 1962,
he gained the insight that shifted his career in a bold new direction. That year he opened a big new store in Saint Robert, Missouri, and discovered that "we could do unheard-of amounts of
business for variety stores, over $2 million a year in sales" even in
small towns.[39]

In 1962 Walton also learned about discounting, which had
begun to sweep the big variety chains. That year F. W. Woolworth
opened its first Woolco store, S. S. Kresge its first Kmart, and
Dayton-Hudson its first Target store. Walton followed suit by
opening his first Wal-Mart discount store in Rogers, Arkansas.
"From day one," recalled his manager Charlie Cate, "Mr. Walton
made it clear . . . he wanted real discounting . . . whatever anybody else did, we always had to sell for less." It proved such a success that the variety stores were soon phased out or replaced with
larger Wal-Marts. In 1970 Walton took the company public, giving him the capital for much faster expansion. Between 1977 and
1987 Wal-Mart averaged a 46 percent return to investors. In 1983
he happened upon the concept of the membership wholesale club
and opened his first Sam's Club. By 1990 he had forged the most
formidable retailing power in America: 1,528 Wal-Mart stores
with sales of $26 billion and 105 Sam's Club stores with sales
exceeding $5 billion. The next year Wal-Mart supplanted Sears as
the nation's largest retailer.[40]

Walton did far more than create a retail empire. He changed the shopping habits and expectations of the American people, as Wanamaker and Penney had before him, by delivering what he promised. Like Penney and Woolworth, he chafed at the arrogance of vendors who "didn't need us, and they acted that way." As his buying power increased, Walton transformed his relationship with major vendors into one that was more like a partnership. He devised a distribution system that became the envy of the industry and, after initial skepticism, invested heavily in computer and other technology to improve efficiency at every level. As Richard Tedlow pointed out, "Discounting is not glamorous. . . . Time after time, discounters have lost that focus and lost their business." Walton never did. Today Wal-Mart remains a giant even as all its major competitors except Target have gone under. As Walton said with obvious pride, "I know one thing for sure. We certainly changed the way retail works in this country."[41]

What Walton did for retailing, Ray Kroc did for fast food. He did not invent fast food or even McDonald's. That honor belonged to the McDonald brothers, who reconfigured their San Bernardino, California, drive-in restaurant in 1948 as a new kind of place emphasizing speed, efficiency, and quality. What Kroc created was a unique franchising system with a remarkable blend of uniform standards, teamwork, loyalty, and individual creativity. Where other franchisers merely looked to grab short-term profits, Kroc envisioned a long-term partnership to the benefit of franchiser, franchisee, and suppliers alike. His gift lay more in building those relationships than in forging the prototype of the modern fast-food enterprise. This approach proved fabulously successful. Kroc opened his first McDonald's in 1955; by 1976 his empire embraced 4,177 stores in the United States and twenty-one other countries with system-wide sales exceeding $3 billion. In 1984 the company opened its eight thousandth restaurant. Two years earlier it surpassed Sears as the largest owner of real estate in the world.[42]

Kroc revolutionized not only the fast-food but also the food-processing industry. As John Love observed, McDonald's "changed the way farmers grow potatoes and the way companies process them . . . introduced new methods to the nation's dairies . . . altered the way ranchers raised beef and the way the meat industry makes the final product . . . invented the most efficient cooking equipment the food service industry had seen . . . [and] pioneered new methods of food packaging and distribution." Kroc managed to impart his vision to employees, managers, franchisees, and suppliers alike. He not only redefined the relationship between customers and suppliers in the commercial food field but created a new breed of suppliers because regular vendors shunned his demands. In his dealings with franchisees he was as tolerant of individual differences as he was intolerant of deviation from the high standards he demanded from every one of them. He took what amounted to 2,500 independent companies and "skillfully bonded them into one family with a common purpose."[43]

The Technologists

The technologists are truly a breed apart in that all but one of them were inventors whose genius at that work thrust them into the larger world of business. They created things in the most literal sense, then had to find ways to make them commercially viable. For this reason, they knew their product far better than ordinary businessmen knew theirs. The one exception, Watson, worked closely with his engineers and learned his machines well. Although every one of these men did well in business, only two of them—Watson and Gates—emerged as superior managers. Not surprisingly, their firms evolved into two of the largest and strongest in the country. Land's firm did well during his lifetime, while those of Edison and Westinghouse endured roller-coaster existences. Both Edison and Westinghouse lost control of the electric companies that mattered most to them.

Of all the technologists, Thomas A. Edison easily ranks first and foremost. No one rivaled him in the sheer output of great inventions or colossal mistakes. He saw early on that technology and invention drove progress and would rule the world. Although many inventors preceded him, he was by far the most prolific at the art and the first to make invention a business in itself. No one even approached him in number of patents, which totaled 1,328 by 1910. Between 1869 and 1910 he averaged one patent every eleven days. In 1911 he incorporated some thirty different enterprises into Thomas A. Edison, Inc., with gross annual sales ranging between $20 million and $27 million. Some 3,600 workers toiled at his West Orange, New Jersey, laboratory complex alone. Even today his hand is felt in nearly every corner of daily life. As Robert Conot wrote, "No other man has been responsible for striking the spring of so much wealth, nor had such influence on the lives of so many people."[44]

Edison created the first research laboratory and thereby made invention a business. Among other things (and there were many other things), he gave the world the incandescent light, the first central electric-power station, the phonograph, motion pictures, an improved storage battery, an electric traction motor, major improvements to both the telegraph and telephone, a prefabricated concrete house, an early mimeograph machine, an improved typewriter, and a host of devices necessary for the creation of the first electric power plant. He laid the foundation for the electric power industry that George Westinghouse and Samuel Insull later developed. Having created the world's first motion-picture studio and the first silent movies, he also tried to develop color film and movies with sound well ahead of their actual appearance. He was one of the first to investigate X rays while seeking to devise fluorescent lamps and fluoroscopes, and also discovered the "Edison effect," which ultimately led to the development by others of the vacuum tube, radio, and television. The lamp he devised using this effect has been called "the first electronic instrument."[45]

If there had been no Edison, George Westinghouse might have been deemed the great American inventor. Over a forty-eight-year career he took out over four hundred patents, an average of one every forty-four days. He profoundly influenced two of the three basic fields of American industrial development, transportation and energy (the third being communication). In the process he created or was associated with 102 different companies, only a few of which bore his name. Like Edison, Westinghouse made a business of invention, and in one notable case he created a giant industry by looking beyond Edison's worst blind spot. The greatest of Westinghouse's many insights was that the future of electric power lay with alternating current. For railroads he invented the amazing air brake, the less celebrated but equally important friction draft gear, and an electropneumatic interlocking system for switches and signals.[46]

His contribution to the electric power industry can scarcely be overstated. Where Edison's system required innumerable small power stations, Westinghouse saw that alternating current allowed for the use of large central stations if ways could be found to transmit the power safely. He and his engineers made this practicable with such inventions as the modern transformer, rotary converter, and induction motor. Two major contracts—lighting the fabulous Chicago Columbian Exposition of 1893 and constructing the first hydroelectric installation at Niagara Falls—clinched the reputation of his system. The Niagara power station in turn gave rise to the world's largest electrochemical complex. It made possible the commercial development of aluminum as well as artificial abrasives, Carborundum, ferrochromium, artificial graphite, chlorine, and phosphorus. Westinghouse's first patent in 1865 was for a rotary steam engine; thirty years later, building on the work of Charles Parsons, he began work on a turbine that in 1899 resulted in a 1500-kilowatt turbogenerator—then the largest of its kind.[47]

Thomas J. Watson was a salesman, not an inventor, yet he created a mammoth technology company. Like his mentor, John Patterson, he understood the need to show customers how much they needed the machines he produced. Taking hold of a failing company called CTR in 1914, he renamed it International Business Machines a decade later and turned it into a giant that in 1967 surpassed United States Steel in size. Watson's great vision was that the rapid growth of American business opened a vast market for tabulating machines with the ability to reduce the cost and human toll of boring, repetitive labor. From this insight grew a company that recorded sales of $734 million and profits of $68 million in 1956, the year of Watson's death. In the process Watson also created a unique corporate culture, a thriving research empire, and a monument to himself in the form of the Watson Laboratory at Columbia University.[48]

From its early foundation of machines—the core of which was a basic rental installation consisting of a key punch, card sorter, and tabulator—IBM gradually expanded into a wide array of business products. During World War II IBM supplied more than three dozen key ordnance items as well as machines that broke codes and "kept toll of the conflict." Watson expanded his operation in foreign markets through a subsidiary, IBM World Trade Company, and eventually reaped large rewards from an electric typewriter company acquired in 1933. Although reluctant to recognize the potential of computers, Watson finally put the company into the business after 1950 and made it the leader in what became the dominant growth sector of the next half century. Unlike the other entrepreneurs, Watson turned his organization into a cult that worshiped at the altar of his image and ideas. It was, said one biographer, "a dynastic empire, in which the qualifications for citizenship were defined by one man."[49]

Something of a cult also developed around Edwin H. Land, but of an entirely different sort. Like Edison, Land was the quintessential inventor who managed to make an enormous business of it. His 535 patents rank second only to Edison in number. Although he was most at home in the laboratory, he ran his company for forty-three years, longer than Eastman, Edison, Ford, or Watson. Land parlayed his boyhood fascination with light and its behavior into the Polaroid Corporation. From his first commercial product, a synthetic polarizing material made of plastic that was given the name "Polaroid" by a Smith College professor, Land moved to create sunglasses, headlights, windows, and the "Vectograph," or 3-D movie system, which he demonstrated at the New York World's Fair in 1939. During World War II he provided the military with a stream of important devices ranging from a tank gunsight to an antiaircraft-gun trainer to "Vectography," a version of which targeted enemy defenses at Guadalcanal, Normandy, and elsewhere. He also formed a research team that produced synthetic quinine in only fourteen months—a major scientific triumph that was crucial to the war effort. Later he became a key figure in the creation of the fabled U-2 spy plane.[50]

All this was prelude to Land's supreme achievement. At a time when Kodak owned 90 percent of the photography market, Land staked the existence of his company on his vision of an instant camera. In 1947 he unveiled the first Polaroid Land Camera, which began a revolution that transformed photography as completely as Eastman had done earlier. He had managed to "compress a whole photographic darkroom into the space between two thin layers of specially coated material." Like Eastman, he followed with lighter, cheaper models, including the first instant camera using color film in 1962. By then Polaroid's stock had a market value exceeding $1 billion, and its products were sold in forty-five countries. A decade later, Land again risked the company's future on a new product, one that required not only "simultaneous path-breaking in chemistry, optics, and electronics" but also a huge investment in new plants and equipment. Solving a welter of nightmarish, seemingly intractable technical problems, he produced the ultimate one-step instant color camera, the SX-70. More new products followed, as Land convinced the public that a Polaroid camera "was not a lifetime acquisition, but an evolving idea." By the time Land retired in 1982, sales had reached nearly $1.3 billion.[51]

Robert Noyce followed in this tradition of inventors turned managers. His critical insight was that an entire electronic circuit could be built on a single chip of silicon. His invention of the integrated circuit in 1959 gave rise not only to a major new industry but also to a region devoted to a new way of doing business. Within a few years this device elevated his firm, Fairchild Semiconductor, into one with $130 million in sales and twelve thousand employees in the United States and abroad. In 1968 Noyce left Fairchild and with Gordon Moore founded a new firm they called Intel. Within two years they perfected the 1103 memory chip, which started a revolution in data storage that elevated Intel into the dominant firm in the industry. The company that started with twelve workers in a "tilt-up concrete building" mushroomed by 2000 into a colossus with a net income of $10.5 billion and facilities in more than thirty countries.[52]

Noyce's legacy extends well beyond these two firms to the world they made. It was his chip that gave Silicon Valley its name, and his first company that spawned a host of ambitious entrepreneurs who left to start their own enterprises. The "Fairchildren," as Tom Wolfe called them, turned the Santa Clara Valley into Silicon Valley, a phrase some children heard so often that they actually grew up thinking it was a place on the map. They brought with them a new corporate culture Noyce had pioneered, one that shouted defiance at the staid, sluggish, class-conscious corporate system of the East he so despised. In Noyce's world, rank had no privileges, doors were always open, dress was as casual as work was intense, everybody had a say, and the young got large doses of responsibility thrust upon them from the beginning. When an acolyte came to him with a problem, Noyce walked him patiently through the possibilities for a solution, then flashed his "Gary Cooper smile" and said, "But if you think I'm going to make your decision for you, you're mistaken. Hey . . . it's *your* ass."[53]

Bill Gates was not one of the Fairchildren but he enhanced the legacy generated by Noyce. Gates had an overriding vision not only of the future of computers but even more so of the destiny of software as the ruling element in that future. As his biographers emphasized, "Software determined what hardware was worth. Software defined hardware . . . *made* hardware. Gates had been instrumental in making this software revolution happen." From a partnership formed with Paul Allen in 1975 when Gates was only twenty, Microsoft evolved into a corporation in 1981, and went public in 1986. Six years later its stock was valued at nearly $22 billion, putting it ahead of such heavyweights as Boeing and General Motors and making Gates the richest man in America at the age of thirty-six. In twenty-seven years Microsoft compiled profits of nearly $50 billion. The software industry, quipped one analyst, had been turned into "Microsoft and the Seven Dwarfs." And Gates did this by creating actual products in an age dominated by "mere money-movers."[54]

Despite his youth, Gates had been present at the creation. "I started the first microcomputer software company," he asserted. "I put BASIC in micros before 1980. I was influential in making the IBM PC a 16-bit machine. My DOS is in 50 million computers. I wrote software for the Mac." He was in fact one of the very few people who had experience with the prototypes of both the

Macintosh and the IBM PC. His genius lay less in inventing new products than in reworking existing ones for other markets. He also had the insight that a huge market existed among computer users who, like drivers with automobiles, used the machine to do things without caring how it did them. Like Carnegie he saw the value of both low pricing and the preemptive strike—the latter a tactic he borrowed from IBM. The corporate culture he created owed something to both IBM and Noyce. In many ways he was to the Age of Information what Rockefeller had been to the Age of Energy. Like Rockefeller, too, he was one of the few entrepreneurs who both created a new colossus and had the talent to manage it at the next level of growth.[55]

The Investor

It is altogether fitting to place Warren Buffett in a class by himself because he has been exactly that in the world of investing. To a world of money movers with inflated egos and perspectives that did not reach the tip of their noses, he brought an improbably old-fashioned philosophy of investment and made it a vehicle for the most spectacular success in the modern financial arena. Where our other entrepreneurs all earned their reputations through some product or innovation, Buffett gained his by picking businesses and stocks. His driving vision was that the evaluation of businesses—and thus the picking of stocks—could be made into an art, if not a science, by thorough study and the rigorous application of principles and criteria. Over a period of four decades, through economies fat and lean and bull and bear markets, he averaged a compounded annual gain of nearly 28.6 percent. This performance earned Buffett a net worth of $9.7 billion by 1995 and made him a regular contestant in the annual race for the title of the nation's richest person.[56]

Starting in 1956 with seven limited partners who put up $105,000 for him to invest, Buffett parlayed his unique approach into an investment empire that became the twenty-fourth largest company, ranked by market value, in the United States, even though the whole operation was run by a staff of twelve from an unpretentious office in Omaha that he wryly called his firm's "world headquarters." His genius lay in an uncanny ability to identify sound companies with stocks that were greatly under-valued because they were going through troubled times, and in the courage to buy the stock heavily even during its darkest hour. Buffett was more the Beethoven than the Mozart of investment; whatever his native talents, his insights flowed from long hours of careful study, close analysis, and sheer hard work. As his biogra-pher wrote, "He read the heavy purple-bound Moody's manuals page for page with the zest of a small boy reading comics." The intensity of his preparation helped explain the paradox of a methodology based on long-term holdings that seemed simple but proved difficult for others to execute.[57]

As he grew older, Buffett turned his annual report to stockhold-ers into a primer on investing, the economy, human nature, and himself. "What set the essays apart," stressed Roger Lowenstein, "was his knack for unbuttoning a complex subject and clearly explaining it." But it was his track record that endeared him to followers, who tended to clutch their shares in his company as financial heirlooms for years. Buffett turned a $10 million invest-ment in the struggling *Washington Post* into $205 million. He put $46 million into the GEICO insurance company during its dark-est days at the edge of bankruptcy and came away with $1.7 bil-lion. Other stocks fetched equally impressive returns. "Price is what you pay," he declared; "value is what you get." No one got more value for the price than Buffett, and he did it far from the coils and rumor mills of Wall Street, which he largely ignored. His view of that place was as down to earth as his investment philoso-phy. Of its machinations he once said, "You won't encounter much traffic taking the high road in Wall Street."[58]

Twenty-six men, twenty-six visions—as diverse as the men themselves yet crowded with similarities and overlapping elements. These men were hardly alone in possessing great dreams or even striking insights. What separated them from ordinary dreamers was the intensity of their ambitions, which drove them steadily onward to the second crucial stage of achievement: execution. Those who lacked this intensity and drive were left to ponder their accomplishments and ask the question that still echoes through every primer on entrepreneurship: How do they do it?

| 4 |

The Talents of the
Great Entrepreneurs

When I go to my office every morning, I feel like I'm going
to the Sistine Chapel to paint.   —WARREN BUFFETT[1]

Any vision, however far-reaching, remains only a fantasy
unless steps are taken to realize it. Far more often than not, these
steps lead to failure rather than fulfillment. Obviously the bolder
and grander the vision, the more difficult is the execution needed
to attain it. What separates the great artist from the ordinary prac-
titioner is not only grandeur of vision but, even more, the ability
to bring it to fruition. As noted earlier, this ability requires a
blend of attributes, of which talent is only one. The others include
energy, determination, competitiveness, ambition, the willingness
to endure failure or scorn, the strength to follow one's own path,
and sheer stamina. Without these elements, talent becomes more
a promise than a product, a tantalizing hint or cruel reminder of
what might have been.

So it is with the great entrepreneurs. All of them share these
qualities in varying degrees. They did not merely engage in business; they stormed it, battered it, tied it in knots of complexity

from which they extracted some advantage, drove it before them like a force of nature or outflanked it with swift and stealthy moves. In the process they destroyed or disarmed competitors, overturned the basic assumptions of their field or industry, aroused fierce protest from foes and the public alike, and transformed the world around them. Some did battle with gusto, others reluctantly. Defeats, or at least setbacks, were frequent and losses often heavy. Some died on their shields; others limped painfully from the fray with serious wounds. Few managed to quit the field and retire to a quieter, more peaceful life. All left behind a monument to their efforts in the form of a large, often giant, and thriving enterprise.

To some degree the energy, drive, and stamina of the great entrepreneurs can be measured by their longevity. Of the twenty-four men no longer living, eighteen survived beyond the age of seventy, twelve made it past eighty, and two—Rockefeller and Penney—lived well into their nineties. Eastman, afflicted by an illness that would soon render him an invalid, shot himself at the age of seventy-eight. Duke barely missed the cut, dying at sixty-nine; Westinghouse lived to be sixty-six and Woolworth sixty-seven. Only three of the entrepreneurs died at relatively young ages. Gould perished from tuberculosis at fifty-six, Harriman of stomach cancer at sixty-one, and Noyce of a heart attack at sixty-two. If it is true that only the good die young, the great entrepreneurs were clearly bad men.[2]

Unlike some artists and other creative people, the great entrepreneurs did not die young. Like them, however, they poured most of their considerable energy into their work for as long as they could. For only a few did the creative fount dry up relatively early in a long life. Rockefeller quietly walked away from Standard Oil while still in his fifties, and du Pont left General Motors at fifty-eight. However, Rockefeller kept busy with philanthropy, investments (many of them poor), the stock market, and a passion for golf, while du Pont lavished attention on his magnificent Longwood gardens among other activities.[3]

They were the exceptions. Gould, Harriman, McCormick, Patterson, Vanderbilt, Wanamaker, Westinghouse, and Woolworth all died while still in harness. Vail and Watson died within a year of leaving their posts. Edison stayed atop his company well into his dotage, as did Ford, who remained in control until two years before his death despite increasing senility. A few men launched second careers after leaving their original firms. Duke left American Tobacco and turned his attention to bringing hydroelectric power to North Carolina. Noyce devoted himself to an organization dedicated to helping American chip manufacturers fend off Japanese competition. Carnegie, Eastman, and Rockefeller made a second career out of philanthropy. Durant kept losing fortunes and starting over; late in life he returned to his hometown, Flint, Michigan, and opened a bowling alley. Carnegie, Rockefeller, du Pont, and Penney alone enjoyed long, leisurely retirements from business, though Penney kept active in company affairs to the very end. "If you are a research scientist," said Land, "what you want is not retirement but another 500 years."[4]

All the entrepreneurs had a zest for work, for the struggle to succeed and the combat it entailed. Jonathan Hughes called Edison a "compulsive achiever," a description that pretty well fits all our entrepreneurs. "I hated to close my desk at night," admitted Duke, ". . . and was eager to get back to it early next morning. I needed no vacation or time off. No fellow does who is really interested in his work." Woolworth agreed that "no man can make a success of a business which he does not like." Wanamaker echoed this sentiment: "No day seems long enough to those who love their work." Patterson and Vanderbilt had little else in their lives and wanted nothing more. Patterson insisted that "Enthusiasm is the biggest asset in business." For McCormick, work embodied the ethos of his Presbyterian heritage. Although Buffett shut down his first partnership at age thirty-eight, protesting that "I don't want to be totally occupied with outpacing the investment rabbit all my life," he soon got back into the race and has never left it. "One of the things that attracted me to working with securities," he admitted, "was the fact that you could live your own life. You don't have to dress for success." Like Edison, Gates became legendary both for the hours he put in and for driving his associates to put in the same exhausting effort. "Even after 20 years," he declared, "I still think I have the best job in the world."[5]

Whether one calls it a talent or merely an attitude, this sheer delight in the act of doing is a vital component in creativity of any kind. "Let us do things—do things," exhorted Wanamaker. "All our confidence has to come from making things," agreed Land. "I don't know," mused Walton, "that anybody else has ever done it quite like me . . . and kept on doing it right up to the end because they enjoyed it so much." Carnegie, too, rejoiced in the challenge. "Take from me all the ore mines, railroads, manufacturing plants, but leave me my organization," he boasted, "and in a few years I promise to duplicate the Carnegie company." Edison had a more earthy view: "As a cure for worrying, work is better than whiskey. Much better." Eastman was virtually alone in demurring. "What makes me mad is that people think I like to work," he once said. "I don't think I have ever taken any pains to conceal my dislike for it. I like to watch other people work." Anyone who looks at his career as a businessman and philanthropist would have a hard time believing him.[6]

Ford expressed his feelings in lofty terms. "When a man is really at work," he wrote, "he needs no title. His work honors him." Harriman, like Carnegie and others, relished the struggle itself. Asked once what he really wanted in life, he replied, "I would rather think of some big helpful thing to be done, get all the people I could opposed to it and to say that it couldn't be done, and then set both feet and go ahead and do it." Kroc recalled, "We were breaking new ground, and we had to make a lot of fundamental decisions that we could live with for years to come. This is the most joyous kind of executive experience." Land quipped of his work ethic that "anything worth doing is worth doing to excess," to which Buffett offered this corollary: "That which is not worth doing is not worth doing well." Penney believed that "success is first of all a matter of the spirit," and for him that spirit was embodied in the most humble task. "I like to remember," he said as a very old man, "that all through my business life I've swept store sidewalks whenever I noticed that they needed it, and I still do it."[7]

The joy of doing did not depend on the scale of accomplishment. In his old age Vanderbilt admitted that "I didn't feel as much real satisfaction when I made two millions in that Harlem corner as I did on that bright May morning sixty years before when I stepped into my own periauger, hoisted my own sail, and put my hand on my own tiller." Land was only eighteen when his "first happiest moment" occurred as he got "suspended polarizing needles to orient in the magnetic field to make the first synthetic polarizer." Wanamaker thought that "the first step toward success in any vocation [was] a willingness to work," and said lovingly of his own effort, "I am glad I will never be through cutting and polishing my store stone. . . . God is good who doesn't ask me to put it aside, unfinished." For Gould, who liked to demur that "I am a mere passenger in all my financial transactions," business amounted to a series of knotty intellectual problems that he thrived on solving with the joy of a chess master unraveling complex positions. Rockefeller saw himself in similar terms: "It has been that way all my life . . . find a problem, solve it as well as I can, put the administration in good hands, and then go on to the next."[8]

Part of this joy sprang from a willingness to take risks and fall flat. The scholars who argue that entrepreneurs avoid rather than incur risk have not looked closely at the lives of the great entrepreneurs. Time and again during their careers they leaped into the void, risking much or all to realize their vision or later to preserve it in the face of threats. Wanamaker, who coined almost as many aphorisms as Benjamin Franklin, observed, "There are too many men who build fences around themselves and do nothing for fear of making mistakes." Duke was not one of them. "I've made mistakes all my life," he said. "And if there's one thing that's helped me, it's the fact that when I make a mistake I never stop to talk about it—I just go ahead and make some more." Land was adamant that "an essential aspect of creativity is not being afraid to fail." Most of the great entrepreneurs did in fact suffer failures during their careers, some of them enormous, but they accepted it as part of the game. "I've been taken to the cleaners often enough to make me a certified cynic," admitted Kroc. "But I'm just too naturally cheerful to play that role for long." An associate said of Walton that he was "less afraid of being wrong than anyone I've ever known."[9]

All the entrepreneurs recognized that losses and setbacks were an inevitable part of the process. What they brought to the game was vision combined with the courage of their convictions and the willingness to back them with action even when the odds seemed long. Many of the entrepreneurs were brilliant, but genius was not a necessary part of the tool kit. "I'm no genius," admitted Watson. "I'm smart in spots—but I stay around those spots." Penney never tired of emphasizing that *"To succeed in life does not require genius."* Persistence, however, was a definite requirement. "Indomitable perseverance in a business properly *understood,*" insisted McCormick, "almost insures ultimate success." Duke believed that he had succeeded in business "not because I have more natural ability than those who have not succeeded, but because I have applied myself harder and stuck to it longer. I know plenty of people who have failed to succeed in anything who have more brains than I had, but they lacked application and determination." On another occasion he put it more succinctly: "While they eat and talk, I work."[10]

Hard work, ambition, and perseverance are common enough qualities to be clichés in the Horatio Alger tradition. To these traits many of the entrepreneurs brought a strong sense of perfectionism. Penney was notorious for being "intolerant of any effort but the best." For Patterson the prime directive was, "Good enough is the enemy of all progress." Any business, he insisted, "that is satisfied with itself . . . is dead. The actual burial may be postponed; but it is dead because it is not going forward. To my mind, nothing can ever be good enough; I am always dissatisfied; I preach dissatisfaction. . . . The throbbing heart of business is the intense desire to do better." Kroc echoed this sentiment. "Perfection is very difficult to achieve," he said, "and perfection was what I wanted in McDonald's. Everything else was secondary for me." Walton attributed this urge for constant improvement in part to his competitors, who "honed and sharpened us to an edge we wouldn't have had without them."[11]

Harriman revealed his version of this trait by insisting that one particular section of the Union Pacific Railroad be made as perfect as humanly possible. Harriman's pride in that accomplishment offered a reflection of his creative vision: "The one perfect section of track became a model for a whole railroad, for entire systems of railroads. It embodied Harriman's demonic urge to transform chaos into order by applying imagination, common sense, and unflagging energy."[12]

This powerful need to impose order on chaos is found in nearly all the entrepreneurs. "If you want order," said Patterson, "you must first put things in order." Most of the entrepreneurs entered a field at its early, formless stage and created dominant firms that forced the industry into a more mature stage. Carnegie did this for iron and steel, Rockefeller for oil, Duke for tobacco, McCormick for farm machinery, Eastman for photography, Vanderbilt, Gould, and Harriman for railroads, Ford, Durant, and du Pont for automobiles, Westinghouse and Insull for electric power, Vail for the telephone, Patterson and Watson for office equipment, Noyce for computer chips, Gates for software, and Buffett for investing. The merchandisers had a similar impact on the retail and fast-food trades. "It is human nature to want to save on purchases," Penney once observed. "I have noticed that, when business principles are explained to some people, they complain of intellectual meagerness. Yet such people would not, when a chemist explained the formula for water as two parts hydrogen and one part oxygen, complain that the formula lacks sophistication. . . . Why, then, do basic truths in the field of merchandising seem too commonplace?"[13]

By the very nature of what they did, the inventors sought to extract order from the chaos of nature. For them, invention became a direct form of creative expression, the equivalent of a painting or symphony or poem. Yet they also sought to impose order in the broader sense of creating techniques and organizations that would enable them to systematize their work. Edison viewed his laboratory as a sort of "factory of creativity." Westinghouse regarded his companies in similar terms, as did Noyce, who followed the same principle of installing bright, creative people in an environment where they could best produce. "We had a lot of creative people," recalled Jean Hoerni, one of Noyce's cofounders of Fairchild Semiconductor, "and he knew how to direct them in general terms, not specific terms. . . . As a result of this freedom came original thinking." In this way Noyce proved more successful than Edison at creating a factory of creativity. Gates created the same free—albeit pressure-packed—environment at Microsoft. "The Microsoft work environment for programmers was deliberately chaotic," wrote his biographers. "The feeling was that with less structure you could be more creative and produce innovative products."[14]

This quality has produced the most direct comparisons of entrepreneurs with artists. Carnegie's biogapher called his organization "the creative building of a great enterprise," while Jonathan Hughes referred to it as "a singular kind of masterpiece." One of Edison's biographers, noting his effort late in life to create synthetic rubber, observed that nothing "could be more characteristic of the artist's psyche than the current passion." David Hounshell said of Ford's company that it "controlled and manipulated information far more creatively" than any other firm in his study. Elsewhere I have described Gould as "a creative businessman who thrived on the challenge of working with unformed clay." Even Buffett's biographer referred to his work as "a 'canvas'—a work of art." Buffett's wife, Susie, once remarked, "Let's face it, I'm married to Artur Rubinstein."[15]

Bringing order out of chaos is, of course, a basic element in what artists do. Unlike the artist, however, the entrepreneur creates not a finished product but a work forever in progress because the context in which it exists is always in a state of change. As Kroc put it, "Business is not like painting a picture. You can't put a final brush stroke on it and then hang it on the wall and admire it." This fact demanded of the entrepreneurs a sensitivity to change and an ability to respond effectively to it. On this point, however, they differ not only from many artists but from one another as well. Some displayed great agility in adapting to change, others responded to it slowly and grudgingly, and a few fought it bitterly. As will be shown later, the consequences for the latter group often proved devastating. What made this attribute especially poignant for the great entrepreneurs is that their resistance to change often stemmed from their devotion to the very creations that had changed the world and elevated them to greatness.[16]

Of all our entrepreneurs, Walton was probably the most nimble in accepting, even welcoming, change to the point of trying to institutionalize it. "One of my assets is my willingness to try something new, to change," he noted. "I think that is a concept we carry throughout the company. We have a low resistance to change. We call it our 'RC factor.'" Carnegie was always prowling about for new means and methods of improving production. So was Kroc, who welcomed input from any source. "As long as you're green you're growing," he said; "as soon as you're ripe you start to rot." Penney liked the aphorism, "Rust never gathers on a sword that is in use." Land argued that "we live in a world changing so rapidly that what we mean frequently by common sense is doing the thing that would have been right last year." Noyce put it another way: "Don't be encumbered by history. Go off and do something wonderful."[17]

In doing their wonderful—and often wondrous—things, our entrepreneurs brought a mixed bag of talents to their work. Carnegie, Duke, Kroc, Penney, Walton, Watson, and Woolworth were masterful salesmen. Durant, Edison, Kroc, Land, Noyce, and Vail had an aura of charm and personal magnetism that drew men to them. Du Pont was the consummate diplomat in a family racked with dissension, an adept, sensitive manager who masked his own strong will behind a rational, levelheaded demeanor. More than most, he showed a willingness to "examine dispassionately views that differed from his own." Gould was a financial wizard. Buffett and Harriman resembled human calculating machines in their remarkable ability to digest data and reach conclusions before most men could even grasp the question. Ford understood "the logic of machines" and was a master at "adapting and improving the ideas of others." Patterson, too, possessed this latter gift, as did Gates, who built his huge empire largely on it.[18]

Gates also has incredible focus and knowledge of his industry. As Ross Perot once noted, "Gates is a guy who knows his product." Like Gould, he used an unimpressive physical appearance to his advantage by allowing rivals to underestimate him. Also like Gould, Gates was persistent if not relentless in getting what he wanted, but there the resemblance ends. Where Gates was a brash, persistent arguer who shouted down opposition, Gould cooed a siren's song and went quietly about undermining rivals. No entrepreneur was more patient in gaining his objectives. "I avoid bad luck by being patient," he explained. "Whenever I am obliged to get into a fight, I always wait and let the other fellow get tired first." Gould also had an uncanny ability to get at the heart of an issue, and to find actions that served several purposes at once. His keen intellect was capable of working on a myriad of complex problems at the same time and producing original solutions to them. More than any of the other entrepreneurs, he possessed a stunning economy of motion.[19]

Insull resembled both Gould and Harriman in some ways. Like Gould, he devoured books and had "a capacity for learning the rudiments of one business which would serve him well in another." Like Harriman, he processed data at lightning speed and had an incredible memory as well as a talent for reducing mountains of data to basic principles. Edison possessed "the gift of total recall" and could carry complex plans in his head for days. Westinghouse, too, was noted for his memory and seldom wrote things down. All of these men—and many of the other entrepreneurs—also had phenomenal powers of concentration that enabled them to shut out distractions and juggle many things at the same time. Often this ability to focus was accompanied by a willingness to make decisions without fretting over their consequences. Eastman and Vail were typical in their apparent lack of fear or worry about the results of their actions. "There has been only one prominent factor in what success I have had," said Vail. "That is to do the best I could and never to worry about the personal outcome."[20]

This ability to make bold moves or commit large resources without hesitation seems the very essence of the great entrepreneurs and underscores their willingness to accept great risks regardless of how many steps they may have taken to minimize those risks. Buffett, the loneliest of the lone wolves, did it again and again in a field where one misstep might mean disaster. Carnegie's biographer marveled at how he could "shut the door on the past with so resolute a slam and with hardly a backward glance." Land bet the company more than once in developing new technologies. "Optimism is a moral duty," he insisted. "There are no problems in science, only opportunities . . . if you [can] state a problem—any problem—and if it is important enough . . . then the problem can be solved." Duke amazed an associate with decisions that, "though seemingly offhand, were as accurate as they were swift." Gould and Harriman were legendary for their ability to deliver the unexpected stroke. Rockefeller did not hesitate to "exhibit visionary daring and undertake colossal gambles," nor did Vanderbilt. The merchandisers all displayed this quality in starting their new enterprises.[21]

Sheer tenacity is another quality that was common to virtually all the great entrepreneurs. At their best, nothing deflected them from their quest. So strong was their faith in the vision driving them onward that they pushed and clawed their way through every obstacle. This quality made them fierce competitors and dangerous rivals. Vanderbilt exemplified this spirit when he discovered that two erstwhile associates had betrayed him. In his barely literate scrawl he sent them a note that read, "Gentlemen: You have undertaken to cheat me. I won't sue you, for the law is too slow. I'll ruin you." Carnegie, a "perfectly ruthless competitor," learned every detail of a rival's business and aimed to outperform him in every area. He embraced Herbert Spencer's social Darwinism in large part because he lived it. "A struggle is inevitable," he said, "and it is a question of the survival of the fittest. . . . One who stops halfway will be crowded out." Rockefeller was no less ruthless and gifted a competitor; one admirer marveled at "his skill in not exposing the slightest surface for attack."[22]

Legendary for his dogged ferocity in any struggle, Duke had what one writer called "a relentlessness that turned momentum into inevitability." His simple formula for victory was one that Rockefeller had already perfected: "First . . . you hit your enemies in the pocketbook, hit 'em hard. Then you either buy 'em out or take 'em in with you." Eastman also proved a savvy infighter in a very competitive business. "Peace . . . extends only to private life," he observed. "In business it is war all the time." Even du Pont had beneath his placid exterior what his biographers called a powerful "determination to succeed." Gould's typically unique way of competing was to destroy an opponent in some undemonstrative way that looked not at all as if he was doing it. By contrast, Harriman competed joyously in everything and was always in his adversary's face. He loved nothing more than driving a hard bargain and was unrelenting on the attack, though he insisted unconvincingly that "I never fight unless somebody fights me."[23]

McCormick, ever the good Calvinist, was renowned for his "bulldog tenacity." As his biographer wrote, "The focus of his endeavor was always the victory to be gained over competitors. . . . He gloried in a fight, neither asked for nor gave quarter, and . . . liked to follow 'the line of most resistance.'" Patterson was no less fierce a warrior; for him it "had to be hammer and tongs all the while." Westinghouse belonged to the same school. His biographer called him "a good fighter—bold, resourceful, and stubborn. He enjoyed fighting." So did Watson, who had the same overpowering urge to prevail. "He always aimed to win," admitted his son. "When he was in a corner, it didn't matter what the rules were; he wanted to accomplish his purpose." Vail and Kroc used a different style. "My way of fighting is the positive approach," said Kroc. "Stress your own strengths . . . and the competition will wear itself out trying to keep up." But Kroc also had his own methods for scouting rivals. "You can learn all you ever need to know about the competition's operation," he observed, "by looking in his garbage cans." Vail perfected the fine art of taking the enemy into his own camp, but admitted to "a stubborn inclination to go through with what I had started to do."[24]

The merchandisers were all tough competitors in fiercely competitive fields. They worked on close margins that left them small room for error. All of them cloaked their strong competitive drives in the garb of service to the community, but their eyes seldom left the details of their operation. "In the face of such a challenge," wrote Penney in words that Carnegie might have penned, "there is justified ruthlessness, akin to the ruthlessness of Nature at the moment when a new life is born." Woolworth thought the same way and seldom strayed far from business, believing that "no one ever built a business on thoughts of having a good time." An associate saw in Walton "a lot of the old yard rooster who is tough, loves a good fight, and protects his territory." Another observed, "What motivates the man is the desire to absolutely be on top of the heap."[25]

The most recent of our entrepreneurs reveal these same qualities. Gates has always been competitive in everything from games to business. In the latter he sought not merely to beat his competitors but to eliminate them from the playing field. "Competing with Bill Gates," moaned Mitch Kapor of Lotus, "is like putting your head in a vise and turning the handle. He doesn't take no for an answer, and he keeps coming back." Philippe Kahn of Borland International was even more explicit. "When you deal with Gates," he complained, "you feel raped." Buffett showed the same competitive stripe at both work and play. The latter revealed itself in his passion for bridge, at which he hated to lose. In the business of investing it can be seen in his desire to succeed on his own terms using his own system. As his biographer concluded, "Buffett very much wanted recognition for being *right*."[26]

Part of what gave the great entrepreneurs an edge in competition was their talent for picking good men and their gift for judging talent. Contrary to what one might think, they did not go it alone. Nearly every one of the entrepreneurs found one or more colleagues who proved indispensable and brought strengths the entrepreneur lacked. For Carnegie it was his brother Tom until his premature death, and then three key associates: Captain William Jones, Henry Clay Frick, and Charles Schwab. Rockefeller collected a stable of key men, foremost among them his brother William, Henry M. Flagler, Oliver H. Payne, H. H. Rogers, Samuel C. T. Dodd, John D. Archbold, and, finally, his namesake son. Duke relied heavily on his father and brother Ben as well as an early partner, George Watts. McCormick, too, worked closely with his father and his brother William, who, like Tom Carnegie, died young. Another brother, Leander, proved equal parts blessing and curse. Later McCormick derived great help from Charles A. Spring, Jr.

Eastman formed a close attachment to his first backer, Henry A. Strong, who was almost a father figure to him and remained a staunch ally throughout his life. Ford had a corps of talented associates, especially Charles Sorensen and William Knudsen, but drove them away. Later he leaned on Harry Bennett, who was little more than a thug, and on his son, Edsel, whom he drove to an early grave. Patterson had the strangest pattern of all. He groomed bright, talented men and then fired them when their star began to shine too brightly, saying he would have no indispensable men about him. One of those stars was Tom Watson, who always revered Patterson despite his harsh treatment. Later Watson followed virtually the same pattern at IBM, promoting and rewarding key executives lavishly, then firing them when they grew too prominent and seemed a threat to the throne. Although he had key executives, Watson ultimately came to rely most on his two sons, Thomas Jr. and Arthur, or Dick, as he was called.

For du Pont the indispensable man was first his cousin Coleman and then John J. Raskob, who became his closest associate. Durant gathered a legion of the auto industry's brightest men around him but never used them wisely or well, largely because he liked to run a one-man show. It is revealing that he is the only one of the entrepreneurs—except possibly Insull—whose career ended in failure. Contrary to the legend of Gould as a lone wolf, he worked closely with several associates, most notably Sidney Dillon, Russell Sage, and Silas H. H. Clark, his top railroad lieutenant. Harriman also had a covey of allies. In financial affairs he formed part of a seamless trio with Jacob Schiff of Kuhn, Loeb and James Stillman of National City Bank. In railroad matters he leaned heavily on Julius Kruttschnitt, John C. Stubbs, and Samuel M. Felton among others. Vanderbilt went through many associates during his career but late in life came to depend on his son William, whom he had once dismissed as weak and inept.

Insull always had a coterie of men on whom he could count, including his brother Martin, John J. Mitchell, William G. Beale, and Harold Stuart. As his biographer wrote, "For thirty of his seventy-nine years Insull had near him at least one man who could say no and make it stick." Unlike some of the entrepreneurs, Vail delegated authority gracefully and freely used the talent around him. He relied especially on the man who succeeded him, Harry B. Thayer. Woolworth desperately needed a good detail man and found him in Hubert T. Parson. Penney recruited Earl Corder Sams early in his career, remained close to him, and eventually put him at the head of the company. Wanamaker used three of his brothers and his son Rodman as key associates along with one talented outsider, Robert Curtis Ogden. Walton leaned heavily on his wife, Helen, and his brother Bud as well as a succession of bright executives, such as David Glass, Ferold Arend, Jack Stephens, Ron Mayer, and Jack Shewmaker.[27]

From the beginning Kroc had two indispensable partners, Harry J. Sonneborn and June Martino. Later he recruited Fred Turner (who succeeded him), Jim Schindler, and Don Conley.

Edison basked in the role of lonely inventor but depended heavily on such associates as Insull, who served as his secretary for a dozen years, Charles Batchelor, and W. K. L. Dickson. Westinghouse did not have any single close associate but did much of his work in tandem with other engineers and colleagues. Land may have been alone at the top, but he leaned on key associates such as Donald Brown, Julius Silver, Meroë Marston Morse, Howie Rogers, and Bill McCune, who succeeded him. "He especially needed Howie Rogers," observed his biographer and associate Peter Wensberg, "the short, unassuming man who had become indispensable to Land." McCune filled a different role: "If Land produced the brilliant theories, McCune had to make things work in the real world."[28]

Both Noyce and Gates had key figures who complemented their talents. For Noyce these men were Gordon Moore, Arthur Rock (who found start-up capital for his companies), and later Andrew Grove. Tedlow described their contributions this way: "Noyce, the visionary, born to inspire. Moore: the virtuoso of technology, the man without a needy ego, the calm at the center of the storm . . . Grove: the technologist turned management scientist . . . who became fascinated with how organizations run and how they interact." From the beginning of his career Gates relied on his partner Paul Allen as the indispensable associate. When illness and battle fatigue forced Allen to leave the company, Gates turned to a corps of capable executives, most notably Steve Ballmer, Charles Simonyi, and Rowland Hanson. Even Buffett, the pioneer investor, found an associate who complemented him perfectly, Charles Munger.[29]

This brief survey reveals an intriguing if unsurprising characteristic of our entrepreneurs. Despite the variety of personalities, the differences in historical settings, and the wide spectrum of business enterprises, virtually all of them required associates with two key attributes: talents that complemented their own, and personalities capable of dealing with or being subsumed to their powerful egos.

Of these twenty-six figures, only du Pont, Gould, Walton, and Buffett did not dominate everyone and everything around them. In four cases—Ford, Durant, Patterson, and Watson—this self-centered dominance became obsessive to the point of emotional derangement. Strong egos drove their work, fueled their vision, and sustained them through periods of adversity and criticism. Gould, du Pont, Walton, and Buffett all had no less strong a sense of self; they simply adopted different styles of dealing with the world. Without this inner strength and confidence, they could not have endured the constant struggles and large risks their work entailed.

It is revealing, too, and hardly surprising, that so many of the entrepreneurs looked first to their own families for helpmates and partners. Fully half of them turned to fathers, brothers, or wives to help them start or grow their business. Walton took advice from not only his wife but her father as well. Penney regarded his first wife as his partner and was crushed by her premature death. Buffett and Gates were both deeply influenced by their fathers even though they did not become partners in their businesses. Not all of the helpmates proved helpful. Insull relied too heavily on his brother Martin, who proved unequal to the task. Tom Carnegie was overwhelmed by the burdens thrust on him, took to drinking heavily, and died relatively young. One of McCormick's brothers, William, did yeoman service for Cyrus until his untimely death; another brother, Leander, served Cyrus well for a time, then fell into a dispute with him that grew uglier over the years until Cyrus finally forced him out of the firm.

One of the strongest qualities the entrepreneurs share is an insistence on doing things their own way. "I really like my life," said Buffett. "I've *arranged* my life so that I can do what I want." Westinghouse was no less adamant. "I had a fixed notion that what I wanted I must have," he admitted. "I have always known what I wanted and how to get it. As a child, I got it by tantrums; in mature years, by hard work." Land received a spanking at age five for taking apart the family's new phonograph. "From then on I was totally stubborn about being blocked," he recalled. "Nothing or nobody could stop me from carrying through the execution of an experiment." Rockefeller was even more blunt: "You can abuse me, you can strike me . . . so long as you let me have my own way." Often this attitude bred conflict born of suspicion and hostility, which required the entrepreneurs to develop tough hides. "It has been my privilege to be called 'crazy' many times during my life," said a defiant Patterson. "It is an epithet which I prize highly."[30]

At the same time, most of the entrepreneurs understood the vital role of having good men in key positions. "I never had much difficulty in working out plans," observed Westinghouse, "but my greatest difficulty seems to have been in finding enough men to carry out such plans." Penney asserted that "in a business such as ours the asset which towers above all other assets is . . . *men.*" Duke agreed that "a man's most valuable capital is the men he picks out to work with him." Watson declared, "Our greatest assets are men." Vail and Durant thrived on recruiting talent from companies they acquired—a game at which Rockefeller excelled. "The ability to deal with people is as purchasable a commodity as coffee or sugar," he said, "and I will pay more for that ability than any other under the sun." Walton described the Wal-Mart success story as "ordinary people joined together to accomplish extraordinary things."[31]

Getting the most from their men required the entrepreneurs to be leaders who knew how to motivate. Their styles ran the gamut of possibilities. A few of them—Durant, Kroc, Land, Noyce, and Watson—cast an almost hypnotic spell with their persuasive charm. Bill McCune thought Land was "an artist . . . in bringing people together to work on one or another technical approach." Others, like Carnegie, Edison, Eastman, Gates, Insull, Patterson, Penney, Vanderbilt, Wanamaker, and Westinghouse, inspired through sheer hard work and force of personality. Rockefeller lacked charisma but handled and motivated people through his "quiet but extraordinary personality." Gould and Walton disarmed people with their unassuming ways and got superb results. Harriman galvanized subordinates with staggering displays of energy and competence. "Buy good automobiles and good men," advised Duke. "Buy good anything. They pay profits."[32]

Motivating people required the entrepreneurs to be good judges of men, which most of them were. Carnegie excelled at finding and promoting bright young men. "Mr. [J. P.] Morgan buys his partners," he boasted, "I grow my own." In 1898 alone he promoted twenty of his young men to partners. Watson shared this belief that "every laborer . . . was a potential executive." Vanderbilt read men well, as did Gould, which made them intriguing adversaries. Insull and Vail took pride in being students of human nature. Insull discovered that newly acquired companies often brought with them talented young men, and he soon devised means of finding them. Before long most of his executives came from the ranks of his growing organization. Land's biographer said that he "enlisted talent like a Toscanini, with concentration and pressure." Gates and Steve Ballmer handpicked all the programmers hired by Microsoft, and Gates learned the name, face, telephone extension, and even the license plate of every one of them.[33]

Durant appreciated talent even if he did not always use it wisely. Penney and Walton shared with Woolworth the principle of hiring good men and letting them manage their stores. "I have never spied on men," said Penney proudly; "I studied them." Woolworth's biographer noted that "In the hiring, coaching and advancement of his men Woolworth displayed a judgment akin to genius." Woolworth himself claimed that he could always size up a man at a glance. Patterson felt the same way, and once gave rein to the views of a man named Palmer, who insisted he could read a man's character from his face. When Palmer turned in negative reports on several executives, they were let go. No one ever quite figured out whether Patterson actually fell under Palmer's spell or simply used him as a device to reorganize the company.[34]

Kroc was an outstanding motivator. "He brought out the very best in people," said Fred Turner, ". . . the best boss you could ever have." He also had a knack for "putting himself in the position of his customers and for addressing their needs and interests, not his own." One of Carnegie's managers admired his ability to "pick a man from one place and put him in another with maximum effect." Land possessed an ability to "select and inspire talented subordinates." Noyce's charm made him a natural leader as well as a natural salesman "who could, in the most casual ways, inspire an interest and faith in his work." Walton said admiringly of Penney that "he could always get a lot of work out of people." So could Walton himself. "He is a tremendous motivator," said one of his executives. "He also has a peculiar faculty for being able to evaluate people." Watson concocted and projected a unique blend of "mysticism, evangelism, nationalism, and faith" that turned his employees into loyal legions.[35]

Most of the entrepreneurs did well at motivating subordinates by giving them free rein to show what they could do. However strong-willed or dominant the entrepreneurs might be, they understood the need not only to delegate authority but also to cultivate talent by letting it grow. Carnegie decreed that "every year should be marked by promotion of one or more of our young men. . . . We can not have too many of the right sort interested in the profits." Duke agreed that "cheap men don't pay. Build up your organization with costly men. Let them make profits. Give them part of yours and you will get it back." Harriman antedated Noyce's "It's your ass" principle by conceiving bold plans and thrusting the responsibility for implementing them onto his subordinates. In the conservative world of railroaders he astounded officers by giving them not only authority but huge appropriations to spend on improvements. In one case a Southern Pacific official, handed approval for spending

$18 million, asked cautiously how fast he should go. "Spend it all in a week if you can," replied Harriman.[36]

The merchandisers subscribed to this principle because they understood how much depended on the manager-partners who operated their stores. "I want my executives interested in every store we own," declared Woolworth. "The prosperity of one is the prosperity of all." For that work he preferred a farm boy to a college graduate because "the college man won't begin at the bottom to learn the business." Penney pioneered in the partnership principle, and Walton insisted that "from the very beginning . . . I have also been a delegator, trying to hire the best possible people to manage our stores." Kroc, too, was an innovator in making his franchise owners genuine partners rather than mere sources of revenue.[37]

To a man the great entrepreneurs knew their product, and many excelled at the art of promoting it. Duke, Eastman, McCormick, Patterson, and Wanamaker rank among the great pioneers in advertising. The first four had to create markets for their products, while Wanamaker had to sell a new approach to merchandising. "There are two things to which I must devote the greater part of my time," said Patterson; "the first is advertising, the second selling." Instead of keeping his list of customers secret, as was the custom, Patterson spent freely to publish their names. He advertised not only his products but even his new factory when it was built in 1888. Carnegie was a superb salesman blessed with "an almost uncanny ability to prognosticate future trends in supply and demand." Eastman excelled at the art of marketing. Explaining the unique name he devised for his camera, he said it was "short . . . not capable of mispronunciation . . . does not resemble anything in the art and cannot be associated with anything in the art except Kodak." Wensberg thought Land was "a great marketer, but he would never admit it." Insull declared himself "a great believer in publicity."[38]

Few men rivaled Wanamaker's skill at the art of advertising. The key, he noted, was "to write the opposite of what is generally understood to be good advertising." As Sobel observed, "Truth in advertising and merchandising hardly existed when he came to retailing. Wanamaker changed this. He earned public trust early and never lost it . . . by advertising his creed widely, to a larger audience than that reached by any American businessman before him." Walton became notorious for the wacky promotions that drew people into his stores. His very first bank loan was for $1,800, to buy a soft-ice-cream machine to put in front of his store along with a popcorn machine to attract customers—which they did. But sometimes his schemes backfired. For one store opening he stacked watermelons on the sidewalk and brought a donkey for kids to ride. As the temperature soared past one hundred degrees, the watermelons began to pop, the donkey "began to do what donkeys do," and the whole mess spilled all over the parking lot, where shoppers tracked it into the store. Walton simply shrugged and moved on to greater feats, saying, "I guess we had very little capacity for embarrassment back in those days."[39]

All of the entrepreneurs excelled at problem solving, and most were inventive if not strikingly original in the solutions they found. Several of them, notably du Pont, Eastman, Gates, Kroc, Noyce, Rockefeller, Vail, Walton, and Wanamaker, excelled at management, a talent conspicuously lacking in Durant, Edison, Land, and Ford. Gould, du Pont, Harriman, Insull, and Rockefeller had strong financial skills, of which Carnegie, Edison, Ford, Gates, Kroc, Land, Noyce, Patterson, Watson, and Westinghouse were devoid. The latter grew touchy about his reputation. "They say I'm no financier," he growled. "So I suppose these great works built themselves." Carnegie hated the whole business of finance and once snapped that he "manufactured steel, not securities." Carnegie, Edison, Ford, Insull, Land, Patterson, and Wanamaker all disliked or distrusted bankers, and other entrepreneurs resented them deeply. Ford, whose loathing of bankers was colored by his anti-Semitism, said that "the very worst time to borrow money is when the banking people think you need money." Insull agreed even though he counted bankers among his associates. "Bankers," he snorted, "will lend you umbrellas only when it doesn't look like rain."[40]

Alfred Sloan, the managerial genius of General Motors, said of Durant that he "possessed rare ability to sense an opportunity in some inventor's attic." Edison had what his biographer called "an instinctive knowledge and discernment of materials." Harriman had a talent for finding larger truths in the smallest incident, Wanamaker a genius for "dramatizing the commonplace." Gould may have been the most inventive financier of all time. Du Pont recognized early on the importance of statistical analysis for planning and made it a central feature in his restructuring of both the Du Pont company and General Motors. Buffett's talent for devouring information about stocks was as awesome as his self-confidence. "One of Carnegie's greatest talents," concluded Joseph Wall, ". . . was his sensitive, almost intuitive perceptiveness of the boundaries beyond which one could not step with impunity."[41]

Although Gould for one thrived on weaving webs of complexity about his affairs, a surprising number of the entrepreneurs excelled at the art of making complex things simple. "People like to look for some obscure or involved explanation for every happening, terrestrial or celestial," said Vail. "Explanations, as a rule, are simple, and because simple, overlooked or regarded with contempt." Edison described the "necessary secret" of illumination, once it came to him, as "so simple that a bootblack might understand it." Tedlow described Ford as possessing "a shrewd simplicity, a mother wit." Even Gould declared that he had "always believed in simple organization. . . . I have found in my management of railroads that I got better results from a simple organization than one too large & complicated." Walton insisted that "there's nothing at all profound about any of our principles. In fact, they're all common sense, and most of them can be found in any number of books and articles on management theory."[42]

But the application of those simple principles was quite another matter. What entrepreneurs often mean by "simple" turns out to be rather the essence of what they do and how they do it.

| 5 |

The Entrepreneurs
at Work

I speak of faith in McDonald's as if it were a religion. . . .
That's exactly the way I think of it.   RAY KROC[1]

The great entrepreneurs were seldom happier than when at work. They believed ardently in what they did and rejoiced in the doing of it. The challenge of creating something, of solving problems or escaping traps, engaged them as nothing else could. They could throw themselves into a project with little consideration for anything else but the task at hand. Whatever great company or product resulted from their efforts became a monument to their dedication—and they savored monuments—but for them the joy was in the doing. When they paused later in life to look back at what they had achieved, their feelings tended to parallel E. H. Harriman's reflection on what his railroad system had wrought:

> Where would have been those whom it serves . . . had we not
> straightened, improved, & improved again, enlarged, made
> better, & so increased its capacity that it permitted the

> enlargement of every enterprise, & establishment of new ones
> in all the territory adjacent to it & the systems under its influ-
> ence. . . . Its method introduced like methods by other impor-
> tant systems. Where would we all now be without them? It
> has all made for advancement in civilization & will someday be
> understood.[2]

Harriman treasured his monuments, as did Thomas Watson, but they cherished even more the creation of them. As early as 1926 Watson prophesied, "This business of ours has a future. . . . The IBM is not merely an organization of men; it is an institution that will go on forever." Edison looked back on his long, long gallery of creations and exclaimed, "Say, I *have* been mixed up in a whole lot of things, haven't I?" Walton admitted that, "Managing that whole period of growth was the most exciting time of all for me personally. Really, there has never been anything quite like it in the history of retailing. It was the retail equivalent of a gusher." Edwin Land could hardly contain his pleasure in recounting the process of creating his instant camera:

> What is hard to convey . . . is the years of rich experience that
> were compressed into those three years . . . as if all that we had
> done in learning to make polarizers, the knowledge of plastics,
> and the properties of viscous liquids, the preparation of micro-
> scopic crystals smaller than the wavelength of light, the lami-
> nating of plastic sheets, living in the world of colloids in
> supersaturated solutions, had been a school and a preparation
> both for that first day in which I suddenly knew how to make a
> one-step dry photographic process and for the following three
> years in which we made the very vivid dream into a solid reality.[3]

For most of the entrepreneurs, the process of transforming their dream into reality followed a strikingly similar pattern of development. The first stage involves recognition of a problem along with a potential solution for it. The solution might be something entirely new (the telephone or electric power), an improved machine or device (the air brake), a different or improved process (alternating current), or some innovation in production, distribution, or marketing (chain stores). The entrepreneur then raises money, often acquires partners to share the load, and creates a simple, often casual organization to carry out this insight. The founders are long on optimism and determination, and usually short on capital and experience.[4]

Beginning on such a small scale, the entrepreneur and his partners have to do everything themselves. Gradually they work out problems of finance, production, technology, and marketing. Their operation is loose and informal; everyone has several jobs to do, and much of the work is improvised because they are new at it and few precedents exist. The partners keep much of the vital information in their heads and operate out of a small, often makeshift office. They make plenty of mistakes and learn from them. If the venture fails, the entrepreneur writes it off to experience and moves on to something else. If it is successful, he thinks at once of expansion, and the process of growth changes the way he must operate. More capital is required at once, forcing him to siphon profits, borrow, and ultimately form a corporation. When that corporation grows even larger, the entrepreneur is obliged to take it public. Suddenly he must then deal with new issues of accountability and stock-market volatility.

Other major changes accompany expansion. A larger, more complex organization is needed, new markets loom, and changes in the competitive arena require new responses. The entrepreneur and his partners must buy new machinery and equipment, hire more people, and install them in larger buildings. It soon becomes clear that the business can no longer be kept in their heads or run casually out of their desks. To cope with new problems, they divide responsibilities and hire people to assist them. A managerial staff begins to evolve that separates the entrepreneur and his partners from the men in the plant. Every staff member takes on some specialized function. A host of procedures such as accounting, purchasing, and marketing become formalized and systematized. Personnel, a virtually nonexistent issue when the operation was tiny, becomes in itself a major concern and potential problem.

If success continues, the operation continues to grow ever larger. New plants and offices are opened and new lines of products are developed that may require separate divisions or even separate corporations to administer. Competing firms are bought out and added to the complex. The labor force mushrooms and grows restive. The amount of capital invested reaches astronomical figures. The company becomes a national concern as salesmen open up new markets. As the economy grows, so does the company. Divisions beget more divisions, many of them with subsidiaries. An organizational monster now sits astride the original idea and the modest firm created to implement it.

By this time the entrepreneur and his partners are long past the point where they can do, or even oversee, everything. They retreat to formidable offices attended by an army of accountants, lawyers, secretaries, clerks, typists, messengers, and junior officers. Relieved of the details of production, they confine their energies to broad questions of policy and strategy while lesser minions handle the routine work. The need to administer the empire supercedes all other considerations, including the promotion of new ideas. Every aspect of the operation falls prey to creeping or galloping specialization. Some officers (and their staffs) devote their entire attention to financial matters, while others tend strictly to production, marketing, transportation, purchasing, research, technology, personnel, labor relations, and public relations. Specialists and experts are hired to study the administrative structure and suggest improvements. At every level coordination and planning are essential to make the operation run smoothly, yet these become ever more difficult to attain as growth continues.

The entrepreneur and his partners, already in their twilight years, reflect in amazement on what has happened. They have nourished the original idea to a destiny undreamed of at the start. The enterprise has taken on a life of its own, one that transcends the founders and the individuals who serve it. It is no longer dependent on any one person. When the entrepreneur and his partners die, their departure is mourned and their accomplishments celebrated, but company operations scarcely feel their absence. Handsome portraits of them are hung in the corporate headquarters, where they gather dust and occasional glances from people of a generation too far removed from their achievement to grasp what it was or what it meant. Like all great artists, they are swallowed over time by the sheer force of their creation. Later, the company may drift from its roots, fail to adapt to changing times, and collapse into the dustbin of failure.

Many of the entrepreneurs not only followed this pattern but understood where it had led them. "A great business is really too big to be human," said Henry Ford. "It grows so large as to supplant the personality of the man. . . . It becomes greater and more important than the individuals." John D. Rockefeller put it even more simply. "The day of combination is here to stay," he observed. "Individualism is gone, never to return." During an interview, Harriman surprised a reporter by pulling out a type-written sheet of data on Union Pacific operations and rattling off some figures. "As he read from it," wrote the reporter later, "I realized it was the apologia pro vita sua." The reporter reminded Harriman that "the public assails and attacks you and impugns your motives and accuses you of all sorts of things. . . . Doesn't the thanklessness of the job ever embitter you?" In response Harriman merely slapped the sheet of statistics and snapped, "That remains."[5]

For every one of the entrepreneurs, "That remains" became the credo of their life, the justification for their work and whatever price it had exacted. "I regard my scientific papers as my essential biography," said Land, who ordered his personal papers shredded after his death. At the same time, many of them looked back fondly at the naïveté and simplicity of their early struggles. "We were all small-town and country boys," James C. Penney recalled, "many of us having made fumbling starts in other work, catching fire now with an idea for which we were suited." Sam Walton chuckled at his early days: "At the start we were so amateurish and so far behind! . . . [we had] an unsophisticated buying program, a less than ideal merchandise assortment, and practically no back-office support." Many of the entrepreneurs cherished these early days with their trials and hard-learned lessons as their "Rosebud."[6]

But learn their lessons they did. All of the entrepreneurs displayed a stunning capacity for growth, climbing the ladder of challenge relentlessly if not always with ease, sometimes falling back, and then doggedly resuming the struggle upward. Each man went his own way, developed his own style, pursued his own vision to its realization. This is why they cannot be stuffed into a formula or pattern for easy summary. However, their work revealed some common themes even though they worked in different mediums. For the producers and merchandisers, the most common ground by far revolved around three key principles: low cost, high volume, and uncompromising quality. Although these factors influenced the technologists as well, the key element for them—the starting point for all that followed—was invention and innovation, the creation of something new and its improvement. For Warren Buffett the key lay in finding high value at low cost.

The railroad men made low cost and high volume a religion. Cornelius Vanderbilt regarded them as basic components of efficient operation, while Jay Gould hounded his officers constantly to "find new sources of income and new ways to cut expenses." It was Harriman, however, who ushered in the modern railroad era based on providing quality service by carrying huge volumes at low rates, which required roads to be in top physical shape. He understood that the way to make money was to spend money—put a railroad in such good condition that its reduced operating costs would undercut any rival line. The key to this policy lay in applying economies of scale with a vengeance by standardizing, rationalizing, and simplifying every practice. Any improvement applied across all his systems could save enormous sums.[7]

A favorite way to get his point across was to find the larger truth in some small example. Walking some Southern Pacific track one day with one of his finest officers, Julius Kruttschnitt, Harriman's restless eye seized on one of the bolts holding a rail in place. "Why does so much of that bolt protrude beyond the nut?" he asked abruptly.

"It is the size that is generally used," replied Kruttschnitt.

"Why should we use a bolt of such a length that a part of it is useless?" persisted Harriman.

"Well," admitted Kruttschnitt, "when you come right down to it, there is no reason."

After walking a bit farther, Harriman stopped suddenly and asked, "How many track bolts are there in a mile of track?" Kruttschnitt did a quick calculation and ventured a figure. "Well," snapped Harriman, "in the Union Pacific and Southern Pacific we have about eighteen thousand miles of track and there must be some fifty million bolts in our system. If you can cut an ounce off from every bolt, you will save fifty million ounces of iron, and that is something worth while. Change your bolt standard."[8]

Andrew Carnegie absorbed the railroads' twin obsessions about costs, which Harold Livesay described as "knowing what they were, and reducing them." He viewed costs and production as the

Siamese twins of success. From his mentor, Tom Scott of the Pennsylvania Railroad, Carnegie learned several crucial lessons: "Install whatever arrangements are necessary to know all costs all the time. . . . Keep the price barely above costs and rely on volume to make a profit. . . . Promote cost-conscious subordinates." James Wall called Carnegie's "constant concern to reduce [costs] in every department" the chief ingredient in his success. He insisted that weekly cost sheets be sent to him regardless of where he was in the world and fretted especially over labor and freight costs. But quality also got high priority. "However sensitive he might be to production costs," Wall added, "he regarded quality of even greater importance."[9]

Rockefeller, too, pared costs to the bone and stressed volume. The larger his operation grew, the more importance these elements assumed. Every cost was computed to several decimal places. Like Harriman, he understood that "a penny saved in one place might then be multiplied a thousandfold throughout the empire." Ford shared Carnegie's belief that a low enough price would find an insatiable market, and cut his prices as fast as he could reduce costs. Buck Duke used the Bonsack machines to slash the cost of making cigarettes. For Cyrus McCormick, George Eastman, and John Patterson, the challenge lay more in getting the best possible product, which meant a primary emphasis on quality. For others it meant using time wisely. "Supervise details but don't allow them to absorb you," advised Frank Woolworth. "Don't waste the time of a high-priced organizer on a clerk's job." Ford went even further. "From time waste there can be no salvage," he said. "It is the easiest of all waste and the hardest to correct because it does not litter the floor."[10]

One key to the equation lay in elevating efficiency to its highest level, which Carnegie, Duke, and Rockefeller did. The ultimate form of efficiency was mass production, which at its best maximized volume and minimized costs by reducing cost per unit.

Eastman delved into it early on by producing a film-roll holder with seventeen standardized and interchangeable parts. By the early 1880s McCormick's reaper works had inculcated the same principle. However, it was Henry Ford who created the modern version of mass production by elevating it to a tempo and scale never known before, and thereby completed the transformation of production methods that began with Eli Whitney's interchangeable parts. The production of the motor of the Model T, for example, was broken down into more than eighty separate actions, and every element was reduced to the utmost simplicity.[11]

Ford carried the ideal of efficiency to its extreme, seeking to make it "the logical and ethical end of human affairs." The Highland Park plant became a marvel of its age, the most innovative manufacturing facility in the world. Opened in 1910, Highland Park had its first assembly line operating by April 1913 and turned out 1,700,000 Model T Fords in 1923 alone. But Ford dwarfed even Highland Park with the monster River Rouge plant, a perfect engine of vertical integration with a factory stretching 1.25 miles long and 1.13 miles wide. As Jonathan Hughes noted, "Raw ore could go in one end on Monday, pass through furnaces, mills, forges, machine shops and, joined by subcontracted components, emerge on Wednesday as a completed automobile."[12]

Historian David Hounshell, in discussing the "ethos of mass production," stressed the revolutionary impact of Ford's methods. "Both the *act* of mass-producing the Model T Ford," he wrote, "and the rapid *diffusion of the techniques* by which it was mass-produced had a profound impact on the twentieth century. Fordism, a word coined to identify the Ford production system and its concomitant labor system, changed the world." *Fordismus,* as the Germans labeled it, also inspired a literature of fear about a future dominated by technology that reduced people to mere appendages of machines. Charlie Chaplin satirized it in the film *Modern Times* while Fritz Lang demonized it in *Metropolis* and Aldus Huxley did likewise in his sardonic novel *Brave New World* (1932). In Huxley's chilling world, Ford has replaced God and people are standardized as types to serve particular purposes. Life is functional, loveless, devoid of emotions, and devoted to pleasures of the moment. One of the most compelling images of Ford's system remains the powerful murals painted by Diego Rivera with the stark title "Detroit Industry."[13]

For the producers, quality consisted of manufacturing the best possible product in the largest volume at the lowest cost. For the merchandisers, it lay in finding the widest variety of goods at the lowest cost, selling the largest amount at the lowest price, and providing quality service in the bargain. All of them shared a repugnance for that oldest of mercantile principles: charging what the traffic would bear. As Penney put it, "The condition for growth . . . was quality for low price." Frank Woolworth started at the other end of the equation by limiting his stock to items that would sell for no more than a nickel or dime, which thrust on him the burden of finding an attractive array of merchandise cheap enough to sell at those prices. His talent as a hard-nosed buyer kept a constant flow of novelties coming to his stores. As his chain of stores mushroomed, he resisted the temptation to go into manufacturing. Instead his buyers used the clout of volume to extract low prices from manufacturers and sometimes—in the manner of Rockefeller with the railroads—also got them to rebate to Woolworth commissions that had formerly gone to jobbers and other middlemen.[14]

Woolworth shared Carnegie's belief that the best time to expand was during hard times, when labor and material were cheap and competitors were cautiously pulling in their horns. He used the depression of 1893–97 to buy large quantities of goods at low prices. Having long hesitated to invade the West because of prohibitive freight charges on merchandise, he did so in 1904 after persuading some of his eastern suppliers to bear the extra shipping costs on the promise of larger orders. To get lower prices, he stirred up rivalries among not only manufacturers but his own buyers as well. He regarded overhead as a mortal enemy and fought it constantly. At first his New York office had only one employee and Woolworth handled all the paperwork—doing letters and orders in longhand—until he finally hired a typist. "The discovery of a wasted penny," wrote his biographer, "never failed to irritate Woolworth even when he had become fabulously rich."[15]

Like all the great merchandisers, Woolworth had an uncanny eye for detail. "We have found on investigation," he once wrote his managers, "that the average customer prefers the small 6 inch nickel shears to the larger ones. Yet inspection shows that only two or three out of thirty or forty stores keep in stock the smaller shears, which give us much greater profits than the larger ones." For Woolworth, detail was a tool and not a harness; his immersion in it never kept him from thinking big or acting boldly. In February 1904, he slipped aboard a train to the Midwest and within two weeks managed to inspect, buy, and pay for twenty-one stores operated by independent merchants in nine states. This coup marked his debut in the region between the Appalachians and the Rockies. As part of his never-ending war on theft, he liked to enter one of his stores wearing no disguise, fill his pockets with merchandise, and dump the loot on the desk of the hapless manager, saying acidly, "I could have filled a delivery truck."[16]

Woolworth also understood the importance of keeping profit margins reasonable. Time and again he warned his managers never to sacrifice sales volume for the lure of larger profits on individual items. "Everybody likes to make a good bargain," he counseled. "Let him. Small profits on an article will become big profits if you sell enough of the articles." He also advised managers not to be afraid of losing a little money through low prices: "First, it prevents your competitor from making money; second, it advertises our stores more than anything else could do and will make people talk about us for years to come." Woolworth also urged managers to "make it a rule not to bore or annoy customers." He admired Wanamaker and Marshall Field for their policy of letting customers shop on their own. "Make your customers feel at home," he added. "Have waiting rooms and rest rooms. Encourage people to meet their friends in your store. Give them something free."[17]

John Wanamaker took a different tack in serving a more upscale market. As early as June 1861 he advertised that "the quality of goods were to be guaranteed," having already promised nothing but all-wool clothing. Four years later he added his money-back guarantee, and in 1874 he formalized the four principles mentioned earlier in the first copyrighted advertisement ever published by a store. Once the public realized that his ads really did mean what they said, his business exploded. In 1881 the Christmas crush of customers became so great that he was forced to shut the doors periodically to protect those already in the store. As the clientele of his "New Kind of Store" grew, Wanamaker steadily expanded his line of goods and began to manufacture his own house brands. The book business began in 1877 with ten dollars' worth of children's books placed on one end of a counter; by 1884 Wanamaker did as much as $10,000 a day in books alone.[18]

His innovations took many forms. Wanamaker was the first to install a restaurant in a general store (1876) and the first to install electric lights—arc lamps in 1878 and then incandescent lamps after they were patented in 1880. Wanamaker even sought out Edison while the latter was working on his light bulb. "His eagerness was like that of a madman," Wanamaker recalled. "He refused to eat or sleep, being infatuated with the idea which he so soon thoroughly developed." Wanamaker had his own infatuation with technology. He installed elevators in 1882 along with a ventilation system. By 1889 he boasted the largest private electric plant in the country. New departments kept coming; in 1880 alone he added furniture, refrigerators, sporting goods, carpets, and jewelry. The expanding store gobbled up buildings on Chestnut Street until by 1883 its forty-six departments occupied eight acres of floor space. Six years later it had nearly doubled again to fifteen acres.[19]

Although he dealt with a different market than Woolworth, Wanamaker was no less sensitive to costs and prices. "The more goods we sell," he announced in 1879, "the cheaper we can afford to sell. . . . Reduced prices to commence and run through the season is a fundamental principle of our business." In carrying out that pledge he created a variety of sales: the February "Opportunity Sale," the July "Midsummer Sale," the September "Early Fall Sale," and, in 1878, the first January "White Sale." In a 1900 speech he declared his belief that "the new American system of store-keeping is the most powerful factor yet discovered to compel minimum prices." But he also demanded style and quality. In 1878 Wanamaker sent his first buyer to Europe; three years later he opened a Paris office to monitor trends in art and fashion as well as to buy goods. By 1884 he had ten buyers making annual trips to the Continent.[20]

James Cash Penney forged a distinctive middle course between those of Wanamaker and Woolworth. Like Woolworth, he concentrated on small towns, where people clutched their money tightly. Like Wanamaker, he sold quality goods only for cash, but he opposed special sales, believing that merchandise "should be sold at the lowest possible price every day." Few merchants understood their customers better than Penney. The folks who lived in and around Kemmerer, Wyoming, where his first store opened, were "people who took the saving of so much as a penny seriously," he recalled. "To save pennies for them I had to save them for myself. We threw away no wrapping paper, no short ends of string, no empty boxes, no nails." Keeping costs down became an obsession with him as it had with Woolworth. "Boys," he told a young Sam Walton among others, "you know we don't make a dime out of the merchandise we sell, we only make our profit out of the paper and string we save!"[21]

His first store could not have been more plain: one room with a single small window that furnished its light, no water or other fixtures. Penney opened at seven in the morning and closed "when no more people in the streets seemed to be heading for the store," which on Saturdays could be as late as midnight. Before opening he saturated the town with flyers and handbills. From the first he determined to sell merchandise of "the best possible value" for less money than anyone else. As his business flourished, Penney worked out the simple but ingenious partnership plan that enabled him to expand rapidly. He put up two-thirds of the capital and the partner one-third, with an important catch: The partner must be a current manager of one of his stores who had already demonstrated his competence. As Penney explained the deal, "When a store manager had enough money out of store earnings to finance a one-third interest in a new store, he was allowed to do so, providing he had trained a man to manage it for him. In this way our personal trainees would become our partners."[22]

What Penney called a system of "enlightened selfishness" proved fabulously successful. Each partner became an entrepreneur but also had to help someone else succeed as well. All the stores followed Penney's guide in avoiding expensive locations, keeping fixtures plain, selling only for cash, and stocking articles that were always in demand. This game plan helped keep prices low and made customers comfortable in his stores. Penney kept his focus on towns of two or three thousand people. He found a man, George H. Bushnell, who developed for him centralized bookkeeping, accounting, and financing systems. Convinced that centralized buying would slash costs even more, he opened an office in New York and trained men as buyers. However, the managers still dictated what merchandise they wanted; in Penney's scheme the buyers were "little more than leg men for the merchants." In 1913 Penney incorporated all his Golden Rule stores into the J. C. Penney Stores Company.[23]

Penney shared Woolworth's disdain for high markups on merchandise and his belief that profits flowed from the quick turnover induced by low markups. He monitored managers to make certain they bought goods "close to the local demand," kept prices low, took advantage of all discounts for cash, and kept stores tidy. Like Woolworth, too, Penney believed in a lean operation. The New York office was as spartan as his first store. He slit his mail to use the envelopes for scratch paper and did all paperwork in longhand. "When a pencil was needed," he noted proudly, "one of us went out and bought it for a penny. We bought ink a bottle at a time, as we did penholders, with pen points by the nickel's worth." Buyers making their first trip to New York were startled to discover that they slept seven to a hotel room, ate at the cheapest restaurants, and walked instead of taking the streetcars.[24]

Sam Walton, the great eclectic, adapted most of Penney's principles into his own system but gave them a unique style imprinted with his own irresistible personality. "There's no question that I have the personality of a promoter," Walton observed. "I have occasionally heard myself compared to P. T. Barnum because of the way I love to get in front of a crowd and talk something up. . . . But underneath that personality, I have always had the soul of an operator, somebody who wants to make things work well, then better, then the best they possibly can." In all three phases of his career—the variety store, discount store, and club warehouse—he kept costs and prices low, pushed turnover, wasted no money on store frills, ran the leanest of operations, and emphasized quality service. As writer Vance Trimble observed, he borrowed "Penney's whole concept of how to succeed by putting customer satisfaction ahead of profit." More accurately, he saw customer satisfaction as the doorway to profit. But Penney was far from his only source.

Like an artist who haunted galleries or a writer who read voraciously, Walton scouted every kind of store that promised even the germ of an idea for improving his own operation. Early in his career he rode the bus all night just to visit two Ben Franklin stores in Minnesota and saw for himself the great advantage of self-service. He returned home and jubilantly turned his Bentonville, Arkansas, store into "only the third self-service variety store in the whole country."[25]

During the late 1950s, Walton began hearing about the early discounters. One of them, Herb Gibson, whose credo was simply "Buy it low, stack it high, sell it cheap," invaded Arkansas and gave Walton a lesson about the future. Walton flew around the country studying the discount store concept, visited stores like the pioneering Ann & Hope in Providence, Rhode Island, and talked with the men who operated them. "There's not an individual in these whole United States who has been in more retail stores—all types . . . than Sam Walton," said his brother Bud. "His mind is just so inquisitive when it comes to this business." In the end the model for Wal-Mart proved to be not Ann & Hope so much as Harry Blair Cunningham, who took dime-store magnate S. S. Kresge into the new world of merchandising with a discount store in Garden City, Michigan, called Kmart. "I have always had the greatest admiration for Harry Cunningham," said Walton, "because . . . that thing was ten or twenty years ahead of its time, and he did it better than anybody else."[26]

Within a remarkably short time that honor belonged to Walton. The first Wal-Mart store opened in Rogers, Arkansas, in July 1962, with only 16,000 square feet of space and no fixtures except tables. "In those days we did not have anywhere near the emphasis on quality that we have today," Walton admitted. "What we were obsessed with was keeping our prices below everybody else's. . . . The idea was simple: When customers thought of Wal-Mart, they should think of low prices and satisfaction guaranteed." By 1966 Walton had eighteen variety stores and four Wal-Marts. To phase out the former and multiply the latter, he needed cheaper merchandise, more good managers, and more capital. Aided by his wife, Helen, Walton found a host of good men, proved as tough a buyer as Woolworth, and raised capital by going public. In seeking men, Walton again did not hesitate to "nose around other people's stores searching for good talent."[27]

He also displayed an instinctive genius for locating stores. The formula was simple: "Put discount stores into little one-horse towns which everybody else was ignoring." Instead of going into cities, Walton threw up stores in a ring well outside the city and waited for growth to come to him—which it did. "We just started repeating what worked," he said, "stamping out stores cookie-cutter style" in one of five sizes between thirty thousand and sixty thousand feet. To stock the stores he created a brilliant distribution system that reversed the usual procedure. Instead of building warehouses to supply existing stores, Walton erected the warehouse first and then spotted locations for stores around it. Later he declared that "the efficiencies and economies of scale we realize from our distribution system give us one of our greatest competitive advantages." The first distribution center at Searcy, Arkansas, became the model for an entire system. "After we proved it would work," said David Glass, "we were able to duplicate the model anywhere, and that's what we've done."[28]

Ray Kroc worked in a different medium from that of the other merchandisers, yet his approach had much in common with them. He emphasized customer satisfaction and devised a formula that stressed quality, service, and cleanliness (QSC). Where Penney and Walton created systems that allowed managers to succeed in an expanding system, Kroc revolutionized the franchise system in a way that enabled franchisees to succeed. Food service franchises arrived on the American scene as early as 1924 in tandem with the mushrooming popularity of the automobile, most notably Ford's

Model T. The early franchisers—A&W, Howard Johnson, and Dairy Queen—set the pattern for the industry by earning their money from license fees and, more important, selling food products and supplies to the franchisees. They did little more than rake in the profits with no responsibility for standards or operations. It was an El Dorado stacked heavily in favor of the franchiser, and for that reason drew plenty of imitators.[29]

This short-term, easy money approach held no appeal for Kroc. "Ray's theory was totally opposite," said Don Conley, one of his executives. "He thought that if franchisers made their franchisees successful, they would automatically be successful. His new idea was to provide the franchisees with enough services to be successful." In short, he would service the servicers. "As simple as it sounds," wrote author John Love, "it was a revolutionary idea in the rapidly expanding food franchising business, and Kroc's notion of a fair and balanced franchise partnership is without question his greatest legacy." To do this required much more control over the system, and to get it Kroc had to sacrifice the quick profits typical of the industry's conventional practices.[30]

Once Kroc gained the right to franchise from the McDonald brothers, he took a different tack by selling only single-store, not territorial franchises. Then he took the major step of refusing to profit from selling products and equipment to the franchisees on the grounds that it amounted to a conflict of interest. "I had to help the individual operator succeed," he explained, ". . . and I couldn't do that and, at the same time, treat him as a customer." He did select the suppliers for the franchisees in order to insure uniformity of quality and gain the price advantages of bulk buying, but he passed these savings along to the franchisees instead of pocketing a rebate from the supplier as was the usual practice. Like the other merchandisers, he exploited the value of volume purchases. Kroc built franchisee loyalty by providing savings on food products, supplies, and equipment; they gained customer loyalty by charging lower prices.[31]

McDonald's set the standards for quality and recommended packaging methods, but the operators did the actual purchasing from suppliers. With a menu of only nine items that required only thirty-five or forty more items to make them, the supply list was limited and large in volume. Kroc also helped suppliers figure out ways to lower their costs, driving down their prices even more. By using a slim list of suppliers, Kroc could develop and enforce rigid specifications to ensure quality. "From an operations standpoint," wrote Love, "McDonald's was introducing not a new restaurant but a food manufacturing system." A key element of that system lay in stringent conformity to standards spelled out in Fred Turner's first operations manual, which appeared in 1958 and was updated regularly to reflect the collective experience of the franchises. The result was a consistency of product and service unmatched in the food industry's history.[32]

Most of the manual's provisions came from trial and error. Kroc had no grand design to impose on the company. "I work from the part to the whole," he said, "and I don't move on to the large scale idea until I have perfected the small details. . . . You must perfect every fundamental of your business . . . to perform well." Once lessons were learned, they were inculcated into the system and expounded in the manuals. In 1961 they became the core curriculum of a training program that evolved into Hamburger University. "Our first class had eighteen students," Kroc recalled. "We awarded them a Bachelor of Hamburgerology with a minor in french fries." By 1963 the training program was launching a steady stream of qualified managers and operators into the McDonald's system. Yet it did not breed mere clones. On the contrary, Kroc relied on the franchisees for new ideas in products and encouraged them to experiment and innovate. The result, noted

Love, was "a corporation of natively intelligent, fanatically aggressive, and extremely divergent personalities" upholding the rigid standards of QSC. "These were not organization men," he added; "they were Kroc's version of corporate entrepreneurs."[33]

The technologists worked in a different world, one in which issues of cost and price matter less at first than quality. Yet they share many characteristics and concerns even though their lives range across 150 years of rapid technological change. The most surprising and striking thing they have in common is that, for all their genius at invention, the major contribution from most of them lay in their ability to organize, lead, and inspire. Had they done nothing more than create new machines or products, their reputations would have been secure. But in every case except one, they built on the foundation of invention to create organizations that, as with the other entrepreneurs, long outlived them. (Obviously, this point amounts to sheer speculation in the case of Bill Gates, who is still living.)

Even Thomas Edison, the one exception, built a large enterprise and ran it for many years before turning it over to his son Charles. "I do not regard myself as a pure scientist," he declared. "I do not search for laws of nature, and have made no great discoveries of such laws. . . . I am only a professional inventor. My studies and experiments have been conducted entirely with the object of inventing that which will have commercial utility." Like so many of the great entrepreneurs, he had the capacity to extract long hours of hard work from his staff through both inspiration and example. No one worked longer or harder than Edison himself did, and, as Harold Livesay observed, "his charismatic, pyrotechnic character generated excitement and kept the staff entertained." But not even these qualities or the dedication of his men succeeded in making either Menlo Park or West Orange the "factory of creativity" that Edison longed to realize. He could lead and inspire, but he did not organize well. Robert Conot described West

Orange as "a veritable cuckoo's nest of learned men, cranks, enthusiasts, ambitious youth, plain mockers, and quite insane people," all inhabiting "an unstructured and disorderly rat's nest." Nor did Edison delegate well; only those projects in which he was personally involved made significant progress. "As a manager of men," wrote Forrest McDonald, "Edison was a driver, not a leader . . . only a few, who could work at his own killing pace, were permitted to exercise initiative."[34]

Tom Watson occupied the opposite end of the spectrum from Edison. The only one of the technologists who was not an inventor, he excelled at the more traditional skills of organization, salesmanship, leadership, and management. Yet he succeeded where Edison failed in building one of the first great technology companies and research laboratories in the nation. Unlike all of the other entrepreneurs except Vail, Watson did not own the company he ran. But after 1924, when he became CEO, he dominated the firm he renamed IBM as completely as if it were his own. Indeed, he created the company in his own image, one that stressed loyalty, unity, idealism, enthusiasm, and conservative social values. Like his mentor Patterson, Watson became a benevolent dictator governing a realm of his own design. He subscribed fully to Patterson's dictum that "business is only a form of teaching. You teach people to desire your product; that is selling. You teach workmen how to make the right product; that is manufacturing. You teach others to cooperate with you; that is organization."[35]

Not being an inventor, Watson had to rely on experts, but he picked them wisely, used them well, and kept himself above them. A consummate salesman, he put together a sales force unequaled in its dedication to the job and the company. IBM salesmen were not merely well trained; they were converted to the gospel of Tom Watson, which had loyalty at its root. He offered worthy employees not just jobs but a life commitment complete with perks reminiscent of a welfare state and high-church rituals that energized and unified the faithful. In return Watson demanded that employees surrender "their right to be different, to question the system that embraced them, engulfed them, rounded off the outlines of their diversity until they became nearly identical reflections in a corporate mirror." They were admonished to avoid doing anything, even in their private lives, that reflected poorly on themselves or the company.[36]

Standards of conduct, written and unwritten, were made clear. Drinking was anathema to Watson, as was dress that departed from his conservative model of white shirt, tie, and suit. "Clothes don't make the man," he once said, "but they go a long way toward making a businessman." Employees were expected to be good citizens, attend the church of their choice regularly, and participate energetically in the songs, slogans, sales pep rallies, and rituals that marked the IBM way of life. Every desk held a sign that said "THINK" in full view of its occupant, and woe to the employee who did not have one in its proper place. Watson especially loved the company songs, which rang out at meetings, conventions, banquets, and company ceremonies. "I used to marvel at how willingly new employees embraced the company spirit," recalled Tom Watson, Jr. "As far as I could tell, nobody made fun of the slogans and songs. Times were different then . . . being earnest didn't seem as corny . . . as it does today."[37]

Watson hardly relied on spirit alone to grow his company. Besides his ferocious drive and uncommon intelligence, he had the salesman's gift for persuasion. He could convince customers to buy his product (and show his troops how to convince them), motivate employees to perform beyond their capacities, and charm powerful men into doing things they did not particularly want to do. He knew how to make decisions, and his judgment was sound. During the Great Depression, for example, while other companies wilted and contracted, Watson followed Carnegie's dictum by expanding. Between 1929 and 1938 he doubled his sales force, told them to take off the kid gloves and be aggressive, and emerged in 1940 as the nation's leading office appliance firm. He also paid close heed to the production forces, touring the factory regularly to see for himself what was needed. After one such tour in 1934 he overruled his managers and abolished piecework, saying it distracted people from producing goods of the best quality. He was in many respects an unmatched executive who took a group of ordinary men and turned them into a first-rate organization.[38]

Andrew Carnegie called George Westinghouse "a genius who can't be downed." Although the creator of numerous major inventions, his influence extended far beyond them. "In the field of electricity," noted a biographer, "he was not an inventor of fundamentals. He invented many useful details, but his great work was in stimulating, combining, and directing the work of other men. . . . He was the captain of them all, the man who received and coordinated and executed." Westinghouse revered basic research. Like Thomas Edison, he gathered about him an all-star team of bright men; unlike Edison, he used them as a team and knew how to lead them. Though somewhat aloof by nature, he could charm and persuade men to do his bidding. His blend of gifts, like those of Watson, made him a benevolent dictator as a manager. Above all, he respected the work of his team. One of the brightest among them, Nikola Tesla, praised Westinghouse for being "one of those few men who conscientiously respect intellectual property."[39]

Edwin Land shared many attributes with Westinghouse, especially his love of pure research and distaste for finance. He, too, combined "inventive genius and personal charisma with a hard-headed business sense that included a shrewd grasp of the market, a conservative approach to business finance, and an ability to select and inspire talented subordinates." Howie Rogers said that "the way he trained me was letting me see the way he operated and then leaving me free to proceed." But where Westinghouse was not the least bit introspective, Land viewed himself as a philosopher-scientist and regarded the two roles as mutually reinforcing. His management style has been described as "unconventional, indirect and elliptical. He seemed able to manipulate parts of his company without managing them." Land always preferred working with small teams and, as the company grew, exhorted, "Let's keep small. Let's keep intimate." He scorned market research, insisted that a good product would create its own market—a view that often brought him into conflict with his officers—and believed firmly that he was creating "the ideal company."[40]

Robert Noyce also found himself pulled out of the laboratory into management and, despite his success, came to understand his limitations at the latter. "One thing I learned at Fairchild," he said later, ". . . is that I don't run large organizations well. I don't have the discipline to do that, have the follow through. . . . My interests and skills are in a different place. . . . Getting people to do something . . . only works for me in a smaller group." Yet he played a major role in the formation and growth of two wildly successful companies. When he and seven colleagues launched Fairchild Semiconductor, none of them had any experience running a business. Noyce emerged at once as the individual capable of doing the job. It helped that he had a gift for salesmanship as well as the kind of charisma that induced people to believe him and follow his lead. As writer Michael S. Malone observed, "It must have taken a remarkable individual to hold together a company perpetually at a flashpoint with dozens of explosive and brilliant personalities." Having cut his teeth on Fairchild's spectacular growth, Noyce applied the lessons learned to Intel and created something more akin to a "factory of creativity" than Edison ever had.[41]

As a manager Noyce thrived in and encouraged an environment where people lived for their work and, as Tom Wolfe noted, "became absorbed in their companies the way men once had in the palmy days of the automobile industry." This pattern of work as a way of life, in which the techies met after hours to drink and swap war stories, soon became the signature image of Silicon Valley. It was, added Wolfe, "not a great way of life for marriages. . . . The second time around they tended to 'intramarry.'" At Intel Noyce removed all the cubicles and put everyone, executives included, in one big room. Levels of management were virtually eliminated in favor of "strategic business segments," which resembled major departments in corporations but with far more autonomy—enough to operate like separate companies. "Councils," composed of line people from the divisions involved in projects, moved from problem to problem and worked them out as coordinating bodies without vested authority.[42]

Noyce's system had at least a faint tinge of Watson's approach. "This wasn't a corporation," wrote Wolfe, ". . . it was a congregation. . . . Everyone—Noyce included—was expected to attend sessions on 'the Intel Culture.'" But it lacked any hint of the authoritarianism and cultlike worship of the leader that came to dominate IBM culture. It was, however, no less performance oriented. Noyce approved Andrew Grove's use of report-card performance ratings on employees, believing that, as Wolfe said, "most of the young hotshots who were coming to work at Intel had never had the benefit of honest grades in their lives." The point always was not only to evaluate but also to encourage self-discipline, which lay at the heart of Noyce's paradoxical management style: The freer the work environment, the more disciplined the worker had to be to benefit from it. But Noyce did not care to devote his life to management. In 1974 he put Grove and Gordon Moore in charge of Intel and retreated to the office of chairman of the board.[43]

Bill Gates, who actually called himself a "technologist," borrowed something from both Watson and Noyce while creating a firm so much in his own image that one executive said bluntly, "We hire little Bills." All three men created companies that existed in their own special worlds, devoted to what one Microsoft executive called a "maniacal work ethic," and all three revered their leaders. Unlike both Watson and Noyce, however, Gates did not come easily to management. The early years of Microsoft were a shambles in which "budgeting and planning were nonexistent. Product pricing was seat-of-the-pants. . . . Until mid-1981 the entire accounting system had amounted to some handwritten ledgers and two checkbooks." But Gates learned quickly how to manage as well as market, and he made superb choices in the men he recruited to help him. He became what even Philippe Kahn of Borland conceded was "one helluva sharp businessman and a top-notch negotiator." Warren Buffett called his business savvy "extra-ordinary," adding, "If Bill had started a hot dog stand, he would have become the hot dog king of the world."[44]

In forging his empire, Gates created a corporate culture that thrived on conflict and confrontation. "Conflict is at the heart of every significant Microsoft decision," said one observer. "This is a company constantly at war, not only with outsiders, but also with itself." To understand the company, added a developer, "you have to understand that we're all adolescents. And proud of it." Gates provided the most pleasant of battlefields at the Redmond campus. Unlike Noyce, he gave people private offices with doors and a view, but he also eliminated virtually all the layers of traditional management. Above all, Gates's own tireless work ethic prevailed. His style of motivating the troops was not pretty. Where Noyce seldom raised his rich baritone voice, Gates yelled and ranted and kept repeating how stupid something was until the victim either persuaded him otherwise or retreated in humiliation to do it better. Gates believed in enlightenment by argument and would hotly contest any issue, but he was also willing to change his mind when shown that he was mistaken. "We never waste a lot of time talking about what we're doing well," he declared. "Every meeting is about, 'Sure, we won in seven of the categories, but what about the eighth category?' . . . Staring out the window and saying, 'Isn't this great?' is not the solution to pushing things forward."[45]

All the technologists could lead because those working with them realized they knew their stuff and were the brightest of the bright. They had all (except Watson) developed technology and were as comfortable—if not more so—in the laboratory as behind a desk. As one Microsoft vice president said of Gates, "Bill is just smarter than everyone else." He had to be, because he worked in an industry that was as savagely competitive as any of the old industrial sectors, one in which the notion of competition took on ominous new dimensions. "You always have to be thinking about who is coming to get you," Gates observed. Mitch Kapor of Lotus said bluntly, "The PC business is *war.* Either you fight or you're a casualty. You have to look the enemy in the eye and never, ever blink." It was an industry, said Ross Perot, "where the faster you run the faster you have to run. . . . There is no halftime in this business. You don't even get to go to the locker room and rest." Management and the creation of new products become even more challenging in an environment where change comes so fast that today's stunning breakthrough is tomorrow's quaint curiosity. Ford and Edison learned that lesson the hard way, but they at least enjoyed years of supremacy.[46]

No one understands this condition better than Gates, who takes nothing for granted. "The entrepreneurial mind-set continues to thrive at Microsoft," he declared, "because one of our major goals is to reinvent ourselves—we have to make sure that we are the ones replacing our products instead of someone else." A Microsoft vice president put it another way: "If Microsoft were a car, it would have a large gas pedal and a small but workable brake. It would not have a rear view mirror." A journalist reported that he "observed no scolding 'THINK!' signs on the wall as in the IBM of yore, but 'THINK' permeated Microsoft's bloodstream through and through." Although Microsoft spends more than $2 billion a year on research and development, Gates realizes that no one wins forever. "Microsoft won't be immortal," he said. "All companies fail. It's just a question of when. My goal is to keep the company vital as long as possible."[47]

This was the lesson Gates learned from Ford, whose spectacular rise to success flamed out when he failed to read a changing market during the 1920s. Ford's failure offers but one example of the final phase of the pattern of development offered earlier in the chapter. At every stage of growth the formula that made the previous stage successful is rendered obsolete by the very nature of that success. This may be the single most important principle in the process. It means that future success cannot be attained by simply repeating past methods or patterns, because those patterns have changed the environment. The company must adapt to the new environment, which may require a new organization, a different approach, fresh skills, new products, or other changes.

Ford is but one of the many great entrepreneurs whose success moved them into a new environment in which clinging to past patterns doomed them to failure. The talents of the entrepreneur who created the original organization may or may not be suited to move the company to this next, or any succeeding, stage. And once he retires or dies, his successor may fail to understand this need. Nothing is more difficult for a firm or its managers than getting away from what made them successful in the first place. For this reason it is instructive to look at the shortcomings and failures of the great entrepreneurs as well as their successes.

| 6 |

Follies and Foibles

Money is only loaned to a man; he comes into the world with
nothing, and he leaves with nothing.

—WILLIAM C. DURANT[1]

Durant understood the truth of this observation better than
most. Few if any of our entrepreneurs made and lost more fortunes
than he did. All understood that, as Land put it, "You must expect
failure after failure after failure before you succeed," and most
agreed with John Wanamaker that "a man who never makes mistakes loses much that it would do him good to know." Like other
great people, the entrepreneurs did nearly everything on an
enlarged scale, including their gaffes. In many cases their misjudgments stemmed from the same qualities that characterized their
successes. Galvanized by some vision, they threw themselves into
the quest, turned a deaf ear to those who said it couldn't be done or
warned that it invited disaster, and pounded relentlessly against
all obstacles. The joy, after all, was in the doing, even when the
doing turned into a grind or turned out badly. Risk and failure are
an indelible part of the creative process. Land, an expert in color,

revealed his true color when he said, "Any market already existing is inherently boring and dull."[2]

The follies of the great entrepreneurs vary as widely as their personalities. Some resulted from misreading the market, others from failing to discern trends or developments. A few involved trying to do too much with too little or doing too little when more was needed. What nearly all of the entrepreneurs had in common was some error in judgment that proved inconvenient to some of them and disastrous to others. For some, the miscues occurred in their primary endeavors; for others the problem lay in areas outside their expertise. James Penney's investment in a Miami bank that failed cost him not only most of his fortune but also his reputation. Cyrus McCormick, John D. Rockefeller, and Theodore Vail were incurable speculators who got burned repeatedly but kept coming back to the fire. "I have a blind spot," admitted Vail; "when I want to do anything I cannot see anything in reasons or in arguments against it. That blind spot has cost me a good deal of money."[3]

Vail had a penchant for investing in new technologies, few of which panned out. "Creating new stock companies was his hobby," observed his biographer. "He created corporations as a farmer makes hen's nests." The analogy was apt. One of his more esoteric but no less expensive flings, an ostrich farm, produced as a dividend a lone ostrich egg. The forlorn stockholders decided to make an omelet of it; when Vail could not be present, they sent him the shell. His most ambitious venture involved the creation of a system for heating cities and towns with superheated water from a central plant. The Prall Central Heating System made its costly debut in Boston. "I had the utmost confidence in the thing," Vail admitted, even though a report by the city engineer pronounced the building of hot-water mains beneath the city streets "extremely dangerous" and unwise. The enterprise failed in less than a year, leaving Vail saddled with debts that forced him to sell his Walnut Avenue mansion and most valuable paintings. Ironically, Vail's fortune rebounded when his shares in a Colorado mine, long considered worthless, turned golden after an unexpected strike.[4]

McCormick "relished a new financial adventure," claimed his biographer, because it "afforded him a release from the humdrum affairs of every day." He did extremely well in Chicago real estate and profited from his investment in the notorious Crédit Mobilier, but he also developed a weakness for mines that nearly always came up empty. A shrewd, hardheaded businessman, he nevertheless could not resist pouring money into faraway claims on nothing more than a prospectus or the report of some distant miner. Rockefeller's financial advisers, once in charge of his portfolio, were astonished to find that he had been duped in many of his investments. His true weakness lay in the stock market, which he played with a "guilty thrill." Even in old age, after Rockefeller had disbursed his fortune to his son and foundations, he kept $25 million as "pocket change . . . for playing the stock market." The crash of 1929 shriveled it down to a mere $7 million.[5]

The stock market was an intersection at which many of the entrepreneurs met. Some merely dabbled in the market and came away the wiser for the experience. Woolworth learned his lesson early. "I had a little experience of speculating in stocks myself," he recalled, "although I have never been guilty of buying stocks on margin. . . . Before I was aware of it I was paying much more attention to the quotations . . . than I was to running the store, and in three months I was losing my trade, and I decided then and there to let stocks alone and attend to business." Although Warren Buffett alone made his living there, others lived and died by the market's vacillations. Both Jay Gould and E. H. Harriman began their careers on Wall Street and maintained close ties to it. Gould depended on the market as a source of capital for his innumerable enterprises and never escaped its clutches. "The harsh truth was," wrote his biographer, "that Jay could not quit the market because his fortune and his empire were inextricably tied to its vagaries."

A serious miscalculation in 1884 nearly cost him that empire, and the ordeal of averting disaster undermined his already fragile health. Harriman worked on Wall Street well into middle age before his sudden and startling leap into railroading. Cornelius Vanderbilt was also tied to Wall Street by his investments and by the need to support the stocks of his railroads.[6]

For Billy Durant, the market became a cruel mistress that alternately rewarded and ruined him. During his peripatetic career in the automobile industry, he first ran General Motors as a one-man operation until he overreached himself and lost control of it to Wall Street bankers in 1910. Six years later he regained control with the support of Pierre du Pont and said laughingly, "If they stab me again, it will be when I am looking right straight at them." Although he shared control with du Pont, the ebullient Durant fell back into his familiar role as a one-man band rushing everywhere with fresh expansion plans. His bursts of creative energy caught up du Pont in the whirlwind of adding new firms to the General Motors stable—some of them thoroughbreds, many of them nags. When American entry into World War I sent the market tumbling in April 1917, Durant plunged in to support GM stock and soon found himself overextended. He was saved from embarrassment only by the receipt of $1 million from du Pont and the other directors.[7]

Bloodied but unbowed, Durant resumed his expansionist binge, confident that the war's end would bring a surge in demand for vehicles of all kinds. A $52.8 million expansion program launched Durant on a buying spree that ended abruptly when a plan to finance the program fell through and a severe recession gripped the nation in 1920. As the price of GM stock sank, Durant again undertook a rash campaign to support it with his own funds, buying heavily on margin using his GM stock as collateral until he had run up a tab of $34 million to bankers and brokers. Fearful that the collateral might be dumped on the market, du Pont and his colleagues joined with the House of Morgan to bail out Durant on condition that he surrender the presidency of General Motors to du Pont. In December 1920 Durant left GM for the second and final time, leaving it to the man who would provide it with the management team it sorely needed.[8]

Six weeks after leaving GM, Durant organized yet another car company, Durant Motors, but it never received the close attention he had given his earlier ventures. Alfred P. Sloan, Jr., who Durant had brought into General Motors and who would ultimately provide it with a successful and enduring organization, wrote the epitaph to Durant's role in the industry: "Mr. Durant was a great man with a great weakness—he could create but not administer." Durant's attention shifted from the industry he had pioneered to the stock market, where his heavy buying and seemingly uncanny judgment earned him a reputation as "king of the bulls" in a market that had begun to march steadily upward during the 1920s. He became a front-page pundit who practiced what he preached. In 1927, for example, he bought and sold over 2.5 million shares of 75 different industrial issues and ended the year owning 805,012 shares of stock with a paper profit of more than $7.5 million.[9]

During the 1920s Durant ceased to be an entrepreneur and became a trader, dealing in the abstractions of the market, which were light-years away from the real product he had helped create and promote for so long. "Money in such quantities," wrote his biographer, "took on a shimmering, impalpable quality, lacking the literal impact of the smaller sums that he had spent his life raising and dispensing for real estate, parts, workers. . . . He was now twice removed from the actual, gritty process of mechanical creation that he had once mastered." As he leaped joyfully into the maw of the boom, Durant Motors faded into failure. The crash of 1929 brought his bullish exuberance to a cruel reckoning that saw his net income shrivel from millions to a mere $3,731 in 1933. Three years later he declared bankruptcy. He returned to Flint, Michigan, his hometown, and in 1939 turned a vacated garage into an eighteen-lane bowling alley to which he added a lunch-room with a horseshoe-shaped counter and drive-in window. Insisting on high standards, he sometimes stepped in to demon-strate personally how to make a good hamburger. In this small way the great entrepreneur was reborn.[10]

While many of the other entrepreneurs dealt in the stock mar-ket, most of them had the bulk of their fortunes tied up in the companies they created. A few, notably Edwin Land, John Patter-son, Thomas Watson, and George Westinghouse, had virtually no outside investments beyond their own stocks. The only one of them to suffer so great a fall as Durant was Insull, who narrowly escaped prison in his twilight years. Unlike Durant, Samuel Insull had built his empire on a firm foundation of organization and sound management. Starting with Chicago Edison, a direct-current (DC) company, he confined its service to an area of about a mile around the Loop while using Commonwealth Electric, an alternating-current (AC) company, to provide service for the rest of the city. As his network expanded into the suburbs and rural areas, Insull gradually merged his mosaic of companies into larger firms such as Public Service Company of Northern Illinois, a 1911 consolida-tion that embraced thirty-nine companies. Another large amal-gam, Middle West Utilities, served 131,000 electric and 43,000 gas customers in thirteen states by 1914 and became the parent company for a growing network.[11]

By then Insull found himself in possession of the Chicago ele-vated transit system, which had floundered financially. He also became chairman of People's Gas, Light & Coke Company and rehabilitated that weak, corrupt firm. During World War I he took charge of the Illinois State Council of National Defense and proved so adept at raising money as to prompt the quip that if he had run the war, it might have turned a profit. But his companies suffered from neglect during the war and required heroic efforts on his part during the severe postwar adjustment that brought down

Durant. When the ordeal was over, Insull had what his biographer called "a thoroughgoing nervous breakdown," from which he recovered by a leisurely trip to Europe with his son. When he returned, Insull caught the rising tide of postwar prosperity and used it to resume his expansionist policy. By the mid-1920s he had emerged as the "one great utility operator independent of New York."[12]

To finance his growing empire, Insull borrowed a lesson from his wartime experience and concluded that he could sell bonds directly to his customers. To do this, he set up security sales departments in each of his major companies and turned to Harold L. Stuart of Halsey, Stuart & Co., who thought that bonds could be mass-marketed through small outlets to a great untapped supply of buyers awakened to securities by having bought war bonds. Stuart earned Insull's respect and all his business, selling as much as $200 million worth of bonds in one year. Insull loved this radical new approach because it bypassed the Wall Street bankers he despised, who had always been wary of utility bonds. As the bond business mushroomed into a mother lode, the New York houses took umbrage at Insull's disregard for their leadership. "These New York fellows were jealous of their prerogatives," said Stuart's brother later, "and if you wanted to get along you had to be deferential to them and keep your opinions to yourself. Mr. Insull wouldn't, and that made bad blood between them. Real bad blood."[13]

No one resented Insull's defiance more than the group of firms led by the House of Morgan, which were eager to organize the utilities industry under their rule. Halsey, Stuart & Co. had snatched from them the lion's share of the utility bond market, which approached $1 billion in new issues by 1926. Insull further outraged them by invading their domain early in 1928 when he acquired two power systems with operations in fourteen eastern states—his first major presence in what the Morgan group deemed "their" region. By then Insull had merged his two Chicago companies into Commonwealth Edison, one of four major pillars of his empire along with People's Gas, Public Service Company of Northern Illinois, and Middle West Utilities—the latter grown into a $1.2 billion colossus operating in thirty-two states.[14]

Although Insull had emerged as a public icon and major player in one of the nation's fastest-growing industries, he had not piled up a fortune. As late as 1926 his net worth was only around $5 million, largely because he showed little interest in making money. He did, however, want to preserve his empire for his son, and he grew suspicious of Cyrus Eaton, a rival who had surreptitiously bought large blocks of stock in all of Insull's major companies. To protect his control, Insull created in December 1928 a new holding company, Insull Utility Investments (IUI), and put all his and his brother's holdings into it. Having ignored the stock market for most of his life, he set the IPO price for the stock at a modest $12 a share just as the Great Bull Market was about to launch its mad acceleration. To his surprise the price of IUI climbed past $80 by the spring of 1929, and the stocks of his other companies soared as well. Between January and August, Commonwealth Edison leaped from 202 to 450 and Middle West Utilities from 169 to 529.[15]

Buoyed and bewildered by the market's overheating, Insull moved to do what he had long opposed: perfect his control by pyramiding his holdings. He formed a second holding company, Corporation Securities Company of Chicago (Corp), secured control of it through a voting trust, and interlocked it with IUI by having each one hold securities of the other. Together they became "the throne room of the Insull empire" with large blocs of stock from all four major Insull companies. As the market soared to dizzying heights, Insull's fortune rose with it. During one frantic fifty-day period in July and August 1929, the value of securities in his firms jumped more than $500 million at a rate of $7,000 a minute. On paper Insull found himself with a fortune of nearly $150 million. Then came the crash, which sent his security prices plunging as rapidly as they had risen. During the crisis he helped his overextended employees by using stock from his own portfolio to provide whatever collateral they needed.[16]

Confident that the aftermath of the crash would be no different from that of other depressions he had faced, Insull made three crucial decisions: He decided to expand while prices were low, use debt financing to do so, and eliminate Eaton as a threat by buying him out. All three policies, which seemed so reasonable at the time, proved disastrous. Recovery never came, the large debt incurred by selling new bonds became onerous, and $20 million of the $56 million paid for Eaton's holdings had to come from the hated New York bankers, giving them a wedge into Insull's empire. Using their market influence to hammer the price of Insull's companies steadily downward, the Morgan group finally brought Insull to his knees by the end of 1931. During the bleak months of 1932, IUI, Corp, and Middle West Utilities all fell into receivership and Insull was shoved out of his other companies much as Durant had been from General Motors. In both cases the Morgan group replaced them.[17]

The worst was yet to come. In 1934 Insull was indicted for mail fraud in an atmosphere that had grown virulently antibusiness. The charges were dubious at best, but they transformed the man who only a few years before had been an icon for the best attributes of business into a scapegoat for its transgressions. Despite the lurid publicity surrounding the trial, Insull was found innocent. A year later the state of Illinois tried him on embezzlement charges but failed to gain a conviction. Although Insull beat the charges, the headlines and notoriety damaged his reputation beyond repair. He spent his few remaining years broke and discredited. As his biographer observed, "For his fifty-three years of labor to make electric power universally cheap and abundant, Insull had his reward from a grateful people: he was allowed to die outside prison."[18]

No such fall from grace befell Thomas Edison, who remained a heroic figure in the public's eyes to his dying day. Still, he remains unique among the great entrepreneurs not only for the breathtaking number of his accomplishments but also for the astonishing number of his failures and gaffes. No man was so right about so many fundamental things and so wrong about so many others. He invented the phonograph but insisted that it was a business machine. "I don't want the phonograph sold for amusement purposes," he said. "It is not a toy. I want it sold for business purposes only." When he returned to the machine decades later and devised several major improvements, he resisted for a long time moving from his once successful cylinders to disks as a recording medium. Then, after making a belated success of disks, he adamantly refused to regard radio as anything more than a passing fad even though it soon devastated the phonograph and recording business with its programs of free music.[19]

Edison's pioneering work in motion pictures, which engulfed him in endless litigation, led to the creation of the "true father of all modern motion picture cameras" and the use of thirty-five-millimeter film, which remains standard. He also erected the first building intended as a studio for making films, and explored the use of color and sound in movies. At the time, however, Edison became best known for devising the kinetoscope, a peep-show machine that exhibited short movies to individual viewers. It was a stunning success and instant moneymaker, and to Edison it represented the future of the industry. To the suggestion that movies ought to go into a bigger hall or theater where large numbers of people could watch a longer version at the same time without interruption, he turned an already deaf ear. No amount of argument could convince him to leave "the narrow world of vaudevillian one-reelers, preachy vignettes, and didactic 'home library' subjects" in favor of full-length feature films.[20]

By far his greatest misjudgment occurred in the very field that brought him immortal fame. His invention of the incandescent light bulb and organization of the first electric power generating and distribution system ranks among the greatest technological achievements in history, and his efforts to expand that system marked the beginning of the electric power industry. It also became a trap that led him into wrongheaded embarrassment, if not infamy. In utilizing direct current for his system, Edison dismissed the potential of alternating current as unsafe despite the severe limitations of DC, which could not be transmitted over an area much greater than a mile. No amount of argument could dislodge his prejudice against AC. Edison had never been able to detach his ego from his inventions or give rivals their due. Of the man who became his bitter rival he once said, "Tell Westinghouse to stick to air brakes. He knows all about them. He don't know anything about engines."[21]

In fact, George Westinghouse knew a great deal about engines and even more about the potential of AC, which he proceeded to develop. His success prompted Edison to launch the "war of the currents," in which he used every means fair or foul to thwart Westinghouse and his supporters, including the charge that they were foisting a lethal technology upon an unwary public. It proved an ugly fight, but in the end Edison's DC was no match for a system that could transmit current hundred of miles compared to mere city blocks. The successful spread of AC forced even the Edison companies to adopt it by the turn of the century. Here, as elsewhere, Edison was spectacularly wrong in his dogged refusal to grasp or accept change in a field he had pioneered. It was as if his genius could take him only so far before becoming an obstacle instead of a beacon. As historian Harold C. Passer observed, "In 1879, Edison was a bold and courageous innovator. In 1889, he was a cautious and conservative defender of the *status quo.*"[22]

All these misjudgments hurt Edison in one way or another, but none did him more severe damage than the utter failure of his ore-operation scheme. During the mid-1870s Edison became aware of the lack of iron ore suitable for smelting in the eastern states. He devised an ore separating machine capable of extracting iron ore from marginal deposits and decided to build an industry on the notion that large profits could be gleaned from ore deposits previously thought worthless. In January 1880 he formed the Edison Ore Milling Company, which soon turned into the inventor's greatest and most fatal obsession. For ten years he poured his creativity, energy, and most of his fortune into the venture while ignoring badly needed work in electric lighting and other areas. He did so, argued one of his biographers, because "a successful ore-extracting operation would be justification for his failure to produce an alternating-current system."[23]

Instead the venture turned out to be the supreme white elephant of his career. "It was an unmitigated disaster," wrote Matthew Josephson, costing Edison "the entire fortune accumulated by his inventive labors." In all, Edison threw $3.2 million—two-thirds of it his own money—into the fiasco. When at last the operation folded, he had wasted half a decade in a struggle that left him heartbroken and slow to recover. "The final years of the 1890s," noted Robert Conot, ". . . were the least creative of his career until the closing decade of his life. . . . His illnesses grew more frequent, and he took longer to recover from them." Although Edison moved on to other successful projects such as the Portland cement business, the poured cement house, the storage battery, the revived phonograph, and the kinetoscope, he never again displayed the level of insight and ingenuity that marked his earlier career.[24]

Henry Ford, who drew early inspiration from Edison and later became his devoted friend, endured an equally harsh fall from grace that was entirely of his own doing. More than any of the great entrepreneurs, he fell prey to what Richard Tedlow called "the madness of great men." The problem was that Ford was far from a great man; he was only a great mechanic with a vision. He understood machines like Yeats understood poetry, and once said, "Machines are to a mechanic what books are to a writer." They were also the only books he read. "I don't like to read books," he declared; "they muss up my mind." That mind was a laser casting strong, brilliant light when focused on the narrow area that Ford understood, but nearly everything in the darkness outside its reach escaped his comprehension and became prisoner to his prejudices. He was at bottom a bigoted, small-minded man driven by dark suspicions and a vindictive spirit who understood neither himself nor the world around him.[25]

None of this would have mattered much had not the spectacular success of the Model T elevated Ford into a national celebrity and source of headlines. Earlier he had been a tough-minded, hardworking man devoted to his craft, easygoing despite his mean streak, and willing to hear the ideas of others. But fame and attention spoiled his essential simplicity. As Tedlow observed, "The 'ocean of publicity' . . . and the thousands of letters he received released something inside him which would have been better kept under lock and key. . . . He soon began to believe that his was a wisdom which surpassed understanding." He developed what David L. Lewis called "an insatiable appetite for headlines" and for attention—all of which confirmed his swelling belief in the infallibility of his own views. During the 1930s he turned Ford Motor Company into a totalitarian dictatorship with its own brand of secret police and purges that emulated the Stalinist regime in the Soviet Union.[26]

The certainty of his own convictions brought Ford both glory and disaster, as it had Edison. It fueled his creation of the Model T, one of the two or three most important machines of the twentieth century, but it also induced him to stay with the car despite an obvious shift in the automobile market. By 1921 Ford owned a 55 percent share of the automobile market. Although he made improvements to the Model T over the intervening years, his market share dwindled to 30 percent by 1926 because both cars and buyers had grown more sophisticated. Thanks largely to Ford, what had been a seller's market became a buyer's market, saturated as well by the accumulation of used cars. The Model T had become outmoded, but Ford remained blind to this increasingly obvious fact. As Jonathan Hughes wrote, "Ford refused to believe that the American public would abandon the glorious utility of the stark Tin Lizzie for the useless gadgetry, color and year model changes of his competition."[27]

But abandon it they did, until even Ford had to face the reality that the Tin Lizzie was doomed. In 1927 he had to shut down the giant River Rouge plant for six months to retool for production of the new Model A—a transition that cost the company anywhere from $200 to $250 million and was unprecedented in the magnitude of the task. While Ford struggled to create a vehicle for which nearly all its 5,580 parts had to be newly created, General Motors surged to the forefront of the industry led by its Chevrolet division, which took an entirely different and more efficient approach to production than Ford did. Ironically, the man who led Chevrolet to its leadership position, William Knudsen, had been one of Ford's most able lieutenants until Ford drove him from the company. The Model A proved to be a winner, but Ford paid dearly for the lag time and enormous cost of its production. From then on he trailed General Motors.[28]

Ford remained a powerful figure in the automobile industry, and with the Model A he adopted many of the policies he had long resisted, such as lavish advertising, installment buying, and model changes. He remained even more an American folk figure to the public, but his company turned increasingly into a nightmare workplace. Once hailed as a leader in labor relations with his introduction of the five-dollar-a-day wage in 1914, he soon developed a reputation for the worst labor relations in the industry—not only with workmen but also with executives, who had to endure constant infighting and regular purges of the ranks that seemed wholly arbitrary in their choice of victims. Having missed the industry's main challenge—the transition from production to marketing—Ford presided over a firm in disarray with a capricious hand and a mind that gradually gave way to senility. To many Americans he became known less for his pioneering automobile than for his bellicose anti-Semitism.[29]

Where Ford blundered by staying too long with the tried and true, Edwin Land erred by betting the farm on new products. As is typical with the great entrepreneurs, he let past performance govern future prospects without looking closely enough at significant differences. He had gambled his company's existence on the development of the first instant camera and won. He did the same thing on an even larger scale with the revolutionary SX-70 camera in 1972, which *Fortune* called "one of the most remarkable accomplishments in industrial history." Like Ford's Model A, Land created a product with virtually all new components, but he also had to create factories to build them. Again he proved successful, although at a heavy cost to himself and the company.[30]

While the development of the SX-70 generated friction within the company, its success reinforced Land's conviction that progress required defying the conventional wisdom in the introduction of new products. He was not above killing off a new product that failed; he had done so with a document copy machine in the late 1960s. But his judgment faltered when it came to Polavision. "The sophisticated simplicity of the Polavision system was one of his cleverest achievements," wrote his biographer. "To Land, it was impossible that such ingenuity would go unrewarded." Polavision was a kind of instant movie using a new type of film invented by Land's team that operated on a small cassette. The feat of creating this film was a tour de force done at enormous cost largely because Land had the same disdain for videotape that Edison had for radio. As a result, Polaroid found itself in the position of "putting a film on the market knowing that it would lose money, no matter how popular it proved to be."[31]

With Polavision, Land completed the cycle of instant photography from sepia pictures to movies. But the new system lacked sound, and the cassette held less than three minutes of film at a cost of $8. For $17, Sony offered a camcorder videotape with sound that played for two hours. The Sony machine was three times as expensive as the $600 Polavision system, but the future belonged to videotape. Polavision made its first appearance in California late in 1977 to a groundswell of apathy. It never caught on, and proved a costly failure at a time when the bloom of instant photography itself had begun to fade. Other technologies, especially smaller, cheaper, and lighter video cameras and thirty-five-millimeter cameras, rose to challenge Land's instant systems. In 1979 Polaroid had to lay off a thousand production workers and write off a $68 million loss. Its decline from greatness had begun.[32]

Polavision became Land's greatest failure. Deeply embittered by it, he blamed associates, marketing, and especially Bill McCune, who had always taken a dim view of its potential. McCune had been made president in 1975 after the ordeal of producing the SX-70 had split the board. When it became clear that Polavision was sinking, Land lobbied the directors to remove McCune. Instead the board, which included many of Land's longtime friends and associates, asked him to step down as CEO. "Oh, you don't want me? The hell with it," Land is said to have responded when the issue was put to him. He left the company formally in 1982 and retired to the splendid laboratory at the Rowland Institute he had created on the Charles River in Cambridge, Massachusetts. He remained a prophet with honor but never went back to the company he had founded. Steven Jobs said of him in 1985, "The man is a national treasure. I don't understand why people like that can't be held up as models."[33]

None of the other entrepreneurs miscalculated on so grand a scale, but nearly all of them had missteps that cost them dearly. Watson had built his career on punch cards and electromechanical machines and refused for a long time to acknowledge the ascendance of the electronic computer. He scorned magnetic tape as Land did videotape. When ENIAC first appeared, he ordered his engineers to build a super calculator in 1947. The resulting Selective Sequence Electronic Calculator cost nearly $1 million and was an ungodly amalgam of electronic and mechanical parts spanning 120 feet with 12,500 vacuum tubes and 21,400 mechanical relays. It became an immediate technological dinosaur unable to match the speed of the all-electronic ENIAC. Only the dogged, often fiery arguments of his son and the coaxing of another executive persuaded Watson that the future lay with the electronic computer.[34]

In a very different context, Walton had his own distrust of computers. "Sam never did like computers," said one of his executives. "He thinks of them as overhead." As his biographer observed, "The electronic age seemed to offer several fancy ways to waste money." It took the persistent arguments of David Glass and Jack Shewmaker, two of his top executives, to convince him of the value of computers. "Everybody at Wal-Mart knows that I've fought all these technology expenditures just as hard as I could," Walton admitted. "I did want it, I knew we needed it, but I just couldn't bring myself to say, 'Okay, sure, spend what you need.'" Once persuaded, however, Walton poured $500 million over a five-year period into a sophisticated system that by 1979 enabled all his stores and warehouses to communicate with headquarters around the clock.[35]

Walton had made a very different error with his very first Ben Franklin store in Newport, Arkansas. Having spent five years making it the largest variety store in the state, he had to surrender it when the landlord refused to extend his lease. The landlord wanted the successful business for his son, and Walton had left himself vulnerable by not demanding a long-term lease. "I had no alternative but to give it up," he recalled gloomily. "It was the low point of my business life. . . . I blamed myself for ever getting suckered into such an awful lease." His wife, Helen, took the loss just as hard. "I hated to leave," she said later. "We had built a life there, and it was so disturbing to have to walk away from it." Nineteen years later, in 1969, Walton opened Wal-Mart No. 18 in Newport. It thrived from the start and soon forced the Ben Franklin store to close. "You can't say we ran that guy—the landlord's son—out of business," said Walton. "His customers were the ones who shut him down. They voted with their feet." Never would the fiercely competitive Walton admit to the satisfaction of sweet revenge.[36]

Ray Kroc made a comparable mistake in the first contract he signed with the McDonald brothers. It ran for only ten years, and contained provisions that later proved incompatible with Kroc's vision of what his enterprise should be. As that vision expanded, he found the brothers unwilling to deviate from the strict letter of the original terms. "The McDonald brothers were simply not on my wavelength at all," Kroc declared. "I was obsessed with the idea of making McDonald's the biggest and best. They were content with what they had." In 1960 Kroc got the contracts extended for ninety-nine years, but to gain a free hand he pushed for an outright purchase. The McDonald brothers agreed to sell for the steep price of $2.7 million and demanded cash. Although

Kroc's projections showed that he could not pay off that amount until 1991, he struggled to raise the money and completed the deal. McDonald's growth was so successful, however, that he managed to pay off the principal in only six years. "The total cost . . . to us—about $14 million—was peanuts compared to what the corporation earned in the years that followed," he said, but at the time it looked to be a steep mountain to climb.[37]

Later efforts by Kroc to expand outside the McDonald's formula all fell flat. He bought a restaurant on Chicago's South Side, but it folded in eighteen months. He tried to start a chain of pie shops in California and a more upscale hamburger emporium called Ramon's, but both efforts flopped. At different times he came close to buying the Taco Bell and Baskin-Robbins chains, and he skated to the edge of plunging into the amusement park business. In 1974 he bought the San Diego Padres because he had always wanted to own a baseball team and would have acquired his hometown Chicago Cubs if Philip K. Wrigley had been willing to sell. But none of his other endeavors or concepts in the food industry, fast or otherwise, amounted to anything.[38]

As might be expected, Kroc was hardly alone in overreaching himself on occasion. Jay Gould's main fault was forever trying to do more than his limited resources would sustain. The problem persisted because his visions grew even faster than those resources. Some of his ventures collapsed because their financing was too feeble; others simply didn't pan out. Such disappointments were inevitable for Gould, who kept the vast part of his capital in play rather than in safe investments. Cornelius Vanderbilt rashly tried to inaugurate a transatlantic mail and passenger service without the government subsidy that barely sustained the existing one. He had much better luck in creating a Panama line. John Wanamaker hoped that buying and renovating the old A. T. Stewart emporium in New York would give him a foothold in that city's retail trade. But the store, built in 1862, had languished as trade moved uptown, and Wanamaker could not reverse that flow even though his operation did reasonably well despite the location.[39]

George Westinghouse tried to make a business out of producing and distributing natural gas in Pittsburgh during the mid-1880s. This led him to form a company to experiment in making fuel gas for heat and power. Both ventures ended in costly failures, as did other Westinghouse brainstorms such as the vapor lamp, but these setbacks never deterred him from trying out some other new idea. In putting together his tobacco empire, Buck Duke labored mightily but in vain to dominate the cigar trade as he did cigarettes, plug, snuff, and pipe tobacco. E. H. Harriman tried to forge the nucleus of a global transportation system but found that his methods could not budge the governments of several key nations such as Japan, Russia, and China.[40]

A few of the entrepreneurs committed the opposite blunder of omission in their slowness to see or grasp opportunities. George Eastman was slow to realize that motion picture film was a major new market and not just another passing fancy. The fact that he also disliked sound movies kept him from moving to the forefront of that market. Andrew Carnegie, burned by earlier ore ventures, was even slower to grasp the potential of the Mesabi Range, which proved to be the mother lode of iron deposits on the entire North American continent. It was Mesabi's ore that finally made Carnegie Steel entirely self-sufficient. "Fortunately," he recalled, "I woke up in time. . . . The truth of the matter is until I went to Lake Superior and saw and studied the question, I was averse to buying ores at all." Bill Gates went so far as to create a memo to himself entitled "Microsoft's Greatest Mistakes." Topping the original list was missing the computer networking market that Novell captured. Later, however, he allowed that the company's slow awakening to the growth and development of the Internet was an even bigger oversight. He was also slow to appreciate the bonanza offered by the retail market for software.[41]

The follies and foibles of the great entrepreneurs can be dismissed as demonstrating that they too were human, or in some cases proving the old moral that pride goeth before the fall, but they reveal something more as well. They show a scope of ambition and depth of confidence that few other people can match, as well as a willingness to take enormous risks. Entrepreneurial theory often posits that entrepreneurs do not take great risks but rather take calculated risks seeking to avoid or minimize losses. While this may be true at the tactical level, it does not apply to the strategic realm. Every one of our entrepreneurs reached points where he had to plunge into the unknown and hew his own path through it. In most cases they put all they had on the line because they believed so strongly in their vision. Failure always revealed the true dimension of risk far more blatantly than success, which often concealed it.

In daring not only to have great visions but to pursue them relentlessly, the entrepreneurs behaved in the same manner as creative people in other fields. Like other creative people, too, entrepreneurs found that success and failure were cut from same cloth. The very qualities that enabled them to succeed usually proved to be the same ones that led them into their worst follies. They believed ardently in a project, pursued it vigorously, threw all available resources at it, refused to be swayed by naysayers or warnings, and could not accept the possibility of failure even when it stared them in the face. The failing, in short, was not one of technique but of judgment. This holds true for their errors of omission as well—those times when they missed important changes or new conditions that offered choice opportunities or threatened their original masterpiece. The very strength of that original vision and their enormous effort in realizing it often blinded them to anything that ran contrary to it.

Few of the great entrepreneurs were flexible of mind, however adaptable they might be in carrying out their own mission. Once they found their medium and style, they tended to stick with them. There are some exceptions. Cornelius Vanderbilt made his fortune on the water, which he had known since boyhood. But at an advanced age when most wealthy men think of retirement, he saw that the future of transportation belonged to the railroads. Without hesitation he left shipping and plunged into this new field, which he soon dominated. Buck Duke excelled in two industries, tobacco and electric power, but not at the same time. In going into the power industry he followed the lead of his brother Ben.

Of all our great entrepreneurs, Jay Gould was the most flexible in both his style and technique. His empire embraced three separate though related fields—railroads, the telegraph, and elevated railways—and his methods varied as widely as the problems he confronted. Before forging his empire he had operated as a speculator on Wall Street and blackened his reputation through such escapades as the Erie War and the Gold Corner. Then he astonished observers by taking hold of the Union Pacific Railroad, itself tarred by scandals and mismanagement, and making it a going concern. To accomplish this, he devised a unique triangular managerial structure that allowed him to shape policy without holding any office other than director. When Congress failed to resolve the government debt that hung like a millstone on the railroad, Gould quietly sold his holdings and put together a new transcontinental system of his own around the Missouri Pacific Railroad. For the rest of his life he devoted himself to developing that system and the territory adjacent to its lines.[42]

At the same time Gould did not neglect his other major enterprises, Western Union and Manhattan Elevated. Keenly aware of the symbiotic relationship between the railroads and the telegraph, he always formulated policy that suited both sectors. In making alliances or arrangements with other railroads, for example, he made sure that a telegraph contract found its way into the deal. "The lack of resources compelled him to devise methods as novel as the conceptions from which they sprang," wrote his biographer. "Through this process Gould inadvertently made a supreme contribution to his age: he imposed upon rival business-man an education in the realities of transportation strategy. For many of them it was a painful and unwelcome lesson." Near the end of his life, having fought bitter railroad wars for more than two decades, Gould understood that changed conditions made real cooperation necessary and turned to the novel role of trying to mediate peace and harmony among the major rail companies.[43]

No other entrepreneur rivals Gould in the number of times he changed roles or in the variety of the methods he employed. A more common pattern for most of the entrepreneurs was a gift for doing one thing well and doing it in one way. They might admire, even envy, people of many talents, but most of them stayed with what they did best. "Leonardo was one of the most amazing people who ever lived," said Bill Gates. "He was a genius in more fields than any scientist of any age, and an astonishing painter and sculptor." But neither Gates nor any of our other entrepreneurs pretended to be a Leonardo da Vinci. "Put all your eggs in one basket," advised Andrew Carnegie in one of his best-known homilies, "and watch that basket." Buck Duke shared that sentiment. "If you like the thing you are doing, it is enough," he said. "You will succeed at it and you don't need anything else."[44]

As usual, Warren Buffett took a detached view of the matter. "I've always felt," he said, "there might be more to be gained by studying business failures than business successes." When our entrepreneurs failed at some venture, then, it was either because they stepped out of their element—their areas of strength—or because they stayed too long with the formula that had worked so well for them and thereby misread changing conditions. The inventors explored many different areas, which explains their greater number of failures. For them, diversity of interest was an occupational hazard. "I always keep six or eight things going at once," Thomas Edison admitted, "and turn from one to the other as I feel like it." That tendency not only led to most of his disasters but also undermined the development of his successful products. He created the phonograph, then turned from it to work on the light bulb and electrical products for ten years. The ore-separating project pulled him away from his work in the electrical industry at a critical time; he lost his leadership in the field and never regained it.[45]

Most of the entrepreneurs understood all too well that even when things looked brightest, failure could descend like an avenging angel at any time. Carnegie, being a devout social Darwinist, understood that survival involved a constant struggle. More than a century later Gates thought in similar terms. "One of the lessons from the Darwinian world," he observed, "is that the excellence of an organism's nervous system helps determine its ability to sense change and quickly respond, thereby surviving or even thriving." But he recognized that the process of survival was in no way automatic. "We come to work every day knowing that we can destroy the company," he said, ". . . and that we better keep our wits about us."[46]

| 7 |

All in the Family

I think Warren [Buffett] has had more effect on the way I
think about my business and . . . running it than any other
business leader.   —BILL GATES[1]

The notion of family has several layers of meaning when deal-
ing with the great entrepreneurs. Most obviously it refers to their
own families and more particularly to the sons they groomed as
heirs to their empire. On another level it suggests the schools and
similarities among them. In the broadest sense it embraces the
company work force with an inherent assumption of mutual loyalties. At still another level it invokes the clusters of disciples many
of them gathered to help with and perpetuate their work. Except
for Warren Buffett, none of the entrepreneurs worked alone, even
though many were loners who, like other creative people, often felt
alienated and misunderstood in their dealings with rivals or society. John D. Rockefeller expressed their sense of frustration when
he declared, "They will know me better when I am dead."[2]

In many cases these entrepreneurs directly influenced one or more
of their fellows, with three figures standing out in this respect: John
Patterson, James Penney, and Thomas Edison. Patterson personally

trained Thomas Watson and maintained his respect despite humiliating and firing him. "Dad never complained of this treatment and revered Patterson until the day he died," said Tom Watson, Jr. "He used to say, 'Nearly everything I know about building a business comes from Mr. Patterson.'" This included even the infamous "THINK" signs, which Patterson plastered on all his factory walls. George Eastman heard a talk by Patterson and learned from it the value of employee suggestions. Sam Walton met Penney and was deeply influenced by him. His biographer argued that Walton borrowed "Penney's whole concept of how to succeed by putting customer satisfaction ahead of profit." Walton himself recalled that "Penney had called his hourly employees 'associates,' and I guess I always had that idea in the back of my head."[3]

Penney also believed in learning the local market by becoming part of it. "We told our store managers," he said, "that, unless they knew their communities and unless they were prepared to enter sympathetically into community life, they could not make a success of their stores." Walton understood this notion thoroughly, not only as a businessman but as a person. He and his family lived by the virtues and verities of small-town life. "That's exactly how we have become a huge corporation," he observed, "by not acting like one. Above all, we are small-town merchants." He subscribed fully to Penney's notion that "there could be no lasting prosperity for us unless the people of our communities were better off and happier for our being among them."[4]

Edison had a direct and compelling influence on Samuel Insull, who served as his secretary for eleven years and used that time to school himself in the electric power industry. While still in England, Insull had read an article about Edison and came to America in 1881 to serve his newfound hero. Edison also left a deep imprint on young Henry Ford, who met him in 1896 and received a few words of encouragement from the inventor. Although it was but a passing moment for Edison, Ford made him his idol and later regarded the meeting as the inspiration that drove him to his later inventions. Much later, *People* magazine linked even Bill Gates to Edison, saying that "Gates is to software what Edison was to the light bulb—part innovator, part entrepreneur, part salesman and full-time genius."[5]

On a broader level, an impressive number of the entrepreneurs revealed similar talents in several areas of business activity. Here is a short list:

DEVELOPMENT: Durant, Eastman, Edison, Ford, Gates, Gould, Harriman, Insull, Kroc, Land, McCormick, Noyce, Rockefeller, Vanderbilt, Westinghouse

MANAGEMENT: Carnegie, du Pont, Eastman, Gates, Gould, Harriman, Insull, Kroc, Noyce, Patterson, Penney, Rockefeller, Vail, Walton, Wanamaker, Woolworth

MARKETING: Carnegie, Duke, Durant, Eastman, Edison, Gates, Insull, Kroc, Land, McCormick, Noyce, Patterson, Penney, Walton, Wanamaker, Watson, Woolworth

ORGANIZATION: Carnegie, du Pont, Durant, Harriman, Insull, Patterson, Penney, Rockefeller, Vail, Vanderbilt, Walton, Watson, Woolworth

PRODUCTION: Carnegie, Duke, Eastman, Ford, Gates, Insull, Land, McCormick, Noyce, Patterson, Rockefeller, Watson, Westinghouse

TECHNOLOGY: Carnegie, Duke, du Pont, Durant, Eastman, Edison, Ford, Gates, Harriman, Insull, Land, McCormick, Noyce, Patterson, Rockefeller, Vail, Watson, Westinghouse

Not every entrepreneur excelled in all of these categories. He could be inept at it, uninterested in it, or the category might simply be irrelevant to his function. The railroad men, for example, did no marketing in the usual sense. The merchandisers did not produce goods but were all superior marketers. The producers of retail products—Ford, McCormick, Duke, Edison, Eastman, and Patterson—obviously had more interest in marketing than Carnegie and Rockefeller, who turned out capital goods. Buffett's activities do not fit any of these categories. The primary skills he brings to his work, analysis and judgment, are also displayed by all the other entrepreneurs, although not always consistently. At least half, and often two-thirds, of the entrepreneurs turn up in every category. Their creativity bred talent along with versatility in business.

As a group the merchandisers had the most narrow focus and therefore the most in common with one another. In their different venues they all emphasized low prices, quality goods, quick turnover, and superior service. The great challenge for each man was to find ways of systematizing these values in an ongoing operation. All of them except Frank Woolworth relied heavily on employee training to get this done and utilized the "family" concept to boost employee morale and sense of participation. James Penney had his Body of Doctrine that he codified into the Penney Principles. Later the principles were embodied in the Store Meeting Manual, which was "designed simply and solely to help," Penney said. *"Doing* is up to the individual." John Wanamaker shared Penney's belief in the Golden Rule as the proper basis for doing business and in making employees feel a part of the concern. His instructional program for employees began in 1882. He also had his list of principles, as did Sam Walton.[6]

Walton admitted that "In the beginning, I was so chintzy I really didn't pay my employees very well. . . . We really didn't do much for the clerks." But he learned quickly. He began holding meetings with the managers once a week to critique performance. Over time these sessions evolved into the Saturday-morning meetings that Walton called "the very heart of the Wal-Mart culture." At them serious business got done in an atmosphere that blended the spontaneity of a revival meeting with the antics of a vaudeville show. Most companies, Walton conceded, "don't have folks like

Mike 'Possum' Johnson . . . safety director . . . taking on challengers in a . . . persimmon-seed-spitting contest, using . . . our company general counsel as the official target." The sillier the business, the more Walton loved it. "My feeling," he said, "is that just because we work so hard, we don't have to go around with long faces all the time, taking ourselves seriously."[7]

Although a young Ray Kroc had played the piano for a living, he didn't bring entertainment to the training of his people—a very different task in a franchise operation. The fast-food business was still so new that no training ground existed for it. Kroc had to gamble on what John Love called "unproved talent and on extremely individualistic and slightly offbeat characters." To maintain the rigid standards he set for every McDonald's, Kroc had Fred Turner compile a seventy-five-page manual after spending a year consulting with the franchise operators. Other manuals soon followed, setting forth in greater detail not only the standards but the experience of different operators for the benefit of others. Turner also devised a grading system that launched QSC, "the universal symbol of performance in the fast-food trade." By 1957 Kroc had begun making crude training films; four years later he launched Hamburger University, the heart of his training program.[8]

The merchandisers were not alone in recognizing the importance of training programs. Cyrus McCormick and John Patterson pioneered in the creation of programs to instruct agents and salesmen for products that the public had to be taught to use. To sell and service his reapers, McCormick recruited good men, devised one of the first training programs for them, gave them brochures that instructed as well as advertised, and even brought them to Chicago to see how the machines were made. Like the merchandisers, Patterson set down his fourteen principles of National Cash Register management. He tried the agency system at first, giving it his own twist by paying commissions and awarding salesmen exclusive territories. Convinced that high-pressure tactics were counterproductive, he opened the nation's first school to train salesmen in 1894 and decreed that all NCR agents had to attend. He wrote *The Primer,* a textbook conspicuously devoid of academic theorizing, and used only salesmen as instructors to teach others how to sell. He is credited with being the first to break the approach to a sale down into steps and to use movies for instructional purposes, saying, "We teach through the eye."[9]

Watson learned these lessons well from Patterson and added to them his own distinctive flavor. "Whatever seemed good about Patterson's way of doing business, Dad copied," wrote Watson's son; "whatever seemed bad, he boldly reversed." The slogans, songs, training school, and newspaper Watson created all came from NCR models. Patterson liked to use his annual conventions for salesmen as a vehicle to instruct and arouse fervor in the ranks. Watson began using his conventions in the same manner and by 1924 had already infused them with an evangelical enthusiasm. To the usual rousing speeches Watson added the famous company songs, which filled every training session, convention, meeting, and ceremony at IBM. He believed ardently in slogans, what his biographers called "those salted-down imperishables of the mind," and the songs became, in effect, slogans set to music.[10]

Marketing was another crucial area in which all five merchandisers excelled. Woolworth was the first to give his stores a uniform appearance. He experimented with a long list of paints and varnishes before choosing a brilliant carmine red as his signature color for storefronts and windows. Penney took another tack. "The effective display of goods always has occupied a good deal of my thought," he said. "Eye appeal draws the customer to the store." The other merchandisers carried this principle to greater extremes. Wanamaker splashed his name everywhere through advertising, using billboards at first, followed by newspaper ads, circulars and other printed matter, balloons, and the store itself: His name ran full length on one side of the building. "I put more money than

I have into advertising," he admitted cheerfully, but he also understood the advertising value of his principles. His large ad stating the famous four points was the first to be copyrighted in this country.[11]

Late in the 1870s Wanamaker shifted his advertising style to the interview and reportorial style. A few years later his ads became single-column "chats." But his true genius lay in turning the store itself into a promotional engine. Apart from its sheer size and astonishing variety of goods ranging from pianos to works of art imported from Europe, the store offered free concerts in its huge auditorium equipped with a pipe organ and a variety of amenities aimed especially at female shoppers. Wanamaker filled his stores with works of art acquired in Paris by his son Rodman, whose tastes baffled his father at first. "We didn't know what to make of it," recalled Wanamaker. "Thomas [his other son] and I began to think Rodman had gone out of his head. . . . We tried to curb him. He wouldn't be curbed. . . . Now, I know what he was about."[12]

Besides turning his stores into museums, Wanamaker knew how to stage his merchandise. "His genius," said Ralph Hower, historian of Macy's, "lay in dramatizing the commonplace." Wanamaker, wrote his biographer, had a gift for "dramatizing" his stores, "making them living panoramas of commerce, colossal productions of the thought and craft of man; with lavish exhibits and decorations and display rooms and auditoriums." Magazine impresario S. S. McClure paid Wanamaker an even higher compliment. "Mr. Wanamaker is a great artist," he said. "All first-class institutions are founded by great artists. If Mr. Wanamaker had not been a great artist he could never have founded this great thing. This is not simply a department store—it is the expression of a great mind in a department store."[13]

Walton followed in this tradition on quite another level. His stores, too, became their own advertisements. But where Wanamaker exuded urban sophistication, Walton perfected the art of country cornball. Both his variety stores and Wal-Marts embodied the best of ordinary folks come to town in search of bargains and a good time. "We have a lot of fun with all this item promotion," observed David Glass, "but here's what it's really all about. The philosophy it teaches . . . is that your stores are full of items that can explode into big volume and big profits if you are just smart enough to identify them and take the trouble to promote them." In the early days Walton and his managers spliced together ads from pieces of ads of competing stores, tacking the Wal-Mart price beneath the picture. It worked, said one of his early managers, because "we made real hot prices. . . . Sam was a dime-store man so at first he wanted to make a certain percentage of profit on everything. But he came around to the idea that a real hot item would really bring them in the store so we finally started running things like toothpaste for sixteen cents a tube."[14]

This approach merely expanded as the stores grew larger and more numerous. One manager, opening a new store in Hot Springs, Arkansas, got a terrific deal on a whopping 3,500 cases of giant-sized detergent, then ran an ad offering it for $1.99 a box instead of the usual $3.97. The huge pyramid of boxes dwindled fast. Another manager found a good buy on riding mowers that normally sold for $447. He bought two hundred of them for $175 apiece, lined them up in rows outside his store, and watched them vanish. Walton relished a mattress pad called Bedmate, which he learned about by talking to a salesman who happened to be waiting in a lobby. On a hunch he bought a large lot of the pads, displayed them prominently, and sold them at a lowered price. Over the years Wal-Mart sold more than 5.5 million of them. "In the early days of Wal-Mart," admitted Walton, ". . . our emphasis on item promotion helped us to make up for a lot of shortcomings we had—an unsophisticated buying program, a less than ideal merchandise assortment, and practically no back-office support."[15]

Kroc also believed ardently in promotion and marketing. "I never hesitate to spend money in this area," he said, "because I can see it coming back to me with interest." In time McDonald's became one of the largest advertisers on television, but Kroc was slow to find his way. The company did not hire an advertising director until 1961 and did not run its first national ad until 1963. A year later, Kroc hired his first major ad agency; in 1967 McDonald's finally formed a marketing department and developed a national advertising program. Kroc encouraged the franchisees to do extensive local advertising. By 1959 operators were required to spend 2.5 percent of sales revenue for promotion; a decade later the figure was raised to 4 percent.[16]

Publicity was another matter. As early as 1957 Kroc retained a public relations firm to get the company's name in the papers. His own colorful personality and shrewd sense of publicity helped enormously. Kroc understood that "McDonald's is not in the restaurant business; it's in show business." The firm he hired, schooled in the tradition of press agentry, used any wacky device to get McDonald's into the papers, including the "burgers-to-the-moon" vehicle of how many times the number of hamburgers sold would reach the moon, or how soon the amount of ketchup used would fill Lake Michigan. The result was to build McDonald's a solid reputation as "the world's unquestioned authority on hamburgers." Kroc himself won over a prominent syndicated writer, Hal Boyle, with a beguiling interview in which he said, "I put the hamburger on the assembly line." From this first national press coverage flowed a flood of franchise applications and free publicity from other national news sources, which discovered in Kroc a sparkling interviewee.[17]

Local charities became another prime source for free publicity and photo ops. They also sparked a growing movement by franchisees to turn community involvement into a promotional bandwagon. Eventually it was the franchisees who developed and expanded the company's most conspicuous charity, the Ronald McDonald houses. The first one opened in Philadelphia in 1974, and others soon followed. The name came from the most conspicuous and successful promotional character created by the company. His origins lay in a Washington, D.C., local television show in which a young Willard Scott played Bozo the clown. The local franchiser recruited Bozo for promotional gigs with fabulous results, but the show was canceled in 1963. In searching for another clown character to serve as McDonald's ambassador to children, Scott came up with the name "Ronald McDonald" and made his debut in October 1963. His appeal was instant, and Ronald went national two years later. As John Love noted, "Network television commercials featuring Ronald would create the only commercial character in the United States with a recognition factor among children equaled only by Santa Claus."[18]

The most revealing aspect of Ronald's success was that the concept and the promotion of it had come from local operators, who continued to play the lead role. The idea spread quickly to other franchises, which gradually began forming regional alliances to advertise and promote. Kroc himself had moved to Los Angeles in 1962 to revive the southern California market that had always disappointed him. A stiff injection of television advertising there paid immediate dividends, sending sales up 22 percent the first year and 21 percent the next. By 1985 McDonald's advertising and promotional budget soared to $600 million, with the local operators using 65 different ad agencies through their 165 regional cooperatives. Kroc's faith in the local franchisees had been rewarded in this area as it was in so many others.[19]

The merchandisers were hardly alone in their talent for marketing. George Eastman's gift for advertising has already been noted. His classic slogan, "You press the button, we do the rest," found an echo in one coined by Edwin Land for his camera: "Touch the button, you have the picture." Buck Duke spent lavishly on advertising from the first and kept adding touches, such as putting into each package the picture of a famous actress or athlete or flag and turning them into collectibles. One dealer thought that "this one stunt, more than any other, really put the cigarette over with the public." Duke hired clever artists to execute the giant billboards, signs, and posters he designed. By 1906 he was spending $10 million a year for advertising and promotion. Cyrus McCormick's promotional work lacked Duke's flair but capitalized on the publicity value of public contests against rival reapers in every venue from his hometown to the great 1851 World's Fair in London. Even his early advertising letters, noted his biographer, "reveal a shrewd appreciation of sales psychology." Forever tangled in patent litigation, McCormick came to realize that even a lawsuit could become a splendid advertisement.[20]

John Patterson scoured the globe for advertising material and soon began to print his own material because he could not get it done the way he liked elsewhere. He had the task of not only promoting NCR products but convincing merchants of all kinds that they truly needed one of these newfangled machines called cash registers. "The advertising differed from any which . . . had been seen," wrote his biographer. "Every piece held a reason why the purchase of a register would make money for the purchaser. It was educational advertising." To make his points, Patterson borrowed from patent-medicine advertisements the technique of including testimonials from satisfied users. He strongly believed that no form of advertising could match word of mouth.[21]

The technologists, also, faced the difficult task of selling unfamiliar concepts and products to a public that didn't know it needed or wanted them. Over time Edison became as much showman as inventor, turning invention into a form of show business, as Kroc did for fast food. Menlo Park served not only as a laboratory but as a theater for the performance of new technology to beguile investors, reporters, and the public alike. Thousands of people flocked to what Matthew Josephson called "the Mecca of a continuous pilgrimage of scientists and curiosity hunters. . . . Like a comedian, Edison entertained the crowds by showing them all sorts of tricks. . . . The great public took him to its heart as it had never done with other men of science or any other inventor." Westinghouse had no such knack for entertainment, but he used his lighting of the spectacular Chicago World's Fair in 1893 to promote his electrical system as no other venue could have.[22]

Land turned the introduction of new products into carefully staged theatrical events designed to garner publicity and whet appetites. In marketing the SX-70 camera he showed an uncanny gift for promotion—finding ways into newspapers and magazines with what his biographer called a "campaign of anticipations and surprises." Gates borrowed this technique of promising more than could be delivered at the time and turned it into an art form. His marketing director, Steve Smith, conceded that "virtually everything we sold was not a product when we sold it. We sold promises." The standing joke in the industry was that every Microsoft product stayed in beta test until version 3. But Gates knew how to roll out a new product, usually at the annual Comdex convention, with a barrage of fanfares, bells, and whistles. For the crucial debut of Windows 3.0 he spent $3 million on a one-day extravaganza.[23]

Teamwork as a key to productivity was a concept that infused most of the entrepreneurs. Inventors are often thought of as lone figures struggling to wrest a workable model from their vision, yet all of our inventors worked best in groups. Edison, Westinghouse, and Land belong to what might be called the heroic school of inventors, who gathered teams around them and attacked one problem after another as defined by the leader. Whether by coincidence or not, all three ran into financial difficulties. Noyce and Gates created a new form of work culture built around creative teams. Carnegie's famous dictum that he could re-create his company if everything were taken from him but his organization got a reverse twist from Gates, who said, "Take our 20 best people away and I tell you that Microsoft would become an unimportant company."[24]

Most of the entrepreneurs strongly believed in putting as large a slice of earnings as possible back into the business. Carnegie was adamant about this policy. He made it a practice to avoid overcapitalization and used most of his profits as a financial reserve rather than fodder for dividends. "The question of dividends versus investment," wrote his biographer, "would always remain the sharpest point of difference . . . between Carnegie and his partners." Rockefeller followed the same policy of distributing only a small part of the profits in dividends. As his biographer observed, "He thought this policy of 'retained earnings,' then unique in American business, the crucial element in his strategy." E. H. Harriman practiced the policy of retained earnings so relentlessly that one critic denounced it as "conservatism run mad." Ford did so out of necessity because he loathed bankers and refused to borrow from them.[25]

Among the merchandisers, both Woolworth and Penney took the different tack of using partnerships to expand the enterprise. In Penney's system the manager got the capital for his one-third interest in a new store directly from his share of store earnings. Wanamaker financed all his expansion out of earnings and short-term borrowing. He shunned Wall Street and never went public with his stock, saying proudly, "My customers, not the bankers, made me." Between 1902 and 1908, when he was rebuilding the Philadelphia store and expanding the New York store, he self-financed the millions of dollars needed and struggled through the Panic of 1907 without resorting to loans or security issues. In 1953, only two years after opening his first variety store in Bentonville, Arkansas, Walton put all his then meager holdings in a family trust that was later incorporated as Walton Enterprises. Each of his four children got a fifth of all stock and property.

Walton then plowed all his later Wal-Mart stock back into the corporation. "We control the amount we pay out to each of us," he said, "and everybody gets the same. . . . That way, we accumulated funds in Enterprises rather than throwing it all over the place to live high."[26]

Family was important to Walton in business no less than life. Fourteen of our entrepreneurs involved members of their families in their firms. Twelve groomed sons to succeed them—though in the cases of Vanderbilt, Patterson, and Edison, "groomed" is too benign a word. Six brought their brothers into the business, and Duke involved his father as well. Walton relied heavily on his wife's good judgment, as did Harriman and McCormick. Rockefeller, Duke, and Wanamaker all worked smoothly with their brothers; the others were not so fortunate. The McCormicks fought and feuded to the point where Cyrus finally kicked his brother and nephew out of the firm. Tom Carnegie disagreed repeatedly with his brother and drank himself to death. Insull placed more trust in his brother Martin than the latter's ability warranted.[27]

The notion of family hit home most personally for the entrepreneurs when the delicate question of succession arose. For most of them, success posed a thorny clash between family and mortality. Like all creative people, they sought a sliver of immortality through their creations, and most kept at it until the end of their lives. On one hand, those with sons waiting in the wings usually beamed proudly at the thought of perpetuating a dynasty; on the other, many of them could not look directly at death or even the prospect of leaving their life's work. There were exceptions, of course, the most conspicuous being Eastman. More than any other of the entrepreneurs he put a sound management team in place and arranged for an orderly transition into retirement in 1925. "What I would like to do is just fade out of the picture and not go out with a bang," he said. "I am trying to organize it so people will say after I am gone that the old man was not the whole thing after all."[28]

This becoming modesty was hardly typical of most entrepreneurs, but Eastman managed to do exactly what he said. Being a bachelor, he had no children and therefore no issues of dynasty. In 1919, when he turned sixty-five, he reorganized Eastman Kodak along functional lines headed by a management team of nine that reported directly to him. When the day of departure came, he packed his bags and headed to Africa for six months. Just as he did not fear retirement, neither did he refuse to face mortality. Late in 1930 Eastman was diagnosed with a hardening of the cells in the lower spinal cord that left him unsteady on his feet and doomed to eventual invalidism. As his condition deteriorated, he had to confront his worst dread—that of becoming dependent and unable to manage his own affairs. Rather than face that ultimate helplessness, he chose to shoot himself in 1932—leaving behind a note that read, "To my friends. My work is done—why wait?"[29]

Of those entrepreneurs with sons, Edison, Gould, McCormick, Vanderbilt, Wanamaker, and Watson handed their companies over to them successfully. Gould, McCormick, Wanamaker, and Insull doted on their sons and longed for the day when the boys could take a place at the father's side. For McCormick, the matter had a special urgency: He was fifty when Cyrus Jr. was born. When George Gould turned twenty-one, his father presented him with his power of attorney, a seat on the New York Stock Exchange, and a position on the boards of his companies. He wanted his younger sons to get a college education, but Edwin quit Columbia and came downtown to enter his father's office. Wanamaker made his son Rodman a partner in 1902, resident manager of the New York store in 1911, and turned the entire business over to him before his death. Wanamaker also put his son Thomas in a key executive position, but Thomas died in 1908.[30]

Young McCormick proved a capable manager, as did Rodman Wanamaker. George Gould lost his way, preferring society to business. However, Edwin Gould and both his younger brothers made fortunes of their own outside their father's enterprises. Rockefeller doted on his children and was fiercely protective of them, but he doubted his son's talent for business. John Jr. graduated from Brown in 1896, the year his father walked away from the direction of Standard Oil. The following year Junior took a desk at the company with unspecified duties that included filling inkwells. In 1904 he was finally elected a director and in 1909 a vice president, but his distaste for what Ron Chernow called the "moral squalor" of the current management led to his severing all ties with the company in 1910. His development came slowly. Until 1912, when Junior was thirty-eight, Rockefeller kept his son in what Chernow called "a prolonged adolescence, paying him a salary that was really a glorified allowance." However, in 1909, he did give Junior a controlling interest in the American Linseed Oil Company. Once Junior began to demonstrate his business acumen, he became his father's chief lieutenant and ultimate heir to the business and philanthropic empires.[31]

Edison, always a neglectful parent, never schooled his son Charles in the business. Nevertheless, the quiet, restless boy quit MIT and went to work for Boston Edison. After some roaming about, he settled in at his father's West Orange facility. In 1918 he took charge of its operation and proved a capable manager. Later in life he turned to politics and served as governor of New Jersey. Vanderbilt was not only indifferent to but often contemptuous of his eldest son, William, whom he banished to a farm on Staten Island. Not until age forty-three was William summoned to manage the Harlem Railroad for his father. He gradually impressed his father with his business ability and became the heir apparent, but the Commodore never let go of the reins while he lived. Not until his death in 1877 did William, then fifty-five, inherit the empire, which he ruled for only eight years before his own death in 1885.[32]

Tom Watson, Jr., and his brother Dick both rose to the top of IBM and performed well, but it did not come easily for either of them. Tom had always had a tempestuous relationship with his father. "I was in awe of the man," he confessed, "yet we both had such hot tempers that it was hard for me to be in the same room with him." As a boy young Watson was known as Terrible Tommy, the one who always got into trouble. During the years after World War II, when Watson was trying to impart his business secrets to the boy, their relationship grew even more stormy. "In public he would praise me lavishly," Junior said. "In private Father and I had terrible fights that led us again and again to the brink of estrangement. These arguments would frequently end in tears. . . . We fought about every major issue of the business." It amazed him that "two people could torture each other to the degree Dad and I did and not call it quits. . . . Those fights were . . . savage, primal, and unstoppable."[33]

Clearly, Watson wanted his sons to succeed him but he was, like Vanderbilt, exceedingly reluctant to surrender power even in old age. He had set IBM's retirement age at sixty-five yet still clung to the top job when he was past eighty and considerably slowed. "Even if Dad had been ten years younger and kept control of the operation himself," young Watson concluded, "he couldn't have made his one-man style of management work for very much longer. Important problems were taking too long to filter through to the top, and we had unmade decisions piling up in every corner." Watson also grew uncomfortable with the prominence his son had begun to garner; he wanted the boys to succeed but hated sharing the limelight. In 1948 he upset young Tom by forming a new subsidiary, IBM World Trade, and putting Dick in charge of it. To Tom Jr., it looked as if he was to have the United States while Dick got to manage everything else. Not until May 1956 did Watson finally make his namesake CEO of IBM and Dick CEO of World Trade. It was, said Tom Jr., "the first promotion I ever got from him without a fight." Five weeks later the elder Watson died.[34]

Harriman did something remarkable and unique for his time. Before his death from stomach cancer in 1909, he made one of the shortest wills ever penned by a prominent figure, in which he left all his holdings to his wife, Mary. Neither of his two sons, Averell and Roland, were ready to assume large responsibilities, and Harriman had always trusted his wife's judgment. In time the boys assumed major roles in the Union Pacific Railroad. Averell, who had become a banker, served as chairman of its board until summoned to diplomatic duty during World War II. In his absence, which proved permanent, Roland took the post and kept it until 1969. He remained on the board until 1978. No other major railroad could boast such continuity in its management. Walton remained active in Wal-Mart until slowed by the hairy cell leukemia that took his life in 1992. His four children at first showed no interest in joining him in the business; they had worked too hard at it as teenagers. Later, however, three of the four became involved in its management and still control the company through the trust set up earlier.[35]

Most of the other entrepreneurs have less happy stories. Ford doted on his son Edsel, yet treated him horribly over the years. In 1918 he made Edsel, then twenty-five, president of Ford Motor Company, a position he held for the rest of his life. But Ford clung tenaciously to power, and Edsel, although he held 40 percent of the company's stock, hesitated to cross the father he revered. He developed legendary patience from dealing with the unpredictable antics of Henry. "I have not worked out a separate business philosophy for myself," Edsel admitted in 1929. "I agree absolutely with my father's philosophy. I do not merely accept his beliefs; I feel as strongly about them as he does." Although they were extremely close, Henry seemed to delight in humiliating or embarrassing his heir in the belief that he needed toughening. He turned Edsel's life into what Robert Lacey called "a never-ending emotional assault course."[36]

The old man's ways of toughening took some odd forms. Once Edsel ordered a new line of coke ovens for River Rouge. His father seemingly approved the move, then had them torn down as soon as they were finished. On another occasion, persuaded that the sales and accounting staffs needed more space, Edsel started work on a new office building while his father was away. When Henry returned and received an explanation, he responded by having maintenance men enter the old building that night and completely strip the fourth-floor accounting offices of everything in them. Later that day Henry announced that the entire department had been abolished. Before doing so, however, he told Edsel with a grin, "If you really need more room you'll find plenty of it on the fourth floor." Edsel managed to find jobs for all the discharged accountants, but his ordeal continued until his untimely death from stomach cancer in 1943, five months before his fiftieth birthday. His friends said he died of a broken heart. Henry, by then a senile old man in failing health, was devastated by the loss but took feeble command of the firm until his grandson Henry II took over in 1945.[37]

Vail lost his only son in 1906, a year before his return to the presidency of AT&T. Insull doted on his son, Samuel Jr., and longed to make him heir to an empire, but he lost the empire. A similar fate befell Westinghouse. Durant also lost his fortune, but his son Cliff lived the high life largely on the proceeds from his own shrewd investments in the market. The elder Durant had always relished power but somehow managed to bounce back from its loss. Duke and Woolworth had only daughters but handled succession in quite different ways. Duke walked away from American Tobacco a few months after its dissolution in 1911, leaving its management to Percival Hill, and shifted his interests elsewhere. His only child, Doris, was born the following year. Woolworth had three daughters and continued to clutch power despite deteriorating health and a string of personal misfortunes.[38]

For Carnegie the issue of succession came more smoothly than most. Like Duke, he had a daughter late in life, and like Eastman, he had a host of outside interests. Lacking an heir and disapproving nepotism anyway, he sold the business to J. P. Morgan when the right moment came and walked away to a second career in philanthropy, as Rockefeller had done a few years earlier. Du Pont had the unique problem of a family firm turned modern corporation. In 1919 he turned management of Du Pont over to his brother before taking up the challenge of General Motors. Nine years later, having put an outstanding management team in place, he retired to a long life of leisure. Penney had four children by three wives, three of them sons, but none were old enough to be considered heirs when he turned the presidency over to Earl Corder Sams in 1917 and became chairman of the board. Although he remained active in the company to the end, his interests gradually shifted elsewhere over the years.[39]

Patterson married late and had two children only to see his wife die six years after their marriage. The children were reared by his sister and other relatives, and Patterson got to know them only after they had grown up. NCR became his only family, one he clung to tenaciously. Work became his life and his solace. "He thought of the human body purely as a machine," wrote his biographer. "He really did not know what pleasure was. He did not know the meaning of the world 'recreation.'" Above all else, he dreaded the coming of death and resolved not to sit still and wait for it. He fired pretenders as they neared the throne and worked furiously until the last year of his life, when he yielded the presidency to his son Frederick and became chairman of the board. It was an unexpected and in many ways ironic conclusion to his career.[40]

Vail, Kroc, and Noyce all handled retirement gracefully. Ever the good executive, Vail had groomed a successor before stepping down in 1919 to become chairman of the board. Aware of his own limitations, Kroc, too, built a capable management team. He had long shared power with Harry Sonneborn, who was "chief executive not only in name but also in fact" from 1962 to 1966. Differences between them led to Sonneborn's departure in 1967. Kroc became president but kept the title only until early 1968, when he handed it off to Fred Turner. For the rest of his life Kroc remained active in the company in many capacities, not the least of which was his "key role in maintaining its image as a colorful and human organization." For Kroc, retirement meant doing the things for the company he liked best to do. Turner was anything but a clone of Kroc and proved an inspired choice. As Kroc said, "He has never disappointed me."[41]

Noyce had the advantage of outstanding partners in Gordon Moore and Andrew Grove, which allowed him to become chairman of the board in 1974 and devote more time to his new wife and myriad other interests. But he did not retire entirely. The threat posed to the American semiconductor industry by the invasion of cheap Japanese chips led to the creation of Sematech, an association designed to foster industry cooperation. Noyce became involved at an early stage and agreed reluctantly in 1988 to head the new organization. His presence gave a dubious undertaking instant credibility. Within two years he achieved his twin goals of assuring strong commitment from the member companies and validating Sematech to the federal government. In June 1990, two days after Sematech held "Bob Noyce Day" to celebrate his contribution to it, Noyce died suddenly of a heart attack.[42]

Land took no smooth road to retirement, largely because he had never dealt well with the issues of succession and mortality. A major point of friction with his board was his failure to groom potential successors. As Peter Wensberg pointed out, "He had always run the company; all the titles of power and command were his." When the time came to surrender them, Land found himself at a loss: "This was not a problem that could be solved by Herculean efforts in the laboratory." Nor did it help that he seemed unable to confront his own mortality. "Land's ideas of organization were naïve," observed Ken Olsen, a member of the board. After grudgingly yielding the presidency in 1975 and the post of CEO in 1980, Land retreated to the Rowland Institute, and by 1985 had sold off his remaining shares in Polaroid. "My wife and I feel," he said, "that the time has now come for a final separation from the company we shall never forget." He was seventy-five years old. Perhaps he sensed that the day of Polaroid had come and gone.[43]

Buffett confronted these issues in an oblique way. His business has relied so heavily on his personal judgment that it would be hard to impart the critical elements to even the most willing of students despite his protestation that anyone who imbibed three basic ideas ought to do reasonably well in stocks. Always somewhat aloof from his children, Buffett doubtless would have taken any one of them into the firm who was eager and willing, but all of them went into other things. Buffett encouraged them to do what appealed to them. "I respect what my kids are doing," he said, "and I don't feel my lifestyle is superior to any of theirs. If they want to get involved in this business, fine, but I don't expect it." Like several of the other entrepreneurs, he has always had trouble confronting mortality. Asked once how he would like to be remembered, he quipped, "Well, I'd like for the minister to say, 'My God, he was old.'"[44]

Although Bill Gates is still a young man, he has already confronted the question of succession. "Gates is to our era," said *Business Week*, "what Rockefeller and Carnegie were to theirs." The comparison is apt in several ways. Like Rockefeller, Gates is one of that rare breed of entrepreneurs who had the talent both to create a great company and manage its growth to fabulous proportions.

Carnegie came close to joining this elite circle but never really solved the problem of efficient organization before selling out. However, both Rockefeller and Carnegie left their creations and went on to second careers in philanthropy. Gates seems to be following that same path. By 1998 the strain of coping with a giant firm besieged by a major antitrust suit and watching talent defect to the mushrooming crop of dot-com companies was taking its toll on him. At one board meeting in January 1998 he complained that "this job is too hard for anybody." A director who witnessed the outburst said, "He was really distraught. He was at his wit's end."[45]

For all his combativeness and drive, what Gates loved most was the development of new products. In recent years his role as CEO has taken him farther away from that function. Gradually, Gates began turning elements of the day-to-day management over to Steve Ballmer. In July 1998 he made Ballmer president of the company; then, in January 2000, he surrendered the office of CEO to Ballmer and moved up to chairman of the board and "chief software architect." The transition did not go entirely smoothly at first. "Bill had to acclimate himself to the idea that he could defer decisions to Steve," said a Microsoft vice president, but gradually Gates has begun to settle into his new role. "I have a strong voice, a strong recommendation," he declared, "but Steve has to decide." Most important of all, Gates freed himself from the daily grind of budgets, schedules, and other managerial pressures. "Steve's promotion," he said, "will allow me to dedicate myself full-time to my passion—building great software and strategizing on the future."[46]

Family had another dimension for creators of great enterprises who were so fiercely devoted to their work. The concept embraced those who worked with and for them. The distinction is important, for in many cases the entrepreneurs had very different relations with their executives than with their workers. The image of entrepreneurs, especially those of the nineteenth century, as ruthless exploiters of their men turns out to be a myth. There were plenty of hard-driving employers, but few of the great entrepreneurs were among them. The worst labor relations in our group belong to Carnegie, Duke, Ford, Gould, Vanderbilt, and Woolworth, but even their records are mixed. All lived in an era when unions were anathema to most businessmen, including themselves. It is important to remember that although unions existed, they had no standing in law until passage of the Wagner Act in 1935. This meant that employers had no legal obligation to recognize any union as a bona fide bargaining agent for their workers. They might choose to do so, but the majority fiercely opposed granting any formal recognition to unions.

It was a labor crisis that exposed Andrew Carnegie's capacity for self-deception more cruelly than any other event in his life. Although he kept a sharp eye on labor costs, he thought he treated his men as well as or better than most employers and was proud of his policy of promoting men from the ranks. "That he could describe himself as being 'Kind Master' to his workmen without understanding the full import of what he was saying," wrote his biographer, "is perhaps more damning than anything that was said about him by others." Carnegie's obsession with costs and loathing of the union led to the worst debacle of his career, the infamous Homestead strike of 1892, which blackened his reputation with denunciations from the press, pulpit, and the entire political spectrum. It also ruptured his relationship with Henry Clay Frick, who had the thankless task of confronting the strike while Carnegie absented himself in Scotland.[47]

Jay Gould showed little interest in his labor force other than to keep their wages down, hours long, and productivity high. In dealing with coal miners he thwarted strikes by playing one ethnic group off against another. Yet prior to the widely publicized strike against his Missouri Pacific Railroad in 1886, for which he received undeserved criticism, Gould did something extraordinary for the times. Amid growing labor strife on the railroad during the mid-1880s, he invited union leader Terence V. Powderly and his executive board to his home to discuss matters. Observers were shocked and horrified that the most formidable railroad man in the nation would deign even to acknowledge the head of a union, let alone sit in the same room with him. Buck Duke treated his men decently but worked them hard for low wages. Early in his cigarette-making career he imported skilled immigrants, mostly Jewish, from New York to work in his North Carolina factory. When the Bonsack machines proved their worth, he replaced them with cheap, unskilled local labor—black and white, male and female—all desperate for work. As historian Robert Durden noted, the newcomers "would long constitute a remarkably vulnerable and unorganized labor force."[48]

Cornelius Vanderbilt treated his men no differently than did other railroad owners. As already noted, Ford was hailed as a pioneer in labor relations early in his career, especially after he introduced the five-dollar-a-day wage in January 1914. But the work in Ford's plant involved mind-numbing repetition, and the turnover rate reached a staggering 470 percent in 1913. Over the years Ford's virulent antiunionism increased until by the 1930s he kept his disgruntled workers in line with thugs and spies. "'Perpetual ferment,'" said Charles Sorensen, "was his scheme for keeping people alert." No one fought unions more savagely than Ford, yet after decades of strife he abruptly caved in and offered the UAW what Richard Tedlow called "the most generous contract in the industry." Woolworth built his entire operation on the premise of low wages. He watched clerks closely for signs of breakage or theft, paid them the lowest possible wages, and worked them long hours. When strikes threatened, he made small concessions, but no one ever called him a friend of labor.[49]

Henry Ford was contemptuous of most employees. "The average worker," he claimed, ". . . wants a job in which he does not have to put forth much physical exertion—above all, he wants a job in which he does not have to think." For obvious reasons Ford scoffed at coddling workers. "I pity the poor fellow who is so soft and flabby that he must have an 'atmosphere of good feeling' around him before he can do his work," he said. "There is altogether too much reliance on good feeling in our business organizations." But this attitude was a minority opinion in our group. Many of the other entrepreneurs took the opposite tack of pioneering in good labor relations, providing their workers not only decent wages but improved working conditions and a variety of benefits. The motives in every case included both a genuine concern for the welfare of employees and a strong dislike of unions.[50]

Cyrus McCormick pointed proudly to the loyalty of his workers and rarely endured strikes except during the Civil War. John D. Rockefeller despised unions and so paid his men well, showed genuine interest in their welfare, stood by them in times of trouble, and even invited them to send complaints or suggestions directly to him. If a strike arose, he crushed it ruthlessly, but few occurred. E. H. Harriman demanded high standards of his men and drove them hard, but he was among the first to introduce a pension plan as well as a Bureau of Information and Safety, which "offered training at company expense in any area and created a separate board to answer inquiries on any aspect of their work." At Pierre du Pont's family firm, the workers had long been a family; they lived on the grounds and many of the sons followed their fathers into jobs with the company.[51]

Eastman, Patterson, Vail, and Insull took the family concept of labor more seriously than most other employers. George Eastman turned Kodak Park into a forerunner of the Silicon Valley campuses. The employees had access to gyms, auditoriums, shooting galleries, bowling alleys, camera clubs, baseball teams, and other amenities. They were well paid and enjoyed pleasant working conditions. Three years before the state of New York passed its Workmen's

Compensation Act, Eastman created a permanent welfare fund and utilized it for sick and disability pay, pensions, and hospital benefit plans. After the company reorganized in 1898, Eastman took $175,000 of his own money and distributed it among three thousand employees. Small wonder that Kodak had one of the lowest turnover rates of any major corporation—about 10 percent a year.[52]

Eastman had taken his cue on the worth of employee suggestions from John Patterson, who came slowly but surely to the value of paternalism and in the end outdid all the others. "Labor is suspicious—and has a right to be," he said. "Generally speaking, it is not fairly treated and it has not been given either its rightful share in industry or its proportion of income. . . . Were I a worker for wages, I should be deeply suspicious of my employer until he had demonstrated to me that he was willing to play fair."[53]

Patterson went a long way to show his workers that he played fair. The NCR Relief Association, created in 1896, provided sick and death benefits as well as cheap medical service. Legend has it that in 1904 Patterson saw a female employee heating a pot on a radiator and learned that it was coffee. A short time later he began offering hot meals for the women and later extended it to all employees. There followed such amenities as dining rooms, rest periods, baths on factory time, medical service complete with a dental clinic, visiting nurses, health education, recreational grounds, movies during lunchtime, night classes, and group vacation trips. To critics of his policy he replied, "It pays. . . . Hungry people, people with bad diets or in poor health, are not good producers."[54]

Patterson then extended his largesse beyond the factory to the city of Dayton, Ohio, opening what he called the "House of Usefulness," which helped turn a rough, shabby neighborhood into a pleasant residential community. He created clubs and started Saturday morning entertainments for children in the NCR auditorium. A vocational school enrolled two hundred pupils, and free baths—the first in Dayton—were opened to the community. During the great flood of 1913, which inundated Dayton, Patterson outdid himself as he turned NCR's factory and grounds into "Relief Central," housing the homeless, feeding the hungry, and tending the sick. His heroic efforts made him a national hero and embellished his company's reputation as nothing else did. Patterson was in position to play this role because he had prudently built his factory on high ground.[55]

Theodore Vail had an unusual number of women employees in the form of operators and went out of his way to accommodate their needs. He implemented dining service and better rest rooms as well as benefits for sickness, old age, and death. For some of the sick or exhausted workers he arranged convalescence at a resort. When AT&T acquired Western Union, Vail "made himself one with the men of the service . . . wrote letters, telling them that the company wished to improve conditions, asking the men to come directly to him if they had grievances. . . . [He] established a pension system . . . [and] organized a loan service." By instituting such innovations as the night and day letters, the cable letter, and the weekend cable, he not only provided new services but filled the once idle hours of operators so well that their pay increased by 50 percent within three years. "The employees of the W.U. owe you a debt of gratitude they can never pay for the Pension and sick benefit scheme inaugurated by you," a grateful employee wrote Vail. "Before the pension scheme . . . Unionism and discontent were more or less prevalent in every large office, but one never hears of either now." This sentiment was music to Vail's ears.[56]

Samuel Insull did not begin to regard his employees in this light until the end of World War I, when he came to the "striking realization" that "his employees were as much a part of his family as his brothers and sisters. . . . Without stopping to ponder what he was doing, he set out to create a new kind of employee, a kind that would one day be styled the organization man." He looked carefully at welfare programs, private and government, across the globe before instituting his own innovations. They included a forty-four-hour workweek (the norm was still sixty to seventy), free medical benefits, unemployment compensation, a profit-sharing plan, night school paid for by the company, voluntary employer liability benefits, a savings and loan association, a retirement plan, and many others. During the 1920s he moved toward employee ownership by fostering employee associations to buy stock in his companies at well below the market price. Insull did more than create new welfare programs for his firms; he actively promoted them to other corporations as well.[57]

George Westinghouse always emphasized safety in his plants and installed what his biographer called "little emergency hospitals, with operating room and pharmacy, all complete and modern, and with surgeon and nurse." The air-brake company created a pension plan in 1906 and paid benefits not only to retirees but to their dependents after death. Westinghouse once assured Samuel Gompers that "all workmen are guaranteed the same rights and privileges with us, whether they are affiliated with organized labor or not." When his air-brake company first opened, Westinghouse invited all fifteen of his workers to Thanksgiving dinner at a local hotel. He kept up this practice until the workforce grew too large, then gave each man a turkey for his own Thanksgiving dinner. He introduced a relief program to provide medical care for employees and a pension plan for those who retired or became disabled. His desire was to "have every person connected with one of his companies . . . feel that he was part of the concern, that its interests were his interests, and that its personnel was one big family." To that end he encouraged the workers to form clubs and provided recreational facilities for them.[58]

Education was another priority for Westinghouse. For a nominal fee, any male employee could get technical training in a variety of night classes ranging from mathematics to engineering. Female employees, of whom Westinghouse had quite a number, could for a small fee get instruction in subjects such as stenography, typing, cooking, sewing, "household art," or music. Earlier than Patterson he saw the necessity of providing better facilities for women workers, including a special lunchroom with two attendants. When the plant at East Pittsburgh was built, he noticed that it lacked sidewalks and overhead protection. Although cost estimates had already been exceeded, he insisted that a walkway be built and enclosed to shield the women workers from rain. "We employ a great many women," he explained, "and when it storms they will be exposed to the rain in their thin dresses, or walk in unprotected shoes. . . . They will catch cold, and if any harm comes to them it will be our fault."[59]

Thomas Edison thought little about welfare programs. He simply expected everyone to work as long and hard as he did. Matthew Josephson called him "a thrifty, honest, and paternal capitalist of the old school," one who could not abide unions. Edison loved to hang out with the boys in the shop, smoking cigars and telling bawdy jokes. But he seldom let feelings impinge on his single-mindedness. As Robert Conot wrote, "Human relationships meant little to him. . . . He never compromised his egocentricity to accommodate himself to anyone." William Durant, too, was entirely at home with the boys in the shops, having come up through the ranks, but he was too busy with his ambitious schemes to pay much attention to such details as working conditions and employee benefits.[60]

As in so many other areas, Tom Watson took his cues from Patterson, who believed that "men work hardest to gain a reward or to avoid punishment," and so deliberately overpaid and just as deliberately overpunished. However, both Patterson and Watson made clear distinctions between executives and workers in their treatment. Anxious to avoid unions, both treated the plant workers well; Watson was hailed as a "model employer to the men in the factory." In the depression year of 1932 he paid wages 50 percent above the industry norm and kept them high throughout the decade. In 1934, after one of his factory tours, he did away with piecework over the objections of his managers, saying it distracted people from producing high-quality goods. He provided a host of benefits, including free concerts, libraries, and night courses, and turned an old speakeasy into a country club that any employee could join for one dollar a year. Unlike many employers, he thought nepotism a good thing and founded a father-son club for employees in the 1920s. "He believed," said Tom Jr., "in management by generosity" in the mold of Patterson.[61]

But that generosity had its dark side, especially when it came to executives. Here, too, Watson took his cue from Patterson, who once told an underachieving officer, "There are only two things the matter with you. . . . Everything you do is wrong. Everything you say is wrong." His treatment of executives who had fallen out of favor could be brutal. One hapless officer arrived back in Dayton from a business trip to find his desk and chair on the lawn in front of the factory. They had been drenched in kerosene and went up in flames just as the man stepped out of his cab. The man got back into the cab and went away. "It was fatal to attract Patterson's attention," wrote Watson's biographers. "He fired some men because he was tired of them, others because they annoyed him, a few probably just for recreation; but he always insisted that he had sound business reasons." Later he admitted to one regret: that he had fired Tom Watson.[62]

Patterson had in typical fashion lavished praise and then humiliation on Watson before eventually firing him. On one occasion Watson learned of Patterson's displeasure by arriving at the office to find his desk occupied by someone else and his staff scattered. He did not react but simply went off to tend company business elsewhere. Day after day the charade repeated itself as Watson worked out of nearby branch offices. At their rare meetings he and

Patterson exchanged only cool civilities. Finally Patterson had to leave for Europe. He said nothing to Watson but had him promoted and moved to New York with other executives. When Watson got married, Patterson gave the couple a summer house he had built near his own home. Five months later he fired Watson, adding him to a list of discharged executives that one wag called "as resplendent as a roll call in the House of Lords."[63]

Watson handled his men with the same bizarre mix of generosity and cruelty, and even played some of the same games with them. Reluctant to delegate authority, he *was* the organization chart; as many as forty executives reported directly to him, and no one could be certain for very long where he stood. Watson was particularly hard on the financial officers because he distrusted numbers—even though they made his living—and thought they distracted executives from the real issues. Without creating formal rules, he absolutely forbade drinking on or off duty and imposed a conservative style of dress, decorum, and behavior expected of all executives and salesmen. As he grew older and more dictatorial, Watson carried these policies and the high-church spirit of the company to extremes that made his son cringe. "The longer I worked at IBM," admitted Tom Jr., "the more I resented my father for the cultlike atmosphere that surrounded him."[64]

Something more malignant than family emerged at IBM that to Richard Tedlow bore "an uncomfortable resemblance to *1984.* …The constant, unending chorus of praise, some of it personally orchestrated by Watson himself, was without parallel." Watson's strong belief in his own vision—a quality so characteristic of all the great entrepreneurs—had ossified into a sense of infallibility. The same disease had infected Edison, Ford, and, to a lesser degree, Edwin Land. Where Watson projected an image of himself as the Great Leader, Land saw himself as the Great Scientist who would lead others in the quest for great inventions. Like Edison,

Westinghouse, and others, he viewed himself as the man with answers—sometimes to questions that had yet to be asked. For the great entrepreneurs, as for all great creative people, the line between self-confidence and hubris proved perilously thin.[65]

Land also worked his assistants to exhaustion, expecting them to match his own tireless pace. He created a democratic and unconventional workplace that included "uniform treatment of all employees . . . in pay practices, bonuses, promotional procedures, career growth opportunities, medical and insurance benefits." Even parking spaces were allocated by seniority rather than rank. As his packet of benefits expanded, Land emphasized education on the premise that growing mechanization was bound to eliminate some jobs and create others. As many as 25 percent of the employees took courses within or without the company. When a union tried to organize Polaroid in 1970, an annoyed Land sent photocopies of a letter to every one of his ten thousand employees. "Our proudest product," he wrote, "is not our film, not our cameras, but is rather a kind of company in which you are not 'workers' but men and women . . . every one different from every other, every one bringing his special talent and his special wisdom to our tasks." The unionizing effort failed.[66]

But in the end so did Land. The very qualities of vision and determination that built his greatness also undermined him and his company. "He's very persistent, and he's very protective of his persistence," observed Bill McCune, who came to know this attribute in Land painfully well. "If somebody . . . wants to tell him why it won't work . . . he will throw him out." Land never lost his concern for his people and their welfare, but toward the end he served them poorly with his insistence on pursuing a product that was doomed to failure, much as Edison had done. In his time, however, he commanded their loyalty and respect, much as Watson had done but without the trappings. "He was revered to an extraordinary extent by most of the people who worked for him," said Peter Wensberg. "That of course made communication difficult. . . . Within the company . . . he seemingly could do no wrong." One sign of this sense of awe was the practice of even older employers calling him "Dr. Land" or simply "Doctor."[67]

Similar trappings of myth attached themselves to Robert Noyce as well, and later to Bill Gates. What Michael S. Malone called the "canonization" of "St. Bob" did not come right away, but when it did Noyce found himself that rare executive admired by business friends and foes alike. "In the Silicon Valley pantheon of Great Men," wrote Malone, "only Noyce has been elevated into the ranks of Hewlett and Packard." A huge part of that growing reputation derived from his handling of people and his influence on them. Many of the men who later became stars in the industry cut their teeth working with Noyce. Virtually all of them agreed that his outstanding characteristic was "trust in his people and respect for their abilities." His charisma did not make him a great or even good manager, but his ability to recognize his own shortcomings enabled him to find the right associates to fill the gaps.[68]

Noyce knew how to handle his people but not how to make hard decisions about them when they fell short. He needed someone to do the dirty work of firing or demoting. At Fairchild that someone was Charlie Sporck; at Intel it became Andrew Grove. Their presence allowed him to be the good cop who praised and rewarded and, above all, created a work environment that encouraged innovation and high performance. In the Fairchild and Intel families Noyce became the parent who seldom punished but always had the final say. Those who worked for him knew that he wanted them to do well for their own sake as well as that of the company. More than anyone else, Noyce created the prototype for the Silicon Valley workplace family that came to be tighter, more dynamic, and closer than any other industry workforce. Younger, brighter, more energetic than most groups, the Valley's kiddie korps lived for work and turned the office into home, which for many proved to be the only one they had for a time. If nothing else, they were family by default.

In time Gates surpassed Noyce in every respect except reputation. The cloud of myth that enshrouded him tended to demonize more than canonize. At Microsoft he took Noyce's prototype and created his own template from it—one that raised the levels of intensity and conflict to new heights. Microsoft's workers were also a family unto themselves, but one that fought and feuded constantly. The programmers were the corps d'elite of the workforce. They "worked hard and played hard. . . . [They] had all been handpicked by Gates and Ballmer. They were special, and everyone in the company knew it." The Microsoft intramural battles took place under the watchful eye of the brightest, loudest, and most confrontational of them all. Unlike Noyce, Gates had no need to be liked, only respected. "If you don't like to work hard and be intense and do your best," he said, "this is not the place to work." He admitted freely that "I like pushing the edge. That's often where you find high performance." But, like Noyce, he gave workers room to show what they could do: "We tell people that if no one laughs at at least one of their ideas, they're probably not being creative enough."[69]

Gates and other technologists became famous for making millionaires out of so many of their workers. In the environment they created, unions had little chance of gaining a foothold. Sam Walton also made large numbers of his employees rich and expanded their ranks by starting a profit-sharing plan in 1971 that proved a bonanza as the stock kept rising and splitting. He made no bones about not wanting unions in his company. "I have always believed that we don't need unions at Wal-Mart," he declared.

"They have mostly been divisive. . . . Anytime we have ever had real trouble . . . or the serious possibility of a union coming into the company, it has been because management has failed, because we have not listened to our associates, or because we have mistreated them."[70]

Walton believed devoutly that "what has carried this company so far so fast is the relationship that we, the managers, have been able to enjoy with our associates . . . those employees out in the stores and in the distribution centers and on the trucks. . . . Our relationship with the associates is a partnership in the truest sense." Penney would have understood this observation well, and would doubtless have shared Walton's concern for the danger of employees being too well off. "A lot of folks in our company have made an awful lot of money," Walton noted. "We've had lots and lots of millionaires. . . . It just drives me crazy when they flaunt it. . . . If you get caught up in that good life, it's probably time to move on, simply because you lose touch with what your mind is supposed to be concentrating on: serving the customer."[71]

Over the course of nearly two centuries, in a radically changing business environment that evolved from owner control to partnership to corporation, the great entrepreneurs gradually devised new techniques of control that emphasized teamwork and cooperation more than dictatorial fiat. "More frequently than a half century ago," noted Penney, "success comes as the result of group endeavor rather than from the dynamic achievement of a single individual." But in every case the entrepreneurs still provided the leadership, vision, direction, and inspiration that others followed. The products and services they created sprang from their own imaginations with the help of talented and dedicated associates. Whether success or failure resulted in any given instance depended on the soundness of their vision and its execution. In this sense they remained peerless leaders relying on their creative instincts to guide their course.[72]

But the entrepreneurs never operated solely in a vacuum of their own enterprise. Like all creative people, they had to struggle against the doubts and hostility of a society lacking their imagination, energy, and drive. Like great artists, they had to not only master their technique or medium but also gain acceptance in the world around them. In the process they often paid severe penalties for being ahead of their time.

| 8 |

The Law and the
Higher Law

This is not a country where success and great products should
be punished. . . . When your own government sues you, it's
not a pleasant experience. . . . I was thinking this is the worst
thing that's ever happened to me.   — BILL GATES[1]

Artists struggle constantly against the bounds of propriety and
taste, seeking to transform or at least expand them. Sometimes
they become social outcasts and run afoul of the law. So it is with
all creative people: They recognize that change is the essence of
creativity, that the two are inseparable and the consequences can
never be predicted. They are harbingers of change, which always
comes hard even in an age where change has become a way of life.
Change upsets people not only because it brings something different but, even more, because it destroys something familiar in the
process. Change unseats habits, disturbs the rituals by which
people organize their lives, and unsettles the certainties that organize their view of the world. John Patterson understood this
process well. "Times change," he liked to say, "but human nature
has not."[2]

This role as agent of change was part of what Fritz Redlich
meant when he characterized the business leader as a "daimonic

213

figure," meaning that "in the economic field hardly any real creation is possible without concomitant destruction," and that
therefore "the destructive power is essentially connected with [the]
creative power." The entrepreneurs conceived and orchestrated this
process, elevated its scale and scope to unprecedented dimensions.
In so doing they created a material civilization that has not only
dominated American life ever since but also transformed its most
basic values and attitudes. Small wonder, then, that they aroused
resentment and hostility especially among those most directly
affected by the changes they wrought. As Warren Buffett once put
it, "It's no fun being a horse when the tractor comes along, or the
blacksmith when the car comes along."[3]

Sam Walton understood this transaction well, having come
under scathing criticism for driving Main Street merchants and
mom-and-pop stores out of existence with his giant discount
stores. "Wal-Mart just cannibalized Main Street," asserted a retail
analyst at Salomon Brothers. The *New York Times Magazine* agreed
that Walton had "incurred the enmity of thousands of Main Street
retailers in hundreds of towns." A 1988 survey in Iowa claimed
that Wal-Mart was also "generally ruining the traditional appearance and character of Iowa's Main streets." Walton dismissed these
charges in language that a social Darwinist like Carnegie would
have applauded. "What happened was absolutely a necessary and
inevitable evolution in retailing," he said, "as inevitable as in the
replacement of the buggy whip makers. The small stores were destined to disappear, at least in the numbers they once existed,
because the whole thing is driven by the customers, who are free to
choose where to shop."[4]

One important aspect of creative destruction is the fact that
economic innovation far outruns the ability of law and custom to
keep up with it. The entrepreneurs who ran afoul of the law and/or
custom were attacked for being lawless and predatory when the
problem was rather that law had not evolved to a point where it

could deal with the innovations they had created. Entrepreneurs, like artists, pay a price for being ahead of their times and for going where others have not gone or fear to go. Sometimes the law was mobilized against agents of change to block their innovations. Sam Walton and other early discounters got a taste of this tactic when they encountered fair trade laws aimed directly at them. Moreover, laws that are passed to do one thing can have unintended consequences. For example, during its early years, the Sherman Antitrust Act was used more against labor unions than against business combinations.

For much of the nineteenth century the legal environment favored innovation. The fundamental goal of American law during that era was to facilitate what J. Willard Hurst called "the release of energy." Where law had earlier favored the protection and preservation of property, it began to help those eager to create something. "We were a people going places in a hurry," wrote Hurst. "Men in that frame of mind are not likely to be thinking only of the condition of their brakes. . . . We did not devote the prime energies of our legal growth to protecting those who sought the law's shelter simply for what they had; our enthusiasm ran rather to those who wanted the law's help positively to bring things about. The sign of this was the overwhelming predominance of the law of contract." Eager to exploit the riches of a vast continent, Americans during the nineteenth century "put little of our creative talent into making the basic framework of law except in areas which we saw most directly contributing to the release of private energy and the increase of private options."[5]

For men in a hurry, this meant an unparalleled freedom from constraints in pursuing their ventures. The development of contracts had the primary effect of increasing the role of the market in social organization and business enterprise. Between 1800 and 1870, Hurst argued, Americans used the law to "enlarge the options open to private individual and group energy." During the next thirty years, as the consequences of that policy unfolded in the form of large corporations and the growing consolidation of businesses, there occurred an "unpatterned, radically important drift and default of policy" that reflected uncertainty over how best to deal with the rapidly changing economic environment. As the century closed, a new concept of law—what came to be known as "sociological jurisprudence"—began to emerge as an approach to many of the problems posed by the mushrooming industrial and urban society.[6]

Oliver Wendell Holmes, Jr., provided the foundation for sociological jurisprudence on the first page of his magisterial *The Common Law* (1881): "The life of the law has not been logic: it has been experience." Roscoe Pound amplified this concept in several works that, as Henry Steele Commager observed, conceived of sociological jurisprudence as "a shift from absolutes to relatives, from doctrines to practices, from passive—and therefore pessimistic—determinism to creative—and therefore optimistic—freedom." Pound himself declared that "in the last century we studied law from within. The jurists of today are studying it from without." In later years the approach found its champion on the Supreme Court in Louis Brandeis, as well as support from Harlan Stone, Benjamin Cardozo, and Felix Frankfurter.[7]

While sociological jurisprudence opened the door to dealing with a myriad of social problems spawned by industrialization, it also became a weapon to be wielded against the growth of large enterprises. Most entrepreneurs were, in Rockefeller's choice phrase, "after something big." It was no coincidence that the jurist most vigorously opposed to bigness per se in business was Brandeis, who made a judicial career of trying to cut giant enterprises down to size. The great conundrum for the courts after 1870 was trying to define the nature of the private corporation. Its twin characteristics of immortality and limited liability posed complex questions that the law never fully answered. Beginning with the

Slaughterhouse Cases of 1873, the Supreme Court groped its way toward a position that defined corporations as individuals and therefore entitled to the protection of the Fourteenth Amendment, which had been created to defend the rights of freed slaves and not giant enterprises. There also arose disputes over vested rights, due process, and the roles of state and federal regulation.[8]

During the turbulent years between 1870 and 1914, when the surging industrial system took shape and began coalescing into giant firms, entrepreneurs perpetually collided with the bounds of law and accepted practice. The collision was unavoidable because the entrepreneurs were creating new conditions to which the law did not fit but must somehow be made to apply. Rockefeller's quest for a viable organization capable of operating on a national scale is a classic example; so was the creation of Northern Securities and other companies that were ultimately dissolved by antitrust suits. The current Microsoft suit is only the most recent example of law groping for a footing in a new context. No less than nine of our entrepreneurs found themselves embroiled in major antitrust suits, many of them landmark cases. Others were subjected to a host of litigation, most notably in the area of patents.

E. H. Harriman was the first to feel the government's wrath when the giant Northern Securities Company, created by James J. Hill and himself as a vehicle to avoid perpetual warfare among their companies by putting the major rail lines of the Northwest into one holding company, was dissolved by the Supreme Court in 1904. It marked the first time the government applied the Sherman Antitrust Act of 1890 to railroads, and it set an ominous precedent in rending asunder companies that decades later would be put back together again. The major lines separated by the Northern Securities case were reunited in 1970 as the Burlington Northern. Harriman received another blow in January 1908 when the federal government brought suit to separate the Union Pacific from the Southern Pacific, a merger he had created in 1901. Harriman did not live to see the resulting breakup of his system in 1912; nor did his sons live to see it put back together in 1996.[9]

John D. Rockefeller jousted repeatedly with the law in seeking a viable organization capable of managing his rapidly expanding empire. His vision had truly outrun the law, which had no provision for corporations operating on a national scale. The railroads, as the first major big businesses, were the first to encounter this problem. The Pennsylvania Railroad, for example, which ran through five states, had to obtain five separate charters from five state legislatures and abide by the provisions of each one. As the system grew, so did the number of charters. Not until 1889, when New Jersey passed a law allowing corporations to hold stock of corporations in other states, was it possible for a company operating on a national scale to manage its operations without resorting to subterfuge. Within a few years Standard Oil of New Jersey became the parent company for the entire Standard Oil empire. Looking back, Rockefeller declared proudly that "all those in the business today are doing business along the modern lines, following the plans which we were the first to propose."[10]

He was correct, but it did not come easily. Before reaching its final form of a holding company, Standard Oil blazed a trail of innovation in seeking vehicles for continental operations. Like most big businesses, it began as a partnership that simply outgrew itself. In bringing rival firms under his control, Rockefeller offered owners—especially those he wanted as partners—stock in Standard Oil, which swelled the number of partners. Rockefeller wanted a central organization capable of managing the business but could not get around state law and charter limitations. Eventually his legal genius, Samuel C. T. Dodd, and his indispensable partner, Henry M. Flagler, found an answer in the form of a trust. In 1881 forty-one Standard Oil partners placed $70 million worth of property in the hands of nine trustees, giving them full authority to manage assets that included fourteen wholly-owned and twenty-six partly owned firms. Two new companies, Standard Oil of New Jersey and Standard Oil of New York, were created as home bases for the combination. Thus arose what became one of the most overused and misused terms of that era and later years: the trust as a synonym for big business.[11]

To manage the giant company, Rockefeller and his associates worked out a brilliant innovation in the form of the committee system, which became a prototype for the management of large organizations. But actual management of the entire operation still had to take place under the table to avoid charges of restraint of trade. No law forbade the Standard Oil trustees from having lunch together at their New York headquarters every day, and these long lunches proved extremely productive. However, the trust posed other problems, and a suit brought by the state of Ohio effectively broke it up in 1892. By that time Rockefeller and his associates were well along in re-creating Standard Oil as a holding company under the laws of New Jersey. In 1906 the federal government targeted the combination in what became the most massive antitrust suit of the era, embracing no less than twenty-one state suits as well.[12]

The procession of suits turned into a cross between a journalistic sideshow and a moral crusade. In one 1907 case Judge Kenesaw Mountain Landis slapped Standard Oil of Indiana with a whopping $29.2 million fine. By that time Rockefeller had long retired from the management of Standard Oil, but he remained the titular head and so found himself dragged into the proceedings. Of this ruling he remarked with rare pique, "Judge Landis will be dead a long time before this fine is paid." He was right; a federal appeals court not only threw out the fine but rebuked Landis for his reasoning in the decision. However, the federal suit came to a climax in 1911 and resulted in the dismemberment of Standard Oil, thus ending what Ron Chernow called "the longest running morality play in American business history."[13]

But not quite, for the moral had some ironic twists. The suit had lasted so long that by the time Standard Oil was broken up for its monopolistic activities, it had already ceased to be as dominant thanks to a flood of new sources of oil and rival firms such as Royal Dutch Shell. Many of the thirty-three newly independent oil companies created by the decision came back together again in later years as the railroads had done. And the last laugh belonged to Rockefeller himself. He owned about a quarter of Standard Oil, which in 1911 made him worth $300 million. After the dissolution he owned a fourth of all thirty-three new companies, the share prices of which climbed steadily as the mushrooming automobile industry fueled a rapid growth in the petroleum market. As a result, Rockefeller found himself on the brink of becoming the nation's first billionaire thanks to a suit meant to punish him and his company for their misdeeds. His fortune peaked at $900 million in 1913, or more than $13 billion in 1996 dollars. Nor did the dissolution stop cooperation among the new companies, which included what later became Exxon, Mobil, Amoco, Chevron, ARCO, and Conoco.[14]

In 1907 the federal government brought suit against the combination Pierre du Pont had put together in the powder industry four years earlier. The decision rendered in 1911 spun two new companies, Atlas and Hercules, off from Du Pont as competitors and required the du Pont family to place their holdings in a single legal framework. More than that, the experience of the suit deeply scarred Pierre du Pont and left him with a profound distrust of all government officials. In 1907, too, a busy Justice Department went after Buck Duke's tobacco trust. Four years of bitter litigation resulted in a landmark 1911 decision that split the trust into the Big Four that became the core of the American tobacco industry: American Tobacco, Liggett & Myers, R. J. Reynolds, and Lorillard, as well as British-American Tobacco and United Cigar Stores. The wicked monopoly was dead, replaced by an oligopoly that, in the most unique feature of the dissolution, was crafted by Duke himself. He alone of the entrepreneurs was asked to author the plan for dismembering his own firm and restoring competition to his industry.[15]

The experience soured Duke on the tobacco industry. Staring at a picture on his desk of the tiny building where he began his amazing career, he muttered bitterly, "In England, if a fellow had built up a whale of a business outta *that*, he'd be knighted. Here they want to put him in jail." After a brief period of perfunctory oversight of American Tobacco and BAT, he left the field he had built up so spectacularly and went on to other things. George Eastman followed the path to New Jersey in 1901 when he incorporated Eastman Kodak as a holding company. For years the Hearst papers howled against the "Kodak Trust." It did not help that Kodak, among all the giant American companies operating overseas, became the first to dominate its field in world trade. Eastman took the charges of monopoly as an affront and tried to modify his policies but admitted that "we don't understand the Sherman Law. . . . I would like to see the man who does." The Justice Department under George Wickersham, which had already gone after Harriman, Rockefeller, Duke, and du Pont, subjected Kodak to a searching investigation that Eastman called "anything but friendly to us."[16]

Eastman managed to stall the instigation of a suit until the administration of Woodrow Wilson came to office. To his chagrin, however, Wilson's attorney general launched an "all-out trust-busting suit" against Kodak in 1913. Eastman could not have been cheered by the round of decisions handed down in 1911, but his case dragged on through various courts until 1921. In the end he settled with the government by signing a consent decree obliging Kodak to sell three plants with the equipment and trade names involved, and to abandon certain brands of equipment. Although Eastman avoided a major breakup of the company, he paid a price for his reluctance to release information about Kodak.

"While there are companies that are nervous and unhappy when being grilled by financial analysts," complained one financial magazine, "Eastman . . . has elevated corporate reticence to a new art form." The experience embittered him as it did the other entrepreneurs.[17]

Thomas Watson's story offers the most unusual experience with antitrust prosecution: He endured the ordeal twice at opposite ends of his career. The first and most traumatic event began in 1912 when the indefatigable Wickersham brought suit against National Cash Register, which was thought to control 90 percent of the cash register market. The suit named John Patterson and twenty-nine other company officers, including Watson. Patterson had given Watson the task of eliminating competitors in the secondhand cash register market, an activity William Rodgers called "clearly illegal under antitrust laws that were extremely difficult to enforce." Patterson made no bones about his way of dealing with competitors, saying, "We don't buy out, we knock out." The government suit indicted NCR and its officers on three counts of criminal conspiracy to restrain trade and maintain a monopoly, which meant that Patterson, Watson, and the others could go to jail if found guilty.[18]

The trial lasted only three months and resulted in a guilty verdict. Patterson, Watson, and another officer received the maximum sentence: $5,000 fines and a year in jail. The others were given the same fine but only nine-month sentences. It was only the second time that jail sentences had been levied under the Sherman Act, and the first case was still on appeal. The decision was appealed, and while it hovered in legal limbo the devastating Dayton flood occurred. Patterson's heroic efforts in that crisis catapulted him to national prominence and led some of his friends to wire President Wilson asking for a pardon. Hearing of this effort, Patterson sent his own telegram to the president assuring him that "these messages and efforts are without my knowledge or consent.

I am guilty of no crime. I want no pardon. I want only justice."
Watson, too, insisted that he had done nothing wrong—though
he did not deny the activities charged against him. In the end the
sentences were quietly suspended and no one served time.[19]

Afterward Patterson wrapped himself even more tightly in
his time-honored cloak of self-righteousness, and a few months
later he fired Watson. Although his painful departure from NCR
became the springboard for his later success, Watson never fully
recovered from the ordeal of the trial. After he had built IBM into
a behemoth, the Justice Department came after him again. When
it first started looking into the possibility of restraint of trade
shortly after World War II, Watson reacted with indignation. Past
experience had taught him to handle his business dealings with a
high degree of rectitude, and he was shocked by any suggestion
that he acted to the contrary. "We have no secrets," he told the
attorney general, "nor is there anything in connection with the
conduct of our business which we are not glad to open to our Government." To another Justice Department official he insisted that
"this business means more to me than you gentlemen can understand. . . . I built it; I am very proud of it. . . . We have done nothing that would violate any antitrust law."[20]

The government rushed very slowly to judgment. A settlement
seemed near in 1950 if Watson had been willing to concede some
changes that would have complicated IBM's business but not damaged it seriously. "If Dad had been reasonable on the subject,"
recalled Tom Jr., "we could have settled the matter then. . . .
Justice . . . wasn't asking for anything drastic, like breaking IBM
up. They thought it would be sufficient if we simply loosened our
hold on the market." But Watson would have none of it. To his
mind, a settlement amounted to an admission of guilt. No amount
of legal advice could get him to see that times had change since
1912—that where the issue earlier had been the *intent* of NCR to
monopolize, it was now the *fact* that a monopoly existed even

though it may have been created by sound, legal business practices. He was hardly the first or the last entrepreneur to puzzle over why the government should find bigness per se an engine for possible illegal activity.[21]

"One of Watson's chief virtues as a businessman," wrote his biographers, "was that he always looked upon problems in simple terms and . . . never complicated the situation. But there was danger in this simplicity, just as there was danger in any virtue. . . . He learned . . . that many of the very attitudes that had accounted for his success now stood in the way of its solution." Convinced of his position much as Patterson had been, he stood firm against a settlement. In 1952 the government finally filed suit against IBM. By that time Tom Watson, Jr., had been made president. He was anxious to settle the suit with a consent decree, but his father, who remained CEO, continued to oppose it bitterly. The antitrust suit became the last of the battlefields over which their tempers raged. Although the proposed consent decree of 1955 was far tougher than the one offered in 1950, Tom Jr. and his advisers all favored signing it. After one last savage argument with his father, he left to negotiate the consent terms. While sitting with the Justice Department officials, a message arrived on a scrap of paper:

100%
Confidence
Appreciation
Admiration
Love
Dad

The consent decree was signed in January 1956. Four months later Watson handed the company over to his son and retired. A month later he was dead.[22]

Not surprisingly, Theodore Vail's AT&T also became a target for antitrust action, especially after its takeover of Western Union. Wickersham suggested the need for an investigation shortly before the end of William Howard Taft's administration but took no action. His interest, however, spurred Vail to a preemptive strike before the incoming Wilson administration took office. He ordered an officer to meet with Wickersham and work out a settlement that would avoid any antitrust suit. The result was an agreement by which AT&T agreed to divest itself of Western Union and terminate the takeover of some independent Midwestern telephone companies. This action earned AT&T praise as a responsible corporate citizen and headed off a potential antitrust suit that it would probably have lost in the climate of 1913. "Take the public into your confidence," he said, "and you win the confidence of the public." Moreover, Vail made no agreement to cease all takeovers of other independent companies, and he resumed his acquisition policy soon afterward.[23]

How Bill Gates will fare in his antitrust suit remains uncertain since the process is still ongoing. His ordeal began in 1991, when the Federal Trade Commission first looked into whether Microsoft had a monopoly in computer operating systems. That probe ended in 1993, but that same year the Justice Department began its own antitrust investigation of Microsoft. The following year Microsoft signed a consent decree agreeing to give PC manufacturers more leeway in using software from other competitors. As complaints mounted that Microsoft was ignoring the terms of the decree, the Justice Department filed suit against the company in 1997 on the charge that it had forced computer makers to promote its Internet browser software. A broader suit filed by the Justice Department and twenty states in 1998 accused Microsoft of illegally using its monopoly power to damage rivals and hamper innovation in the software industry.[24]

Resentment against Microsoft's growing power had been boiling up for well over a decade. Critics tagged the company with the nickname "Big Green," the heir to "Big Blue," which had dominated the industry for so long. As *Business Week* observed in March 1993, "Such a concentration of clout and power has not been seen in the computer industry since the glory days of IBM." Some computer executives accused Microsoft of doing what IBM had done in the 1970s: "Big Green bullies partners, withholds vital information, disparages competitors, and stalls the market by announcing products long before they're ready." Gates called the charges ridiculous. "Our success," he insisted, "is based on only one thing: good products. . . . We're not powerful enough to cause products that are not excellent to sell well." Nor did he accept the view that sheer size was the decisive factor for Microsoft's success. "This is a hypercompetitive market," he pointed out. "Scale is not all positive in this business. Cleverness is the positive."[25]

The investigation dragged on for three years, its tortuous meanderings complicated by a controversial judge who in 1999 issued a finding of fact that Microsoft was a monopoly that did bully competitors and stifled competition. In November 2001 the Justice Department and nine states reached a settlement with terms that fell considerably short of what Judge Thomas Penfield Jackson had tried to impose a year earlier. However, nine other states refused to accept the settlement on the grounds that it was inadequate and offered no protection against future antitrust violations. Their suits continue as of this writing. Afterward, a subdued Gates conceded that the long experience had had "a profound impact on me personally and on our company."[26]

The early stages of the struggle reveal a pattern similar to that faced by the other entrepreneurs. During the long struggle Gates was alternately belligerent and defensive but rarely conciliatory. It did not help that news of the investigation triggered a frenzy of

Gates-bashing by the national media. Like most of the other entrepreneurs he has shown a strong sense of the righteousness of his cause and bitterness over the government's decision to go after his creation. "A monopolist, by definition," he argued, "is a company that has the ability to restrict entry by new firms and unilaterally control price. Microsoft can do neither." Much of his resentment sprang from the view—typical of other entrepreneurs—that his company was being punished for what amounted to superior performance. "What you have here," he said, "is, basically, the U.S. government saying our products are too capable."[27]

The antitrust suits comprised only one legal arena in which the entrepreneurs found themselves doing battle. A far more common one was that of patent law, which engaged many of them in dozens of suits for much of their careers. The inventors, of course, were forever in court defending their creations or attacking alleged infringements on them. Cyrus McCormick spent much of the decade between 1850 and 1860 vainly seeking to get his patent of 1834 extended or fending off suits by rivals poaching on that patent or claiming infringement on their creations. Thomas Edison and George Westinghouse had long days in court, sometimes against each other. Edison fought what was called the "Seven Years War" over his carbon-filament lamp patent and spent another decade defending his motion-picture patents of 1891. He won both cases; the first was a Pyrrhic victory, but the second led to a 1908 trust agreement among the disputants.[28]

It was the carbon-filament lamp patent suit that pitted Edison against Westinghouse in a prelude to the war of the electricity currents. Westinghouse entered the electrical field by buying up patents and incorporating Westinghouse Electrical & Manufacturing Company in 1885. When he moved into the incandescent-light field the next year, Edison countered with a series of suits against the companies controlled by Westinghouse. The Seven

Years War became a three-sided struggle that included Thomson-Houston, which acquired virtually all the patents not owned by Edison or Westinghouse. Few corporate wars matched the bitterness of this one, and the animosity only grew worse when the dispute moved into the contest between AC and DC current. The contest so soured Edison that he refused to meet Westinghouse despite the latter's conciliatory overtures to him.[29]

George Eastman also spent what seemed like a career in court struggling over patent suits as well as antitrust action. One battle with the Goodwin Film & Camera Company involved a decade of legal and other maneuvering that dragged on for yet another decade after suit was finally brought in 1903. "If this case should go against us it would be a most serious thing," Eastman admitted at one point. "I should have no fears if it were not for the present attitude of Judges against big corporations." He finally settled out of court in 1914. Twenty years earlier Eastman had won a decision in a crucial roll-holder suit. His biographer called it "perhaps the high point in Eastman's use of patents. Once the court decisions began to go against him or the cost of enforcing them became prohibitive, he would shift his emphasis from patent protection to product innovation in the ongoing struggle to stay on top of the heap."[30]

Few legal fights grew as tangled and bizarre as that of Buck Duke and his rights to the Bonsack machine. In 1885 Duke bought out a disingenuous partner named Richard H. Wright, who promptly invested his proceeds in the Lone Jack Cigarette Company. Some of the latter's officers were also executives in the Bonsack Machine Company, which used the Lone Jack factory for some of its experimental work. This connection enabled Wright to get from D. B. Strouse, the head of Bonsack, a secret contract for a royalty rate on the machines even lower than the secret rate Duke got from the company. At the same time, Strouse was embroiled in fights to protect his own patents and engaged in a quarrel with Duke over their contract calling for reduced royalties over time.[31]

All these issues came to a head in 1890, just as Duke was working to put together the American Tobacco Company. Lone Jack sued the Bonsack Company, Duke, and other cigarette manufacturers. Duke demanded a refund from Bonsack of $237,000 in excessive royalties because of the lower Lone Jack rate and refused to pay any royalties until agreement was reached. The Bonsack Company sued Duke and another firm, and Wright leaped into the fray with a suit against Duke and his partners charging fraud because he had not been told of the secret contract between Duke and Strouse. A protracted legal battle followed that resulted in a victory for Duke. But Wright appealed, hoping to obtain a settlement, and the fight dragged on. "The mating dance of the whooping crane," wrote historian Robert F. Durden, "could not be more elaborate or humorous than the tortured negotiations that ensued." The man who stepped forward to play a key role as intermediary was none other than Strouse, who had negotiated all the contracts under dispute in the first place. Finally, in 1897, Duke rid himself of Wright by agreeing to pay him $50,000.[32]

The great patent fight in which Henry Ford found himself had enormous stakes. In 1895 George B. Selden, a brilliant patent attorney who became an early mentor to Eastman, had patented for himself an internal combustion engine that he thought gave him the sole right to license all future automobiles using such an engine. A few years later Selden sold the rights to his patent to a Wall Street group headed by William C. Whitney for $10,000 and a fifth of any royalties collected. The Whitney group persuaded a large number of automobile manufacturers to join them rather than risk a protracted legal fight. In 1903 they formed the Association of Licensed Automobile Manufacturers and set out to enlist other manufacturers. A few weeks after formation of the association, Ford Motors was incorporated. Ford tried to join the group but was rejected, leaving him with the option of going out of the car business or defying the association.[33]

Predictably, Ford chose defiance. In July 1903, with his company scarcely under way, he put an advertisement in a Detroit paper
aimed at "Dealers, Importers, Agents and Users of our Gasoline
Automobiles" assuring them that "We will protect you against any
prosecution for alleged infringement of patents. The Selden patent
does not cover any practicable machine, no practicable machine can
be made from it, and never was." The association promptly brought
suit, which dragged on until 1909, when Judge Charles Merrill
Hough upheld the Selden patent. It was during this long legal
hiatus that William Durant, who had also held out from joining
the association, tried to put together the combination that included
Ford and nearly succeeded. When Hough's decision was handed
down, however, Durant and nearly all the other holdouts conceded defeat and joined the association. Durant was reputed to
have paid $1 million in back royalties.[34]

But Ford stubbornly refused to submit. "There will be no let up
in the legal fight," he vowed, and promised to carry it to the
Supreme Court if necessary. Selden's patent, he insisted, was nothing more than "a freak among alleged inventions . . . worthless as
a patent and worthless as a device." Already he had put up a total
of $12 million in bonds to protect any Ford dealer or customer
from the association. It was one of Ford's finest hours and marked
his entry onto the stage of public figures. The Detroit *Free Press*
applauded his stand in an editorial titled "Ford, the Fighter." In
January 1911 he gained complete victory when the appeals court
reversed the decision in such complete terms that the association
gave up the fight and disbanded. At its height the association had
enlisted seventy-three domestic and seventeen foreign manufacturers and collected just under $6 million in royalties. Although
the patent was due to expire in 1912 anyway, Ford had insured the
future of the automobile industry.[35]

Like Eastman, Edwin Land occupied an industry buttressed by
patents that had to be defended and multiplied. The greatest legal

ordeal of his career came near its end, when Polaroid sued Kodak for patent infringement. After considerable hesitation, Kodak had finally gone into instant photography in 1976. Polaroid argued that its rival had done so only by infringing patents. The trial began in October 1981 and lasted seventy-five days, during which time Land testified for three days and withstood ten days of cross-examination. Peter Wensberg called Land's preparation "more meticulous than for any public appearance he had ever made." On the stand he was brilliant, giving a tutorial on the development of instant photography and then fending off opposing counsel in masterful fashion.[36]

Three years passed before Judge Rya Zobel, working without a jury, rendered a decision in the complex case. Her 122-page decision declared that Kodak had infringed seven Polaroid patents, and she followed a month later with an injunction halting further sales of Kodak instant cameras and film. Land and his company had won a complete victory, but he did not live to see its fruits. Kodak appealed, but the higher courts upheld both the decision and the injunction. In 1991 Kodak finally settled by paying Polaroid $900 million, a pittance compared to a potential liability that might have approached $10 billion. But the outcome had a greater significance in refusing to allow a giant company, the dominant presence in its industry for most of the century, to appropriate for its own use the creations of a much smaller firm.[37]

Bill Gates, too, found himself embroiled in patent suits. This was hardly surprising given his reputation for borrowing the ideas of others and improving them. In March 1988 Apple filed a copyright suit in federal court accusing Microsoft of stealing certain visual-display features from the Macintosh computer for use in the latest version of Windows. The suit blindsided Gates; only two days before he had met with John Sculley of Apple, who said nothing about the suit or hinted at any problems with Microsoft. The action rocked the entire computer industry, which feared the chilling effect it would have on software development for Windows. Microsoft countered with a suit charging Apple with breaking their licensing agreement of 1985 and seeking to damage Microsoft's reputation with negative publicity. The case dragged on until 1992, when a judge ruled in favor of Microsoft and Gates and Sculley mended their fences.[38]

For most of the entrepreneurs, the law represented not only boundaries but a nuisance or obstacle that had to be overcome. However, a few of them became masterful at using the law as a tool. Foremost among them was Gould, who used the law to obfuscate and delay much as a chess master creates complex positions to baffle his adversary. As Julius Grodinsky observed, Gould was a genius at the "art of judicial interference. . . . By the fall of 1881 Gould was probably the most successful litigant in American history. His court suits had been almost phenomenally successful." The law was for him an instrument wielded for both offense and defense. He understood its nuances well enough to walk the finest of its lines and skirt its borders with uncanny precision. This ability, combined with his extraordinary financial talents, enabled him to perfect the art of controlling large properties with a minimum of actual holdings. To gain command or retain it, he utilized every device from equity control and funded debt to floating debt, contractual flaws, receiverships, and a host of legal technicalities. No businessman has shown more diversity in his techniques.[39]

After the notorious Gold Corner of 1869, Gould used suits to delay settlements for several years until he had the means to pay them. In seeking control of an obscure railroad, he managed to get its stock released from trust by bringing suit and completing "the entire machinery of complaint, answer, trial, decree, and execution" in only ten days. To keep his hands free for whatever action was required, he avoided signing agreements in his own name but operated through the instrumentalities of bankers, brokers, promoters, and corporations or their officers. To spur action by a rival,

Gould might lay down a barrage of suits to bring him to the table. During a struggle to retain his control of the Wabash railroad, he managed to secure a friendly receiver for the railroad before it had even defaulted, prompting one critic to ask "whether the federal judiciary . . . is really the law department of Mr. Gould's southwestern railroad system." In defending a verdict for $240,000 in a suit against his Western Union, Gould wrote, "We will of course appeal. . . . We can carry it to the U.S. Court at Washington which will take 7 years before Mr. Stokes will see any cash."[40]

These prolonged struggles with the law have both steeled and scarred the entrepreneurs who engaged in them. The antitrust suits especially rankled. The entrepreneurs expected rivals to resort to any device, but most seemed surprised that the government would come after them for doing what they were supposed to do and doing it better than anyone else. After all, the ground rule was to compete, and competition created winners and losers. In business the winners grew larger by the very momentum of their success, which made them even more formidable competitors and therefore dominant in their field. Dominance, if not monopoly, was the logical outcome of the game. The paradox of the free market was that sooner or later it sowed the seeds of its own destruction in any given field. Once the winners emerged, they gained the power to rig the game unless someone intervened to level the playing field, in which case the market was no longer free but regulated and therefore subject to endless debate over the nature and degree to which it should be regulated.

During the late twentieth century the concept of markets was not only debated but expanded, twisted, perverted, and distorted into all kinds of shapes and roles. The result was what Thomas Frank called "market populism," a notion rooted in the premise that "markets were a popular system, a far more democratic form of organization than (democratically elected) governments. . . . That in addition to being mediums of exchange, markets were

233

mediums of consent. . . . In the nineties these ideas became canonical, solidified into a new orthodoxy that anathematized all alternative ways of understanding democracy, history, and the rest of the world." This occurred in part because the society embraced probusiness attitudes with a fervor not seen since the 1920s, but also because American life had moved into an unprecedented era in which virtually everything in everyday life had become a business.[41]

The business of America has become big business far beyond what Warren Harding or Calvin Coolidge ever imagined. Commercialization has rolled like a tsunami into every corner of American life with a force and decisiveness that has radically affected every aspect of the culture yet has drawn astonishingly little attention. Try to think of any human activity—or some inhuman one—that has not become a business in the past twenty years or so. Defenders of this new order hail it as the triumph of the market and in some ironic ways it is, but even more it is the demise of culture in the name of profit. Like the Gilded Age, it has created fertile ground for both entrepreneurs and mere profit mongers who extract their pound of flesh while giving nothing of lasting value in return. These modern robber barons differ little from their historical counterparts except in their scale of operations. Buffett took their measure well. "Boone Pickens and Jimmy Goldsmith and the crew . . . aren't creating value," he said; "they are transferring it from society to shareholders. That may be a good or bad thing but it isn't creating value—it's not like Henry Ford developing the car or Ray Kroc figuring out how to deliver hamburgers better than anyone else."[42]

In a culture dominated by business, every field has its own peculiar stripe of robber baron whose only gift is to exploit rather than create. Whatever else the great entrepreneurs did, they gave the world creations of lasting value. It is this quality more than any other that separates them from ordinary businesspeople or entrepreneurs, just as it separates the greatest creative people in other fields from their peers. They understood this distinction better than most, having often dealt with predators in the course of their careers. Theirs was not a moral superiority but one of vision and accomplishment. Like other creative people, this sometimes led them to the belief in a higher law consisting of their own vision and the means, however unsavory they might be at times, to fulfill it.

For the religious among them, it was easy to enlist God on their side. "But for the fact that Providence has seemed to assist me in our business," said McCormick, "it has at times seemed that I would almost sink under the weight of responsibility hanging on me. But I believe the Lord will help us out." McCormick also saw a moral dimension in courting the Almighty. "Business is not inconsistent with Christianity," he declared, ". . . but the latter ought to be a help to the former, giving it a confidence and resignation, after using all *proper means.*" For other great entrepreneurs, however, the choice of proper means lay within their own superior judgment. Harriman exemplified this attitude on an occasion when he nearly broke the spirit of his most trusted adviser, Judge Robert S. Lovett. [43]

The high-minded judge agonized over whether to reveal something to Harriman in the strictest confidence. Honor demanded that he protect the source but also that he inform Harriman. Finally he told Harriman but only on condition that the confidence be strictly honored and not be broken in any manner that harmed the original source. To Lovett's chagrin, Harriman promptly went out and used the information. "I don't see how you could have done such a thing to me," said the mortified judge, who considered resigning as Harriman's legal counsel. "I understand these things so much better than you do," replied Harriman in a tone much like that he used to scold his sons. "Of course, I can't respect a confidence that ties my hands in a matter of momentous consequence to the operations in which I am engaged. I must be the judge of what is right and wrong in these things."[44]

In this exchange can be found two of the three attitudes common among businessmen (and others) across the years. All three types consider themselves ethical, upright persons. To the Lovetts of the world, right was always right and wrong always wrong regardless of the circumstances or the stakes. A second type was no less rigid in his sense of integrity, but he assumed that because he was a man of strict honor, anything he did must be honorable; because he would not knowingly commit an unethical act, any act he committed must be ethical. People like Harriman belonged to a different breed altogether. They believed in honor and integrity but even more in the superiority of their own judgment to define what behavior those qualities entailed in a given situation. Others, of course, did not bother with any of these distinctions but simply did what needed to be done with little or no concern for ethical niceties, but that category does not include many of the great entrepreneurs. Their greatest strength—and sometimes their fatal flaw—was their utter faith in the higher law of their own judgment.

No one exemplified this attitude better than John D. Rockefeller, who insisted that "There has been nothing in my life that will not bear the utmost scrutiny." He confessed to a strong admiration for Napoleon, whom he thought "would have been the greatest businessman the world has ever known. My, what a genius for organization! He also had what I have always regarded as a prime necessity for large success in any enterprise . . . a thorough understanding of men and ability to inspire in them confidence in him and what is of equal importance, confidence in themselves. . . . It is by such traits as these that men get the work of the world done."[45]

During the late nineteenth century it was the fashion to refer to leading entrepreneurs as the Napoleons of their field, whether it be railroads, iron and steel, manufacturing, or food processing. The reference was apt in the sense that the true Napoleons in each field possessed the same qualities of creativity, leadership, and belief in themselves as well as their vision. They were all men who created their own destiny of greatness, and who tended to believe in the superiority of the higher law of their own judgment over the strictures and obstacles of the law. That was how they not only got the world's work done but also changed the world in the process.

| 9 |

The Entrepreneurs
Off Duty

What you do in your working hours determines what you
have. What you do in your play hours determines who
you are.   —GEORGE EASTMAN[1]

The old argument over whether money can buy happiness goes nowhere unless it begins by defining what is meant by happiness. Few things are more individual or idiosyncratic than the particular activities that make a person happy. For some it lies in the ability to do what they wish and to have control of their life. Most if not all of the entrepreneurs shared this desire, yet all of them were in some way prisoners to an obsession that drove them relentlessly. They did not leave work easily, and their work seldom left them. Although most of them managed to have other interests and find enjoyment when off duty, they seldom led what might be called a balanced life. Obsessions do not encourage balance or foster a rich variety of experiences. What is most remarkable about many of the entrepreneurs is how much activity they managed to cram in while off duty, given how seldom they were off duty.

One of the most persistent clichés about creative people, especially artists, is that they tend to be neurotic or unbalanced individuals driven by some obsession or compulsion. Debate has raged over whether these qualities are somehow essential to their creativity or merely a by-product of it. One element of this debate involves the question of whether truly creative people can lead "normal" lives, however "normal" is defined. Historical evidence can be cited on both sides of the question, but the argument is a fruitless one in that anyone who achieves creative greatness in any field is by definition something other than normal. Great accomplishments set anyone aside, as do the characteristics that make great achievements possible. But this does not mean that such people fit a common profile or even have much in common with one another.

Edwin Land had an original slant on this question. He rejected the notion that creative individuals had to be neurotic or radical in their behavior. "No person could possibly be original in one area," he said, "unless he were possessed of the emotional and social stability that comes from fixed attitudes in all areas other than the one in which he is being original. . . . I doubt whether any person can be happy who rejects this structure of society—intellectual and social." Creative people depended utterly upon the "fixed attitudes" of society, which always pressed one toward conformity. "You need a tremendous amount of literary, political, industrial sophistication when you are young," Land added, "in order to free yourself of the load of disapproval of your novel undertaking." On another occasion he observed, "The test of an invention is the power of an inventor to push it through in the face of the staunch—not opposition, but indifference—in society."[2]

Put another way, the entrepreneurs—and other creative people— found themselves early in life swimming upstream against the powerful currents of conformity, indifference, hostility, and derision for being different. This posed an especially peculiar problem for Americans because no other society worships individualism so ardently and yet is so deeply suspicious of it. A large part of the strong competitive streak the entrepreneurs have may well derive from their experience of being apart and different from other people. Even those who seemingly grew up in the most "normal" of circumstances had characteristics that set them apart from their peers, not the least of which was their strong drive to succeed. For some of them that overpowering determination became an obsession that absorbed nearly everything else in their life. For others, it became a force that expanded to embrace other interests as well.

Since none of the entrepreneurs except du Pont were born into wealth, their attitude toward the accumulation of a fortune offers an intriguing insight into their personalities and lifestyles. "I always knew I was going to be rich," said Warren Buffett. "I don't think I ever doubted it for a minute." Yet the acquisition of a huge fortune scarcely changed his lifestyle. He continued to live in Omaha and to eat the same foods he loved as a kid even though he has become a celebrity who hops around the country on his one extravagant toy—a private jet. "I've fallen in love with the plane," he admitted. "It's going to be buried with me." He attributes his ideas about food and diet to a "wildly successful party that celebrated my fifth birthday." Chided for his decidedly non-master-of-the-universe wardrobe, he insisted that "I buy expensive suits. They just look cheap on me."[3]

Money to Buffett has always been a by-product of his work. "I don't measure my life by the money I've made," he said. "Other people might, but I certainly don't." What he claims to enjoy is "the fun of making money and watching it grow." Like Carnegie, he takes a dim view of people who inherit wealth, which he called "food stamps for the rich. . . . All those people who think that food stamps are debilitating and lead to a cycle of poverty, they're the same ones who go out and want to leave a ton of money to their kids." Land's lifestyle scarcely changed as he grew wealthier. Sam Walton also maintained his simple lifestyle and pleasures as his fortune swelled and admitted that he had "done everything I can to discourage our folks from getting too extravagant with their homes and their automobiles and their lifestyles." Kroc thought that "money creates problems, and the more you have, the bigger the problems, not the least of which is how to spend it wisely." John Patterson spent money on clothing but little else. Henry Ford's tastes remained simple and idiosyncratic all his life.[4]

Most of the entrepreneurs elevated their lifestyles as their fortune grew but managed to retain relatively simple tastes. Fine houses and landscaping became a common theme. John D. Rockefeller lavished money on houses, but they were for him retreats rather than showcases and he remained a homebody whose social life revolved around family and church functions. He revealed a talent for landscape design and believed in the "dignity of manual labor." John Wanamaker bought ever larger town houses in Philadelphia but still preferred the church to the social scene. Like most of the other entrepreneurs, he also had a place in the country. George Eastman lived well but not ostentatiously. He built the largest and finest mansion in Rochester but, like Rockefeller, utilized it to suit his needs and tastes rather than to impress. His home included an organ to satisfy his love for music. Robert Noyce kept his house in the Los Altos hills and devoted a fortune to landscaping it, complete with a pond and waterscape "elaborate enough to put on a bus tour."[5]

Not surprisingly, the push for larger and more elaborate houses often came from wives rather than from the entrepreneurs themselves. Thomas Edison tended to be oblivious of his surroundings but indulged the whims of both his wives for opulent homes and trappings. George Westinghouse maintained homes in Pittsburgh, Washington, and Lenox, Massachusetts. The latter became a special pleasure for his wife, who made a hobby of raising livestock. Cornelius Vanderbilt cared little for frills until prodded by his second wife, Frank, who undertook the arduous task of civilizing his tastes. Buck Duke had a mansion on Fifth Avenue and a three-hundred-acre farm in New Jersey that he converted into an "Elysian showplace." But even this showcase did not satisfy his second wife, Nanaline, who preferred the elegance of Newport society. In 1922 Duke indulged her by buying a Newport mansion, but he built a house he liked in Charlotte, North Carolina, the center of his growing power system. He swallowed Newport society in small doses, saying, "I like those old ladies in Newport, but I don't want to sit by them every night."[6]

William Durant also created a showplace estate for his second wife in the aptly named Deal, New Jersey. Walter Chrysler came away from Raymere murmuring, "I had never experienced luxury to compare with Billy Durant's house." It became, said Durant's biographer, "a palace whose major statement about its royal couple was simply that they could afford it. It devoured money." Penney's lifestyle also grew more elaborate with remarriage. For his second wife he acquired an estate in White Plains, New York, and a fine house on Belle Isle, near Miami Beach. Thomas Watson proved a conspicuous exception to this pattern. He preferred living in fashionable areas such as Short Hills, New Jersey, and acquired a thousand-acre estate nearby. His wife, however, was a frugal woman "strong on prairie virtues" who cringed at the money he poured into their lifestyle.[7]

Some of the entrepreneurs needed no help in acquiring fine homes. Andrew Carnegie might reminisce about the virtues of poverty and scorn the customary social ambitions of his day, but in 1897 he purchased a castle in the Scottish Highlands and poured money into its restoration. He also erected a fine mansion on Fifth Avenue and 91st Street in New York City. Jay Gould owned a brownstone in New York City but loved much more Lyndhurst, his estate on the Hudson, where he filled his giant greenhouse with rare and exotic plants. Pierre du Pont lavished both money and affection on his Longwood estate and gardens. E. H. Harriman had the usual brownstone in Manhattan and near the end of his life

built a magnificent house to crown his Arden estate in Orange
County, New York. Theodore Vail had his splendid Walnut
Avenue house in Boston. When he had to sell it, he began developing Speedwell, his farm in Vermont, into a glorious 2,500-acre
estate that became his pride and joy. There he entertained on a
lavish scale the parties of friends that journeyed up from Boston
and New York.[8]

Frank Woolworth, who had lived the life of a skinflint for so
long, indulged himself handsomely as his fortune piled up. In
New York City he joined the parade of the wealthy who built mansions on Fifth Avenue's Millionaire's Row. His wife, still a creature
of simple tastes, longed for the "more homely comforts of their
earlier dwellings." The new mansion featured in its luxurious living room a player piano at which Woolworth sat for hours, turning
the rolls and beating time while his mind turned over business
problems. He also erected fine mansions for two of his married
daughters and acquired a country estate at Glen Cove on the north
shore of Long Island. When the latter house burned down in 1916,
he rebuilt it into an Italian Renaissance palace and in the process
developed a passion for decorating. Cass Gilbert designed the
house, which included a $100,000 pipe organ equipped with spe-
cial storm effects, and ten master bedrooms.[9]

Even Bill Gates has joined the procession and possibly jumped
to its head. His fabulous mansion in Seattle, built at an estimated
cost of $50 million, became a technological as well as architectural
wonder. Its unique forty thousand square feet includes seven
"pavilions" terraced into a hill above Lake Washington. Like all
the entrepreneurs, Gates embodied in his compound the latest
technologies. In this case the result went beyond mere creature
comforts to the creation of what his biographers called a "Virtual
Xanadu." Software would run everything, including the images of
artwork (Gates purchased the electronic rights from museums
around the world) drawn from a huge database. The walls of each

pavilion consist of video screens capable of being programmed to display whatever works of art the viewer prefers. Music of choice is also piped in; other amenities included a waterfall-spa with pool, large reception hall, library, game room, and trampoline room. A central computer room controls everything from climate to personal preferences. The place, said *The New York Times,* "is not a mansion, or even an estate; it's an organism."[10]

Comparisons with the Newport mansions, William Randolph Hearst's imposing Xanadu, and other great houses of the rich arose at once. "There is a huge amount of solipsistic fantasy in the Gates house," declared Nancy Koehn of the Harvard Business School. Gates declared that his ecologically friendly dwelling "is a house of the future, a test site for computer-assisted living." The parade of jokes and serious scholarly analysis about what the house *really means* has buried some obvious points. Every great house has been a monument of sorts and a showcase to the public, but most of them have meant something quite different to the owner. Like Rockefeller and Eastman before him, Gates paid close attention to the details of his home. It is essentially another form of creative achievement, both palpable and functional to his specific wants. As Margaret Talbot pointed out, "What great wealth procures for itself is not, in fact, Pharaonic excess . . . but insulation, carefully calibrated, from the contingencies and disruptions of daily life as most people live it. That's why the Gates house is the perfect symbol of the new elite. It is not a monument to excess so much as a monument to control."[11]

Apart from such obvious trappings of wealth, many of the entrepreneurs used their fortunes as springboards onto the highest rungs of society. Cyrus McCormick did little in this regard until his marriage, after which he allowed his wife to draw him into society. He bought homes in both Chicago and New York, yet did not build his Chicago mansion until 1879 even though he and his brothers were the largest owners of real estate in the city. Samuel

Insull, who cared less for money than for status, parlayed his modest fortune into a role as a civic and cultural leader in Chicago. In this role he did much for the city even while arousing resentment among some elements of the Gold Coast elite. A lover of opera all his life, Insull conceived a brilliant plan for erecting a new opera house at the base of a forty-two-story office building. When completed in the unfortunate fall of 1929, it was hailed as a marvel in every respect except one: Unlike most opera houses, it had no prominent boxes in which society's leaders could display themselves.[12]

Insull was one of a handful of our entrepreneurs who became civic leaders in their communities. By far the most dedicated in this role was George Eastman, who remained in Rochester all his life and devoted much of his time to its needs. Few events revealed his influence more clearly than the "tonsillectomy marathon." Accepting the medical belief that children with infected tonsils and adenoids were thought to be more susceptible to infectious diseases, Eastman orchestrated a campaign to remove the tonsils of all the city's children. Special clinics were set up, transportation provided, and a publicity campaign launched. "No other Rochesterian," said his biographer, ". . . could have closed all the schools for half a day and moved their population en masse into a makeshift operating theater where 7,833 sets of tonsils were summarily removed." For Eastman it was merely one more civic duty.[13]

To a lesser extent, John Patterson played a comparable role in Dayton and John Wanamaker in Philadelphia. Sam Walton was always active in the affairs of the town in which he lived but rarely extended his reach beyond its modest borders. Few of the others showed any strong interest in civic affairs beyond their philanthropic endeavors, which often benefited their city. Philanthropy posed a challenge to all the entrepreneurs except Durant and Insull, who lost their fortunes, and Vail, who never accumulated wealth comparable to the others. "I never saved a dollar in my life," Vail admitted. Yet at the age of seventy he donated his beloved Speedwell Farm to the state of Vermont, reserving only the right to occupy the main house during his remaining years. Buffett observed that "it's easier to create money than to spend it." Gates echoed this notion, saying that "spending money intelligently is as difficult as earning it." Ray Kroc once exclaimed that "I never realized it could be so damned difficult to give away money." Carnegie said repeatedly that he had not worked one-tenth as hard making his money as he did giving it away.[14]

The possession of great wealth imposed on most of the entrepreneurs the burden of what to do with it. Philanthropy offered one obvious outlet, but fewer than half our group chose this route to any large degree and fewer still subscribed to Eastman's maxim that "the rich man never gives anything . . . he only distributes part of his surplus. The credit to him lies in the distribution of that surplus." Only four of them became great philanthropists, although Buffett stands waiting in the wings. Carnegie made the dispersing of his fortune a credo and a career during the last eighteen years of his life in his determination to make the process as rational and careful as possible. Libraries became his first business, which he dispatched in a manner "as efficient and standardized . . . as the filling of orders for steel billets," utilizing an architectural style that became popularly known as "Carnegie Classical." In all he created 2,811 free libraries (1,946 in the United States) at a total cost exceeding $50 million; every state in the Union except Rhode Island got a Carnegie library. His anti-imperialist views and advocacy of peace led to the creation of his Hero Fund, which always remained his pet project. In 1910 he created the enduring Carnegie Endowment for International Peace.[15]

But it was in higher education that Carnegie made his greatest impact. Although he took a dim view of higher education that lacked some technical or vocational bent, he ultimately exerted a greater impact on its standards than any man before him. In 1904 he created what became the Carnegie Foundation for the Advancement of Teaching with a $10 million endowment, hoping to provide for those who reached the end of their careers without any support for their old age. Within a dozen years it proved infeasible as a pension plan, but by 1909 the Carnegie Foundation had emerged as "the unofficial accrediting agency for colleges and universities." Two years later Carnegie transferred most of the $125 million remaining in his fortune to the first giant philanthropic foundation, the Carnegie Corporation, intended to "promote the advancement and diffusion of knowledge among the people of the United States." It became not only the first "super trust" in philanthropy but also a model for many that followed. In all, Carnegie gave away about $350 million.[16]

No American practiced philanthropy longer or more deeply than John D. Rockefeller. When he first started work in September 1855 he spent a dime for a small book he called Ledger A, which became his most precious relic because it held the record of his giving. During his first year of work Rockefeller donated about 6 percent of his earnings to charity; three years later he upped the figure to 10 percent. Although the Baptist church received most of his attention, other beneficiaries of his generosity ranged from the Five Points Mission in Manhattan to a black church, a Catholic orphanage, a Methodist church, and a black man seeking to buy his wife out of slavery. Throughout his business career the amount going to charity rose sharply along with his income. He took a special interest in the problems of poverty wrought by industrialization and the welfare of blacks. His large contributions to a black seminary in Atlanta did not induce him to put his name on the place; instead Spelman Seminary (later Spelman College) received his wife's maiden name.[17]

Once Rockefeller enlisted Frederick T. Gates to oversee his philanthropic efforts and retired from Standard Oil, he launched a second career that produced creations as spectacular as that of Standard Oil. He did not follow Carnegie's path but carved out his own sphere of interest. As Ron Chernow noted, "The most perplexing issue for Rockefeller was how to square philanthropy with self-reliance." His solution was to promote pure research, especially in medicine, where the findings could result in broad social benefits. What followed can only be summarized here. Rockefeller founded and sustained the University of Chicago; endowed the pioneering Rockefeller Institute for Medical Research (later Rockefeller University); funded the General Education Board to promote black education and later medical education; and underwrote the landmark campaign to eradicate the scourge of hookworm in the rural South. No other philanthropist had poured big money into the areas of medicine and medical education. Carnegie had shunned giving money for hospitals, believing they "should be city institutions, like prisons."[18]

By 1922 Rockefeller had spent a staggering $475 million on charitable causes, but his influence went far beyond money. Far more than Carnegie, he transformed philanthropy into a business. Using the Johns Hopkins Medical School as his prototype, he raised the standards of medical research and education by giving funds to schools that used the Johns Hopkins model. Borrowing from his own business model, he moved to create a philanthropic trust on a scale that dwarfed any earlier effort. In 1913 he secured a charter for the Rockefeller Foundation, which he endowed with $183 million. The move both insulated most of his fortune from inheritance taxes and maintained his close control over the recipients of the foundation's bequests.[19]

At an incredibly early age Gates not only made a fortune that exceeded those of Carnegie and Rockefeller but also created a foundation with assets that dwarf all others. "Giving away money in meaningful ways," he had said, "will be a main preoccupation later in my life—assuming I still have a lot to give away." He set up his first foundation in 1994, the year he got married. Then only thirty-nine years old, he began a career as a prodigy in philanthropy comparable to that in software. Three years later he started a second foundation aimed at reducing the "digital divide." In 1999 the two were combined and moved into new headquarters in Seattle. Gates entrusted the management not to professionals but to his father, Bill Senior, and a trusted former Microsoft executive, Patty Stonesifer. As of February 2002, the Gates Foundation boasted assets of $24 billion. By comparison, Carnegie gave away the equivalent of $3 billion and Rockefeller $6 billion in today's dollars. Under current regulations, the foundation must disperse 5 percent of its assets, or $1.2 billion every year.[20]

Like his predecessors, Gates brought to his foundation the same focus as he did to his work. One program echoed Carnegie in high-tech fashion by providing libraries in low-income communities with computers and Internet access along with training and technical support. By far the most ambitious programs, however, involve world health issues. Like Rockefeller, Gates sought to underwrite research in relatively neglected areas of public health. But he soon moved toward the more ambitious goal of mass prevention of diseases for which vaccines already existed. One pledge of $750 million went to a newly created group called Global Alliance for Vaccines and Immunization; other efforts have attacked AIDS and cervical cancer, the leading cause of cancer death among women in developing nations. A deluge of three thousand proposals swamps the foundation every month. Gates and his wife, Melinda, discuss all those on the short list and personally approve any grant exceeding $1 million. They also try to leverage their dollars and prominence into more funds from other sources.

Newsweek praised Gates for helping to create "a whole new model of philanthropy—a spare, lean, entrepreneurial model that employs leverage instead of largesse to make things happen." But others have criticized Gates's philanthropy as they have everything he does. One historian of American foundations suggested that Gates trade his wife and father to the Ford Foundation for people with more experience, and that he set up an executive board balanced in race and gender. "Before he began giving money away," observed Jean Strouse, "people complained that he was a miser. Now that he *is* giving money away, they complain that he is doing it too late, that he isn't giving enough, that he hasn't a clue about what he's getting into, that the projects . . . are too conservative, too liberal, too big, too small, too safe, too risky, too conventional, too splashy. Or they say he's only doing it to avoid taxes, or to expand Microsoft's markets, or, especially, to improve his image in the light of the government's high-profile antitrust suit."[21]

This pattern has thrust Gates squarely in the footsteps of his predecessors, whose motives and choices were always questioned. However, Gordon Conway, head of the Rockefeller Foundation, lauded the Gates Foundation's leadership for being "extraordinarily well focused in the health field." Another foundation president admired the ability of the small Gates management team to make quick decisions and added, "I hope Gates will continue to maintain personal control—that he really gets and stays involved." Gates himself remains philosophical about the critics and the surprisingly immense difficulties of giving away huge sums of money usefully and intelligently. "Having so much in the way of resources," he observed, "can make it hard to tell what people actually want."[22]

Warren Buffett, who is a quarter century older than Gates, divided $134 million among four organizations but has yet to take the plunge into philanthropy on a scale comparable to his younger friend. "The idea of bestowing a handout—even to charities— made him edgy," wrote his biographer. Persuaded by a friend to become a trustee of Grinnell College in the 1970s, he soon gave the school an impressive financial base. To his astonishment, however, the college proceeded to spend some of its windfall and thereby soured Buffett on giving to higher education. Certain causes have gained his support, most notably population control. In Omaha itself he has compiled a curious record. He has taken great pleasure in giving annual awards of $10,000 to each of fifteen local teachers but has absented himself from most local charity drives. Not until 1990 did he create the Sherwood Foundation, earmarked solely for Omaha charities.[23]

Whether Buffett will follow Gates's example remains to be seen. He has told Gates and others that any major plunge into philanthropy will not happen until he has retired from earning money. "Warren thinks it's very tricky," observed Gates, "to be in a meeting one minute where you're talking about giving away lots of money, and then in the next minute you're thinking about making money. . . . He thinks that's a little schizophrenic." In that respect Buffett is following the model of both Carnegie and Rockefeller, who retired from business before taking up philanthropy as a second career. Gates is unique in tackling both not only at an early age but at the same time.[24]

For George Eastman, even more than Carnegie, Rockefeller, or Gates, philanthropy was a deeply personal occupation. "He attended to the details . . . himself," wrote his biographer, "rather than hiring a squad of bureaucrats." Like them he carefully oversaw the good works he underwrote, but he had no desire to create a foundation for the ages. "Men who leave their money to be distributed by others" he said, "are pie-faced mutts. . . . I want to see the action in my lifetime." In 1924, eight years before his death, Eastman signed away most of his remaining fortune to four educational institutions and gave another $9 million worth of Kodak stock to company employees. Prior to that time, however, he had already done a great deal, especially for the city of Rochester. Part of the $51 million he ultimately put into the University of Rochester went to the creation of a medical and dental school, the Eastman School of Music, and the Eastman Theatre, which sought to combine his two great loves, music and film, by showing silent movies as well as hosting concerts. "His influence over the cultural, economic, and political life of Rochester was considerable, and in most cases definitive," wrote his biographer. "Yet he recognized no contract to appear in public, and the fact that he chose not to lent an aura of mystery to his image of unequaled wealth and power."[25]

Rochester's parks, schools, YMCA, and public buildings also received support from Eastman, and his shyness extended beyond the city to other philanthropies. One of the most remarkable instances involved his gifts to MIT. Between 1912 and 1920 he donated nearly $20 million to the institute's building fund but insisted on anonymity and was known only as "Mr. Smith." Not until 1920 was the true identity of Mr. Smith revealed. Eastman also provided generous support to two black schools, the Hampton Institute and Tuskegee Normal, and endowed a professorship at Oxford. When Rockefeller agreed to help support Eastman's medical school, which used Johns Hopkins as its model, Eastman wrote him that "for many years I have considered you the foremost philanthropist of the age and have admired the wisdom with which your vast wealth is being distributed." Although Eastman lacked Rockefeller's huge fortune, he took a backseat to no one in the fullness of his philanthropy.[26]

The music school especially delighted Eastman, who said it "has given me more fun in my old age than anything I ever tackled. . . . It is a joke that one who is totally devoid of all musical ability is trying to steer one of the biggest musical enterprises that has ever been proposed." He claimed to be tone-deaf, but Howard Hanson, the great composer and conductor who turned the school into a major institution during his long tenure, thought otherwise. "He desired [music] in an elemental way, like food and water and air," Hanson recalled. "He did not probe or analyze; he merely listened. . . . Of his many interests, art and music were the only things he did not pursue or dissect intellectually. He knew instinctively what he liked or disliked. . . . I can't imagine anyone with his sensitivity to music being tone deaf."[27]

Other entrepreneurs made important philanthropic gifts, some of which bore their names, to posterity. Cornelius Vanderbilt, probably at his wife's influence, gave tiny, obscure Central University $500,000 in 1873 and a like amount in installments before his death in 1877. It was hardly a personal passion for the old semiliterate, who never visited the renamed Vanderbilt University. Buck Duke came slowly to philanthropy, pulled there largely by the influence of his father and brother Ben. In 1887 Ben donated $1,000 to help nearly bankrupt Trinity College in Durham, and thereby started an enduring pattern of family support for the place. For many years Ben and his father helped keep the college going. Buck made an occasional contribution at their request but did not really become interested until 1914, when he began thinking about the creation of a foundation devoted to the needs of his native region. From this modest beginning arose the Duke Endowment of 1924, a $40 million trust that was more than doubled by the terms of Duke's will.[28]

Duke also admired Rockefeller and used him as a model for putting his money into education, health, and religion. The income from the trust went to support the Methodist church in North Carolina, hospitals and orphanages for both races, and four educational institutions. Nearly a third went to Trinity, which became Duke University; the rest was allocated to Davidson College, Furman University, and a black institution, Johnson C. Smith University. None of the recipients except Furman lay outside North Carolina; in giving as in personality, Duke remained a homeboy. "I was born in North Carolina," he declared. "I want to leave something in the State that five hundred years from now people can look upon and say that Duke did that." Despite his slow start, Duke took a keen personal interest in the development of the university and involved himself in a host of decisions. He was very eager to select stone of just the right color for the buildings, and his choice of Olmstead Brothers of Boston to design the new campus and redesign the old one revealed his passion for landscaping. He cared little about academic programs or faculty recruitment, being content to oversee the buildings and grounds.[29]

Cyrus McCormick's largesse went chiefly to the Presbyterian church and its seminary, which received about $550,000. Like Rockefeller, he gave to the church not only money but considerable time and energy. He also supported the Chicago YMCA and made numerous gifts and loans to individuals in the South to help them recover from the devastation of the Civil War. He turned a cold shoulder to appeals from southern colleges except for Washington College at Lexington, Virginia, in the county of his birth, but did give to secular schools established for the newly freed blacks. Individual southern ministers and congregations also received his support. His biographer estimated that "about one dollar of every twenty that he made was given away." McCormick shared with Carnegie the belief that it was wasteful if not sinful to leave a large fortune for someone to inherit. "I am in favor of using means while one lives," he said, "rather than leave all to be lost or squandered, as it *may be,* after death."[30]

Henry Ford's notion of giving was also intensely personal and devoted to causes. His most notorious gesture, the peace ship sent to Europe in 1915 to persuade the belligerents to stop fighting, became the butt of innumerable jokes. However, Ford had his triumphs as well. In 1919 he created the Henry Ford Hospital, which served people of all incomes and gave estimates much like a garage. "It is my shop," declared Ford, "where I hope people can get well as rapidly as possible and have their injured parts repaired." Later it pioneered in open heart surgery and creation of the first heart-lung machine. In the dreary depression fall of 1931, Ford targeted Inkster, a wretched Detroit shantytown, and gave it a store to sell food and clothing at near wholesale prices as well as reopening its school, giving people seeds for gardens, buying sewing machines for women, and paying electric bills so they would have light. Ford believed not in charity but in helping people stand on their own two feet. Like Patterson, he saw himself as a catalyst for reawakening dormant neighborhoods. "I have no patience with professional charity or with any sort of commercialized humanitarianism," he said. "The moment human helpfulness is systematized, organized, commercialized, and professionalized, the heart of it is extinguished, and it becomes a cold and clammy thing."[31]

Although Ford created one of the great philanthropic foundations in 1936, he did so as a device to avoid inheritance taxes on his and Edsel's holdings of Ford stock while still maintaining control of the company. By one estimate Ford saved $321 million in taxes through the move; he also created what became the largest American foundation. Compared to the Rockefeller and Carnegie foundations, observed Dwight Macdonald, it was "a whale among a school of tuna fish." But it did not begin to operate until the 1950s, long after Ford's death. George Westinghouse shared Ford's belief in self-help. "As a rule," he said, "a dollar given to a man does him ten dollars' worth of harm, while a dollar honestly earned by his own efforts does him ten dollars' worth of good; so my ambition is to give as many persons as possible an opportunity to earn money by their own efforts."[32]

James Penney's concerns, like those of most wealthy givers, centered on those issues dearest to him. In 1925 he created a foundation and a corporation to carry out the mission of creating a rent-free retirement community for indigent church workers as well as a cooperative farm community in Florida. His Memorial Home Community cost him nearly $1.2 million. But the Florida banking disaster and the depression left Penney, in his own words, "flat broke, touching bottom." He managed to repair his fortune, created a new foundation in 1954, and worked at the business of philanthropy on a relatively modest scale until his death. Before losing his fortune, Samuel Insull was generous in giving money on a personal basis but not to formal charities. "I specialize in individual cases," he said, and especially enjoyed doing it anonymously. The list of pensioners he supported cost him $50,000 a year. Robert Noyce made generous gifts to his alma mater, Grinnell College, but did little else before his sudden and untimely death.[33]

Ray Kroc came late to philanthropy and, like many of the other entrepreneurs, found it as much a burden as a blessing. His own medical problems spurred him to establish the Kroc Foundation. "I had resisted the foundation proposal at first," he said, "because it was presented as a tax shelter. I'm not interested in that sort of thing. . . . That's a peculiarity of mine that runs against common business practice. It's the same thing with expense accounts." In 1969 Kroc persuaded his brother Bob, a Ph.D. who was head of the physiology department at the Warner-Lambert research institute, to move to the Kroc ranch in southern California and oversee the new foundation. It specialized in research in three diseases that had touched Kroc's life personally: diabetes (which killed his daughter), arthritis (which Kroc had along with diabetes), and multiple sclerosis (which afflicted his sister Lorraine). Later it added a public awareness program dealing with the effects of alcohol misuse on the family.[34]

"I have always enjoyed helping other people," Kroc observed. "It's the reason for my interest in the work of the foundation." On his seventieth birthday in 1972 he decided to celebrate by giving a large amount of money to some worthy cause in Chicago. He had planned on a million dollars, but the list of recipients kept growing until finally he bestowed $7.5 million on a variety of institutions. Kroc also distributed another $8 million worth of McDonald's stock to select friends and employees at all levels, taking care to give equal amounts to wives as well as husbands because "all of them make great sacrifices to allow their husbands to succeed, and I wanted to be sure that these women knew my concern and appreciation." However, he remained steadfast in his refusal to give money to institutions of higher education.[35]

Thomas Watson created no foundation but, as his biographers wrote, "gave his fortune away in bits and pieces to institutions already in existence. . . . And he gave money to people—friends, nieces and nephews, first and second cousins, Irish relatives he had never seen." Like Ford he grew nostalgic about his own past. Where Ford created the elaborate Greenfield Village as a shrine to his boyhood, Watson redid the family farm near Painted Post, New York. Later he donated it along with a million dollars to the Methodist church for use as a recreation and rest center. Once possessed of a fortune estimated at $100 million, he died with only $3.5 million of it still remaining and left most of that to various charities. By one estimate he contributed more than $15 million to the Watson Fund, established for the benefit of IBM employees. Edwin Land and his wife donated $12.5 million anonymously to Harvard for construction of a science center for undergraduate students.[36]

The remaining entrepreneurs did little or nothing in the way of formal philanthropy. Jay Gould left nearly all his fortune to his children in a complicated will intended to hold them together. Unfortunately his hopes were shattered by prolonged and bitter bickering among them in later years. E. H. Harriman simply left everything to his wife, who did undertake a number of philanthropic efforts. Neither Thomas Edison nor Frank Woolworth showed any interest in or inclination for philanthropy. John Patterson confined his largesse to employees and his hometown, as did John Wanamaker and Sam Walton. None of these men felt obliged to disperse their wealth as part of some contract incurred in the accumulation of it. Nor did they feel the slightest bit apologetic about having piled up such riches.

Several of the entrepreneurs feared what the possession of wealth would do to their children. Rockefeller, said Chernow, "wanted to accumulate wealth while inculcating in them the values of his threadbare childhood." He did not allow the children to visit his office or refineries until they were adults, and required each child to keep careful account books as he had done. They earned pocket money by doing chores, and had the gospel of economy drummed into them by a father who, whenever a package arrived, conspicuously saved the paper and string. Carnegie was adamant on this subject and formalized it in his Gospel of Wealth. Buffett has always worried about his fortune spoiling his children and warned them repeatedly not to expect a penny of it. As he viewed it, the only way to give them normal, independent lives was to deprive them of financial support. However, they inherited some money from Buffett's father, which Buffett invested for them in his own company and thereby made them quite well off. Gates agrees with Buffett on this point as on so many others. "One thing is for sure," he has said. "I won't leave a lot of money to my heirs because I don't think it would be good for them."[37]

At the other extreme could be found entrepreneurs who did spoil their children. Most of them could not resist giving their children the best things money could buy, yet a surprising number proved to be good parents despite the distractions of their work. Most of the entrepreneurs, especially those who lived in the nineteenth century, left the main burden of parenting to their wives, as was the custom. Their record as parents, like that in other areas, runs the gamut from attentive to indifferent. Only a few fit the cliché of neglecting their families to pursue their work. Noyce admitted to being one of them. "I spent too little time at home," he said after his divorce. "I made the mistake most people make—I thought that by working hard I was providing for my family." But, he added candidly, "if I had to do it over, I think I'd do it the same way."[38]

Edison was possibly the worst of the lot with both his broods. Most of the time he simply ignored the children, especially when they were small. His daughter Madeleine recalled a time when the children were taken to the ore separating mine. "We drove up," she said. "It took us two days to get there. That was the first time I ever realized I had a father. He used to be away all week except Saturday when he'd come back." Edison wanted the children to do well but did not know how to interact with them. On the rare occasions when he tried to play the role of father, he was clumsy and often cruel, frightening the children with his temper. The three children by his first wife grew up wholly without discipline and utterly innocent of how to handle money or cope with life's problems. Charles was the only one of them who got along with his father but had to fight his own uphill battle against alcoholism.[39]

Although Vanderbilt left the upbringing of his twelve children to his wife, he was a harsh and tyrannical father. He was contemptuous of his eldest son, William, and despised his namesake son, who was riddled with personal problems. The son he loved the most, George, died young. As for his daughters, he simply ignored them most of the time. Wanamaker remained close to his two sons and happily took both of them into his business. Patterson played little part in the rearing of his two children but grew closer to them after they had grown up. Penney did not seem especially close to any of his children. The two sons of his first marriage were reared mostly by his mother and sister. His second wife died when their son was only three, and his third wife survived to raise their two daughters. He spoke glowingly of these two girls, both of whom went to college.[40]

Most of the other entrepreneurs had close, devoted relationships with their children even though they may have been remote figures. No less than seven of the twenty-four entrepreneurs with children had only one child; four had sons and three daughters. Of the latter, Carnegie became a father at sixty-one and Duke at fifty-six. Both doted on their daughters and lavished affection and attention on them. Not surprisingly, Carnegie named his daughter after his beloved mother, Margaret, and lived to see her married in 1919. Duke left enough of his fortune to his daughter, Doris, to make her one of the great heiresses of the twentieth century. Kroc had his daughter, Marilyn, when he was only twenty-two and starting out. She was grown and married before he took the plunge with McDonald's, and died of diabetes in 1973.[41]

Insull had a deep love for his only son, whom his biographer called "an institution first (until proved otherwise), a human being only second." Never a demonstrative man, Insull nevertheless played a strong role in the rearing of his only child. Junior became "an added bond of affection between his parents, and later a bridge whenever they seemed about to grow apart." Westinghouse also had a namesake son, but little is known about their relationship. Vail, a devoted family man, remained close to his son, Davis, whose health had been fragile since his college days, and was crushed by his death at the age of thirty-six. By far the strangest relationship belonged to Ford and his son, Edsel, whom he loved not wisely but too well. Few fathers and sons were closer than they were, yet Ford was, as a company executive observed, "unmerciful in embarrassing Edsel."[42]

Henry was an engaging and indulgent parent when Edsel was young, clowning around with him and showing him gadgets. He loved children in general, and Edsel became devoted to the father he adored. He got his first car at the tender age of eight and began driving himself to school. But as he grew older, Edsel's blind devotion to his father became an anchor. As Robert Lacey observed, "He was totally incapable of resisting his father's will, even on matters that related to his most cherished principles, and he paid a painful price for this." They remained close, talking to each other almost every day, but as the darker side of Henry's personality became more dominant, the strain of coping took its toll on Edsel's health. After his death in 1943, his long-suffering widow, Eleanor, devastated Henry by saying in a fit of anger that he had killed his son.[43]

Gould, like Rockefeller, insulated his six children from the world but doted on them and took great joy in his close-knit family. So did Harriman, who did everything with his children and took them everywhere—including his fabulous Alaskan scientific expedition in 1898 and his trip to Japan in 1905. He also developed in his family a tight-knit bond that closed ranks against outsiders. Land, too, was fiercely protective of his family and close to his two daughters, who cared for him in his old age. Little is known about Woolworth's relationship to his three daughters other than that he indulged them as well as himself. Durant gave his children the best of everything but did little to prepare them for a life of wealth in the frantic new era of the 1920s. His daughter Margery ran through four husbands as a free spirit, while his son Cliff lived "in a steady condition of high combustion" on a twenty-six-thousand-acre estate in the Michigan woods.[44]

Although McCormick married late at forty-nine, he fathered seven children, of whom five survived. He and his wife believed strongly in a strict religious upbringing on the premise that "the children should be taught, sternly if necessary, the meaning of duty and the value of money. . . . They must never deserve the title 'idle rich.'" But McCormick, for all his aloofness, was no remote patriarch. He loved romping with his small children and delighted in playing croquet and other games with them. As they grew older, he challenged them in billiards and saw to it that the boys learned to ride horseback. Like many other children of the entrepreneurs, his were provided an education through tutors and private schools. Only his eldest son graduated from a city high school.[45]

Watson's relationship with his four children was predictably complex, shaped by his own inner demons. The two girls adored him; the boys feared his temper and abrupt mood swings, which caused him to be curt and unforgiving. He expected much of his sons and did not mask his disappointment when they fell short. "When we were very young he knew how to loosen up and have fun with us," recalled his namesake son. "But for some reason his playfulness gradually diminished, and by the time I was ten or eleven, Dad acted quite formal and aloof. . . . I think the cause was mainly age." The children found their mother much more accessible, though Watson left her the thankless task of inflicting punishment when it was needed. The constant, unpredictable bouncing between love and conflict grew even stronger as the boys turned into adults.[46]

Walton was a devoted family man who believed with his wife in raising their four children by the small-town values they both loved. Remembering the friction between his own parents, Walton "swore early that if I ever had a family, I would never expose it to that kind of squabbling." He also took great pride in never pushing the children too hard, and in having fun with them. "He traveled a lot, but I never really felt like he was gone much," said his daughter Alice. "He went out of his way to spend time with us, and he was fun to be with." They grew up "mannerly, polite, 'churchy' like their mother, but also full of vim and vigor like their father." For Gates, parenting is a new and refreshing experience. Being married and the father of two seems to have mellowed him somewhat. "I knew I'd enjoy parenthood," he said after his first daughter was born, ". . . but I guess it surprises me just how much fun it really is."[47]

Taken as a group, all but four or five of the entrepreneurs enjoyed stable, fulfilling family relationships. Only four of them—Duke, Durant, Kroc, and Noyce—underwent divorces, and all four remarried. All of them had children except du Pont and Eastman. Their careers and creative drives doubtless took some toll on their family life but did not separate them from it. For many of them the key lay in finding the right woman who understood and accepted the over-powering forces that impelled them to the pursuit of their vision. Edison offers a classic example of this point. Where his first wife never comprehended his admittedly bizarre ways or came to terms with his neglect, his second wife "accepted the fact that she was not going to have a conventional marriage; and she made the best of it." She then developed "an ironclad rule that whatever Edison wanted, Edison got. . . . The less he needed to concern himself with the problems of daily living, the happier he was."[48]

Not every wife could make so drastic an adjustment. Kroc's first wife, Ethel, was appalled when he gave up a high-paying job with all its security to strike out on his own and extended their mort-gage to help his first venture. She balked entirely when he pro-posed making the leap into McDonald's. The result, he wrote, was "a veritable Wagnerian opera of strife" that led to their divorce. Far more typical, however, were wives who, like Mina Edison, served as helpmates regardless of the toll it took on them personally. Woolworth's wife, who had been a poor Canadian girl, never adjusted to a life of opulence, and her mind failed in her early six-ties. Gould's wife, a delicate woman fraught with inner tensions, died of a stroke before she was fifty. Watson's wife struggled under the strain of his demands and temper to the point of once asking for a divorce. "He looked so shocked, so upset," she said much later, "that I realized how deeply he loved me—and I never brought it up again."[49]

However different the rich may be from the rest of us, the entrepreneurs seem strikingly similar to other people when off duty. As Land suggested, most of them found a sturdy stability at home that allowed them to soar in other activities. Eastman, the sole bachelor, found it first in his mother and then in the company of his numerous married women friends, with whom he could chat amiably about babies, women's clothing, or the latest articles in *Vogue.* "This," noted his biographer, "from a gun aficionado who stalked elephants and grizzlies and endured privations in the wild with a cheerful machismo." Eastman took his pleasures as seriously as his work. "I never smiled until I was forty," he once said. "I may have grinned but I never smiled. Since then I've tried to win back something of the fun that other men had when they were boys."[50]

The popular image of creative people—especially artists—as uninhibited radicals living unconventional lives does not at all fit the entrepreneurs. The only one among them who developed unorthodox relationships was one of the most conventional in his habits. Buffett was shocked when in 1977 his wife, Susie, left him to live in an apartment in San Francisco, saying she wanted to live on her own. But they remained close, talked nearly every day, and came together with the kids at Christmas. Less than a year after Susie's departure, Astrid Menks came to live with Buffett. She became his companion but not Susie's replacement. Somehow he managed to keep both women in his life, and the two women became friends as well. "However much it perplexed his friends," noted his biographer, "the fact is that Buffett found, or contrived, a solution that worked for *him*. . . . Typically, he was not concerned with appearances, even now, when flouting social conventions."[51]

Although some of the other entrepreneurs, notably Gates, ignored social conventions, most led lives while off duty that were surprisingly mundane. They had a wide variety of hobbies, interests, and pleasures, but none that defined their gifts. The peculiar form of creativity that drove each of them might be a way of life, but it was never a lifestyle.

| Epilogue |
Profiling the Great Entrepreneur

I think business is very simple. Profit. Loss. Take the sales,
subtract the costs, you get this positive number. The math is
quite straightforward.   —BILL GATES[1]

If this survey has revealed anything, it is that great entrepre-
neurs are as distinctively individual as other creative people, and
no less idiosyncratic. Every man had his own vision, his own style,
and his own obsessions. Their common ground seems little more
than a series of intersections where their ways of doing business
crossed. No single explanation could embrace their roads to success or the routes by which they reached their destination. No formula or set of rules can transform one into a great entrepreneur any
more than it could produce a great artist or scientist.

However, the great entrepreneurs do share some qualities that
illuminate both their lives and their work. Foremost among them
are persistence and determination, a fierce drive to succeed and to
let no obstacle bar their path. A few lines of doggerel, supposedly
written by Calvin Coolidge of all people, captured this unquench-
able push to achieve:

267

> *Nothing in the world can take*
> *The place of Persistence.*
> *Talent will not; Nothing is more*
> *Common than unsuccessful*
> *Men with talent; Genius will not;*
> *Unrewarded genius is almost a proverb.*
> *Education alone will not;*
> *The world is full*
> *Of educated derelicts.*
> *Persistence and Determination*
> *Alone are omnipotent.*[2]

For the great entrepreneurs, the qualities of persistence and determination were necessary but not sufficient. In addition to driving ambition, they all had some supreme talent. To that gift they added a joyous zest for their work, a sheer delight in the doing of it. Nearly all of them plunged into work early in life and developed a strong work ethic. To their work they brought amazing reservoirs of energy as well as an overpowering desire to succeed. They also possessed strong wills and were fiercely competitive. But the world is full of ambitious people with dreams of great achievement, and it has no shortage of competitive people striving to be the best at something. What is it that separates the great entrepreneurs from the rest of the pack?

One indispensable quality is their need not only to make their mark but to do so in their own way on their own terms. "It has always been my rule in business," said Rockefeller, "to make everything count." All of them regarded their undertakings as a personal creation, an expression of themselves. "I use the Harlem road just as though it all belonged to me," Vanderbilt declared, "and that is the way I shall control every other road as long as I control any, as though it all belonged to me." His observation amounts to a credo for the entrepreneurs in spirit if not always in practice. Edison once invented a device and then jotted in his notebook, "Invented by & for myself and not for any small-brained capitalist." By putting this personal stamp on whatever they did, the entrepreneurs revealed their individual style and creative impulse.[3]

The desire to follow one's own path regardless of the consequences required other qualities common to our entrepreneurs. The most obvious is an ability to escape the clutch of habit—what Arthur Koestler called the "'code' of fixed rules"—and frame problems in ways that suggested new kinds of solutions. Buffett once warned that "Chains of habit are too light to be felt until they are too heavy to be broken." The entrepreneurs did not buck or discard conventional wisdom so much as transcend it. To do this, they had to be knowledgeable in their fields yet innocent of or unmoved by what could not be done. They relied on intense study and preparation but did not allow themselves to be trapped by its limitations. This required supreme confidence in their own judgment, and the entrepreneurs all displayed a stunning capacity for growth—at least to a certain level. Most of them probably had a strong fear of failure, yet one of their most striking qualities is a willingness to take large risks and court failure with an impressive confidence that they would succeed.[4]

This paradox is but one of several that separate the great entrepreneurs from other people. They feared failure yet incurred great risks when the crucial moment arrived and did not shrink from the consequences. They displayed an incredible ability to grow yet often tended to stay with the tried and true when it proved successful. They tended to do one thing extremely well, and did it in one way, yet often had the ability to extend their reach into more than one medium. They viewed their creations as intensely personal yet believed ardently in teamwork and relied heavily on others to help them realize their visions. Like the great artists, they conceived and executed an expression of themselves yet sought to make it something greater than the self. Their flaws were often as magnified as their abilities.

All of the entrepreneurs combined some compelling vision with a rage for order and an overwhelming desire to realize the one by imposing the other. Most of them were perfectionists—at least in their work—who were never satisfied with anything less than maximum effort and results. They sought always to improve what they and their associates did, and could not imagine resting on their laurels. They excelled at problem solving and possessed a remarkable gift for making complex things seem simple. This clarity of understanding derived from a clarity of vision and became the polestar by which they guided their course. They believed in teamwork as a key to accomplishment and found associates who possessed two crucial attributes: talents that complemented those of the entrepreneur and personalities that allowed or encouraged them to play second fiddle to the main man. For this to happen, the entrepreneurs obviously needed a strong talent for motivating others, and they had it.

Whatever their field, the great entrepreneurs knew their product and excelled at promoting it. They dedicated themselves to the work at hand and let nothing distract them from it. Partly for that reason, their mistakes were often as spectacular as their triumphs. For all the hoopla surrounding their huge fortunes, they usually plowed profits back into the business before investing in themselves. They took defeat hard and did not surrender power easily. For most of them, work was their life and they regarded death as a dreaded interruption of what they loved best. In many cases they paid a stiff price either for being ahead of their time or for succeeding on so colossal a scale. As Rockefeller said of himself, most of them came to be known much better after they were gone.

Many people had some of these qualities, yet they did not become great entrepreneurs or creative persons. The difference evidently lies in some peculiar blend of them coupled with distinctive talent(s) and a unique personality that enabled the entrepreneurs to achieve on a scale that dwarfed the efforts of ordinary people. But, as has been shown, their personalities did not come in one size or shape. Put our twenty-six entrepreneurs together in the same room and you will find similarities and common traits but no clear pattern. Nor did they insist on reaching for the moon. "I don't try to jump over seven-foot bars," said Buffett. "I look around for one-foot bars that I can step over." The two entrepreneurs still at work continue to regard what they do with joy. "Today, I work because it's fun," said Gates. "Life's a lot more fun if you treat its challenges in creative ways."[5]

That remark may stand as the essence of what separates the great entrepreneurs from other aspirants. Whatever their gifts or talents, most of them were not men for whom success came easily or quickly. They paid their dues in years of hard, painstaking preparation. As Kroc put it, "I paid tribute, in the feudal sense, for many years before I was able to rise with McDonald's on the foundation I had laid." Even Gates, the child prodigy among them, put in years of intensive effort before achieving success. In retrospect the entrepreneurs often marveled at what they had managed to accomplish. "Almost every day last fall [1962]," Land once observed, "we took on things which people might think would take a year or two. They weren't particularly hard. What was hard was *believing* they weren't hard." But of course they *were* hard, and success was by no means assured at the time.[6]

All of the entrepreneurs possessed this ability to pursue the solution to a problem doggedly and maintain their focus on the proper goals. Those, like Durant, who lost it along the way, paid a stiff price in the form of failure. After the collapse of his empire, Insull said ruefully, "I worked with all my energy to save those companies. I made mistakes, but they were honest mistakes. They were errors of judgment but not dishonest manipulations." Time seems to have verified his statement. Vail was fortunate enough to understand at least one of his limitations and abide by it. "I have been as much interested in machinery as in anything," he noted. "I never saw a machine that I did not try to think of an improvement on it. But I should not have made a great success as an inventor. An inventor must be a man of single purpose, a one-sided man. I was not of that kind." Edison might have benefited from this observation.[7]

Who or what, then, are these great entrepreneurs? Like all creative people, they are people with one or more extraordinary talents who possessed the ability not only to conceive of a creation but to pursue it to fruition. In a chicken-and-egg sense it comes back again to persistence and determination—not only the gift but the ability to realize its full potential. Walton put it as succinctly as possible. When people asked him how Wal-Mart became so astounding a success, he'd reply, "Friend, we just got after it and stayed after it." Beethoven or Picasso or Einstein could not have said it any better.[8]

| Notes |

INTRODUCTION

1. Quoted in Robert Sklar, *Movie-Made America* (New York, 1994), 49.

PROLOGUE: SAY GOOD-BYE TO THE ROBBER BARONS

1. Peter C. Wensberg, *Land's Polaroid* (Boston, 1987), 248.
2. Jonathan R. T. Hughes, *The Vital Few* (New York, 1986). This is an expanded edition of the 1965 book.
3. Janet Lowe, *Bill Gates Speaks* (New York, 1998), 160.
4. Justin Kaplan, Introduction to Mark Twain and Charles Dudley Warner, *The Gilded Age: A Tale of Today* (Seattle, 1968), vi. Hughes described the work of the muckrakers as "a baffling morass of special pleading and bias which is great fun for the reader but which is largely incoherent except as entertainment." Hughes, *Vital Few*, 403.
5. Harold C. Livesay, "Entrepreneurial Dominance in Businesses Large and Small, Past and Present," *Business History Review* 63 (Spring 1989): 5.
6. Michael Novak, *Business as a Calling* (New York, 1996), 75; Joseph Frazier Wall, *Andrew Carnegie* (New York, 1970), 640.
7. Janet Lowe, *Warren Buffett Speaks* (New York, 1997), 164.

8. George Gilder, *The Spirit of Enterprise* (New York, 1984), 19; Robert L. Shook, *The Entrepreneurs* (New York, 1980), vii–viii.

9. Peter F. Drucker, *Innovation and Entrepreneurship* (New York, 1985), 22; Gerald Gunderson, *The Wealth Creators: An Entrepreneurial History of the United States* (New York, 1990), 6; Richard S. Tedlow, *Giants of Enterprise: Seven Business Innovators and the Empires They Built* (New York, 2001), 92, 334, 424; Rosabeth Kanter, *The Change Masters* (New York, 1983), 27.

10. Gilder, *Spirit of Enterprise*, 93; A. David Silver, *The Entrepreneurial Life: How to Go for It and Get It* (New York, 1983), ix, 5, 18. The *Newsweek* special issue has no date but appeared in 2000.

11. Silver, *Entrepreneurial Life*, vii, 2, 4, 38–39, 40, 50, 51, 59, 76, 83.

12. Ibid., 76, 82.

13. Drucker, *Innovation and Entrepreneurship*, vii–viii, 11, 17, 25–26, 254. Emphasis is in the original. Drucker considered the emergence of a "truly entrepreneurial economy" in the United States to be "the most significant and hopeful event to have occurred in recent economic and social history."

14. Kanter, *Change Masters*, 23; Robert Sobel and David B. Sicilia, *The Entrepreneurs: An American Adventure* (Boston, 1986), 127; Thomas C. Cochran, "Entrepreneurship," *International Encyclopedia of the Social Sciences* (New York, 1968), 5:90.

15. This material on the origins of the term is drawn from the excellent essay by Cochran, "Entrepreneurship," 5:87–91.

16. John E. Sawyer, "The Entrepreneur and the Social Order," in William E. Miller, ed., *Men in Business: Essays in the History of Entrepreneurship* (Cambridge, Mass., 1952), 7–8.

17. Joseph A. Schumpeter, *The Theory of Economic Development* (New York, 1969), ix, 74–77. This is a reprint of the 1961 paperback edition, which was a reprint of the original 1934 English version.

18. Ibid., 78; Joseph A. Schumpeter, "The Creative Response in Economic History," *Journal of Economic History* (November 1947): 151.

19. Ibid., 75–80, 88–89; Schumpeter, "Creative Response in Economic History," 151–52.

20. Schumpeter, *Theory of Economic Development*, 65–66. In a later work Schumpeter defined the function of an entrepreneur as "to reform or revolutionize the pattern of production of exploiting an invention or, more generally, an untried technological possibility for producing a

new commodity or producing an old one in a new way, by opening up a new source of supply of materials or a new outlet for products, by reorganizing an industry, and so on." Joseph Schumpeter, *Capitalism, Socialism, and Democracy* (New York, 1950), 132. This is the third edition of the 1942 original.

21. Schumpeter, *Theory of Economic Development*, 6, 80–81.
22. Ibid., 84–94. The following paragraphs draw from this same source.
23. Henrik Ibsen, *Three Plays* (London, 1964), 61.
24. Schumpeter, "Creative Response in Economic History," 150. Emphasis is in the original.
25. Ibid., 154–58.

1: THE ENIGMA OF CREATIVITY

1. Dedication in John Chamberlain, *The Enterprising Americans: A Business History of the United States* (New York, 1963).
2. Arthur Koestler, *The Act of Creation* (London, 1964), 330; Albert Rothenberg, *The Emerging Goddess: The Creative Process in Art, Science, and Other Fields* (Chicago, 1979), 138.
3. Koestler, *Act of Creation*, 264; Rothenberg, *Emerging Goddess*, 103–13.
4. Rothenberg, *Emerging Goddess*, x, 330. Emphasis is in the original. "Only the products of genius," Rothenberg added, "are widely accepted as unquestionably valuable and truly new."
5. Robert Grudin, *The Grace of Great Things: Creativity and Innovation* (Boston, 1990), 3; Jacob W. Getzels and Mihaly Csikszentmihalyi, *The Creative Vision* (New York, 1976), 236–37; Rollo May, *The Courage to Create* (New York, 1994), 36–38. This is a paperback edition of the 1975 original.
6. Victor K. McElheny, *Insisting on the Impossible: The Life of Edwin Land* (Reading, Mass., 1998), 233; Wall, *Andrew Carnegie*, 393; Maury Klein, *The Life and Legend of Jay Gould* (Baltimore, 1986), 111.
7. Maury Klein, *The Life and Legend of E. H. Harriman* (Chapel Hill, N.C., 2000), 125.
8. Neil Baldwin, *Edison: Inventing the Century* (New York, 1995), 102, 104; Wensberg, *Land's Polaroid*, 26; Novak, *Business as a Calling*, 72.
9. Rothenberg, *Emerging Goddess*, 282; Koestler, *Act of Creation*, 161; Eugene K. von Fange, *Professional Creativity* (Englewood Cliffs, N.J., 1959), 97.

10. Fange, *Professional Creativity,* 5, 8, 25, 81, 97, 117. All emphases are in the originals.

11. Getzels and Csikszentmihalyi, *Creative Vision,* 246; Rothenberg, *Emerging Goddess,* 131, 133.

12. D. N. Perkins, *The Mind's Best Work* (Cambridge, Mass., 1981), 2, 4, 38, 91, 97, 101, 256, 274.

13. Ibid., 64–66, 71, 90, 99–100.

14. Ibid., 247–48. There are other objections that can be raised to Perkins's argument, but to detail them would require a separate essay.

15. Koestler, *Act of Creation,* 172–77, 208.

16. Ibid., 346.

17. Ibid., 113, 145, 647. See also Grudin, *Grace of Great Things,* 20–25; Rothenberg, *Emerging Goddess,* 123.

18. Rothenberg, *Emerging Goddess,* 69, 110–13, 255–56; McElheny, *Insisting on the Impossible,* 35. Emphases are in the original. The term *janusian* derives from the two-faced Roman god Janus, who was capable of looking forward and backward at the same time.

19. Ibid., 69–71, 115, 268–69. Emphasis is in the original.

20. Koestler, *Act of Creation,* 38–44, 178.

21. Ibid, 190; Fange, *Professional Creativity,* 224; McElheny, *Insisting on the Impossible,* 45, 374; Wensberg, *Land's Polaroid,* 127.

22. Rothenberg, *Emerging Goddess,* 126; Fange, *Professional Creativity,* 59, 104–5; James Wallace and Jim Erickson, *Hard Drive: Bill Gates and the Making of the Microsoft Empire* (New York, 1992), 119.

23. Koestler, *Act of Creation,* 45, 118–19.

24. Ibid., 108, 120; Rothenberg, *Emerging Goddess,* 237–39; Wensberg, *Land's Polaroid,* 31; Grudin, *Grace of Great Things,* 242.

25. Koestler, *Act of Creation,* 154–55, 625, 705; McElheny, *Insisting on the Impossible,* 245.

26. Getzels and Csikszentmihalyi, *Creative Vision,* 4–6, 243; Max Wertheimer, *Productive Thinking* (New York, 1945), 123. See also Rothenberg, *Emerging Goddess,* 244. Perkins declared that "problem finding is a way of using your abilities, not an ability in itself," but here too his argument is unconvincing. Perkins, *Mind's Best Work,* 249.

27. Quoted in Getzels and Csikszentmihalyi, *Creative Vision,* 4.

28. Grudin, *Grace of Great Things,* 9; Wensberg, *Land's Polaroid,* 235; Lowe, *Buffett,* 113; Tedlow, *Giants of Enterprise,* 395; McElheny, *Insisting on the Impossible,* 86.

29. Norman Beasley, *Main Street Merchant: The Story of the J. C. Penney Company* (New York, 1948), 196; Ray Kroc (with Robert Anderson), *Grinding It Out: The Making of McDonald's* (Chicago, 1977), 167.

30. Koestler, *Act of Creation*, 393, 402, 704.

31. Ibid., 233–35; Thomas S. Kuhn, *The Structure of Scientific Revolutions* (Chicago, 1970). This is the second, enlarged edition.

32. Grudin, *Grace of Great Things*, 27–28; Koestler, *Act of Creation*, 200–201.

33. Kuhn, *Structure of Scientific Revolutions*, 97; Grudin, *Grace of Great Things*, 28–30.

34. Drucker, *Innovation and Entrepreneurship*, 35. Emphasis is in the original.

35. Grudin, *Grace of Great Things*, 35–40.

36. May, *Courage to Create*, 43; Hughes, *Vital Few*, 149, 162, 173.

37. Matthew Josephson, *Edison: A Biography* (New York, 1959), 198, 227; Robert Conot, *A Streak of Luck* (New York, 1979), 377.

38. McElheny, *Insisting on the Impossible*, 1.

39. Gilder, *Spirit of Enterprise*, 17, 145; Novak, *Business as a Calling*, 121.

40. Silver, *Entrepreneurial Life*, 84, 92; Lowe, *Gates*, 70; Lowe, *Buffett*, 65; McElheny, *Insisting on the Impossible*, 393.

41. Roger Angell, *Late Innings* (New York, 1992), 30. This is the paperback edition of the 1982 original.

42. McElheny, *Insisting on the Impossible*, 233; Koestler, *Act of Creation*, 329; May, *Courage to Create*, 68; Drucker, *Innovation and Entrepreneurship*, 191.

43. Grudin, *Grace of Great Things*, 201; May, *Courage to Create*, 27. In this vein Robert Hughes titled his survey of modern art *The Shock of the New* (New York, 1991).

44. May, *Courage to Create*, 59–60, 71; Koestler, *Act of Creation*, 659. In both quotations the emphasis is in the original.

45. Schumpeter, *Capitalism, Socialism, and Democracy*, 83. Emphasis is in the original.

46. Fritz Redlich, *Steeped in Two Cultures* (New York, 1971), 34. Redlich borrowed the "daimonic" notion from theologian Paul Tillich and expanded on it.

47. May, *Courage to Create*, 77, 85. Emphasis is in the original.

2: PORTRAIT OF THE ENTREPRENEUR AS A YOUNG MAN

1. Joseph H. Appel, *The Business Biography of John Wanamaker: Founder and Builder* (New York, 1930), 227.

2. Several books have provided profiles of entrepreneurs but made little effort to connect them or derive themes from them. See, for example, Hughes, *The Vital Few;* Harold Livesay, *American Made* (Boston, 1979); Robert Sobel, *The Entrepreneurs* (New York, 1974); Gunderson, *The Wealth Creators;* and Tedlow, *Giants of Enterprise.*

3. Silver, *Entrepreneurial Life,* 8–9, 23–24. Silver emphasizes that he attempts only to describe these aspects of the typical entrepreneur; he does not pretend to explain them.

4. Ibid., 3–4, 31, 37.

5. Ibid., 3–4, 42–43.

6. See Maury Klein, *The Flowering of the Third America* (Chicago, 1993).

7. Thomas J. Watson, Jr., and Peter Petre, *Father, Son & Co.: My Life at IBM and Beyond* (New York, 1990), 8; Thomas and Marva Belden, *The Lengthening Shadow: The Life of Thomas J. Watson* (Boston, 1962), 4–6; John K. Winkler, *Five and Ten: The Fabulous Life of F. W. Woolworth* (Freeport, N.Y., 1970), 20. This is a reprint of the 1940 original.

8. For details, see Ron Chernow, *Titan* (New York, 1998), 1–59.

9. Roger Lowenstein, *Buffett: The Making of an American Capitalist* (New York, 1995), 14–15.

10. Arthur D. Howden Smith, *Commodore Vanderbilt: An Epic of American Achievement* (New York, 1927), 18–19; Wallace and Erickson, *Hard Drive,* 14, 274; Lowe, *Buffett,* 33. Buffett's mother added that "Warren and his father were always the best of friends. . . . Howard . . . never found it necessary to punish the children. His method was to use reason and persuasion." Ibid., 34.

11. J. C. Penney, *Fifty Years with the Golden Rule* (New York, 1950), 150–60; Mary Elizabeth Curry, *Creating an American Institution: The Merchandising Genius of J. C. Penney* (New York, 1993), 269; Appel, *Wanamaker,* 39; McElheny, *Insisting on the Impossible,* 15; Stephen Manes and Paul Andrews, *Gates: How Microsoft's Mogul Reinvented an Industry—and Made Himself the Richest Man in America* (New York, 1993), 451.

12. Samuel Crowther, *John H. Patterson: Pioneer in Industrial Welfare* (Garden City, N.Y., 1926), 29–30.

13. Henry G. Prout, *A Life of George Westinghouse* (New York, 1921), 7; Wensberg, *Land's Polaroid,* 20, 28; Wallace and Erickson, *Hard Drive,* 53; McElheny, *Insisting on the Impossible,* 41–47.

14. Appel, *Wanamaker,* 19; Albert Bigelow Paine, *Theodore M. Vail: A Biography* (New York, 1929), 343; Lowe, *Gates,* 20–21; Lowe, *Buffett,* 123. Gates also said that he "loved my years at college."
15. Beasley, *Main Street Merchant,* 121–22; Kroc, *Grinding It Out,* 187.
16. Paine, *Vail,* 11.
17. Lowenstein, *Buffett,* 12, 23; Lowe, *Buffett,* 67; Sam Walton with John Huey, *Made in America: My Story* (New York, 1992), 4, 16.
18. Tom Wolfe, "The Tinkerings of Robert Noyce," *Esquire* (December 1983): 353, 374; Michael S. Malone, *The Big Score: The Billion-Dollar Story of Silicon Valley* (New York, 1985), 76–79.
19. Manes and Andrews, *Gates,* 40–41; Lowe, *Gates,* 8; McElheny, *Insisting on the Impossible,* 14–17.
20. Beasley, *Main Street Merchant,* 18; Penney, *Fifty Years with the Golden Rule,* 13, 74; David Freeman Hawke, *John D.: The Founding Father of the Rockefellers* (New York, 1980), 12–13; Chernow, *Titan,* 18, 25, 40.
21. Klein, *Jay Gould,* 30; Chernow, *Titan,* 33; Wallace and Erickson, *Hard Drive,* 41, 51; Penney, *Fifty Years,* 68.
22. Paine, *Vail,* 36; Belden and Belden, *Lengthening Shadow,* 17; Hughes, *Vital Few,* 238; Livesay, *American Made,* 112; Chernow, *Titan,* 32.
23. Albert D. Chandler, Jr., and Stephen Salsbury, *Pierre S. du Pont and the Making of the Modern Corporation* (New York, 1971), 38; Hughes, *Vital Few,* 165; Josephson, *Edison,* 181; Sobel, *Entrepreneurs,* 194; Klein, *Harriman,* 37–38; Walton, *Made in America,* 11; Lowe, *Gates,* 156; Hawke, *John D.,* 18.
24. Lowe, *Buffett,* 17; Walton, *Made in America,* 145.

3: THE ENTREPRENEURS AND THEIR VISIONS

1. Lowe, *Gates,* 225.
2. Wall, *Andrew Carnegie,* 585; Hughes, *Vital Few,* 230–31.
3. Hughes, *Vital Few,* 234–35, 238.
4. Wall, *Andrew Carnegie,* 333–34; Hawke, *John D.,* 93, 97, 106–07, 121–23, 187; Chernow, *Titan,* 169–71, 179, 205–06, 257–58.
5. Chernow, *Titan,* 223–29, 249, 332–33; Hawke, *John D.,* 164–67.
6. John K. Winkler, *Tobacco Tycoon: The Story of James Buchanan Duke* (New York, 1942), 111–12, 147; Sobel, *Entrepreneurs,* 150.

7. Winkler, *Tobacco Tycoon,* 48–56, 129, 145–46; Richard Kluger, *Ashes to Ashes: America's Hundred-Year Cigarette War, the Public Health, and the Unabashed Triumph of Philip Morris* (New York, 1996), 22, 47; Sobel, *Entrepreneurs,* 179. Duke got two-thirds of the BAT stock.

8. Elizabeth Brayer, *George Eastman: A Biography* (Baltimore,1996), 67, 70, 206.

9. Ibid., 26, 62–70, 163, 204, 216. The Kodak featured a clever and convenient developing scheme. The owner simply returned the camera with the exposed film inside to Rochester with ten dollars; the film was developed and sent back with the camera loaded with fresh film.

10. Hughes, *Vital Few,* 291, 294; Maury Klein, *Rainbow's End: The Crash of 1929* (New York, 2001), 30. Emphasis is in the original.

11. Drucker, *Innovation and Entrepreneurship,* 77; Livesay, *American Made,* 176; Tedlow, *Giants of Enterprise,* 127; Hughes, *Vital Few,* 325. Work on the River Rouge plant began in 1917, and production activity was gradually shifted from Highland Park to the new facility over the next decade.

12. William T. Hutchinson, *Cyrus Hall McCormick: Seed-Time, 1809–1856* (New York, 1930), 52, 71–73; Sobel, *Entrepreneurs,* 43–44, 72.

13. David A. Hounshell, *From the American System to Mass Production: The Development of Manufacturing Technology in the United States* (Baltimore, 1984), 159; Hutchinson, *Seed-Time,* 327–35, 353–58, 468.

14. Crowther, *Patterson,* 22, 80–82, 94. The honor of inventing the first cash register belongs to a Dayton café owner, James Ritty, and his brother. See Isaac F. Marcosson, *Wherever Men Trade: The Romance of the Cash Register* (New York, 1945), 7, 58–59.

15. Marcosson, *Wherever Men Trade,* 1, 44, 109, 114–16, 134; Crowther, *Patterson,* 88–91, 137–54, 161–63.

16. Wheaton J. Lane, *Commodore Vanderbilt: An Epic of the Steam Age* (New York, 1942), 184–85, 288–90.

17. Ibid., 231.

18. Hawke, *John D.,* 59, 191; Chernow, *Titan,* 112; Alfred D. Chandler, Jr., *The Visible Hand: The Managerial Revolution in American Business* (Cambridge, Mass., 1977), 148–49; Klein, *Jay Gould,* 93–94, 147, 264–65, 269, 340–46, 405.

19. Klein, *Jay Gould,* 220–91, 346, 474.

20. Klein, *Harriman,* xiii, passim.

21. Ibid.
22. Klein, *Rainbow's End,* 31–41; Bernard A. Weisberger, *The Dream Maker: William C. Durant, Founder of General Motors* (Boston, 1979), 93; Chandler and Salsbury, *Pierre du Pont,* 440.
23. Drucker, *Innovation and Entrepreneurship,* 78; Livesay, *American Made,* 232; Weisberger, *Dream Maker,* 234–35.
24. Klein, *Rainbow's End,* 33.
25. Chandler and Salsbury, *Pierre du Pont,* 24, 36–37, 47–54, 75, 123, 323, 430; Livesay, *American Made,* 197–202. Pierre bought the stock of his cousin Coleman du Pont in 1915 and thereby gained personal control of the Du Pont Company.
26. Chandler and Salsbury, *Pierre du Pont,* 125.
27. Ibid., 493–97, 504–10, 516–17, 591–92.
28. Forrest McDonald, *Insull* (Chicago, 1962), 68–70, 103, passim.
29. Ibid., 70–73, 92, 98–106, 137–41.
30. Paine, *Vail,* 121–69, 238; Sobel, *Entrepreneurs,* 211–24.
31. Paine, *Vail,* 240–61; Sobel, *Entrepreneurs,* 195–96, 232–40; *National Cyclopedia of America Biography,* 28:52.
32. Appel, *Wanamaker,* xv, 51, 54, 65–72; Sobel, *Entrepreneurs,* 75–76, 86.
33. Appel, *Wanamaker,* 61, 74, 79–84, 138, 155–56, 397; Sobel, *Entrepreneurs,* 89, 97–100, 107. At one point, Wanamaker even tried to sell airplanes in his store.
34. Appel, *Wanamaker,* 60, 121, 145, 410, 414–15; Sobel, *Entrepreneurs,* 90, 100–06. For more detail, see William Leach, *Land of Desire: Merchants, Power, and the Rise of a New American Culture* (New York, 1993).
35. Winkler, *Woolworth,* 40–51, 227.
36. Ibid., 52–72, 105, 109–10, 121, 149–61.
37. Beasley, *Main Street Merchant,* 49, 60–61, 73, 144; Penney, *Fifty Years,* 45, 70; Curry, *Creating an American Institution,* 117.
38. Penney, *Fifty Years,* 54, 85–86, 102–04; Vance H. Trimble, *Sam Walton: The Inside Story of America's Richest Man* (New York, 1990), 34; Beasley, *Main Street Merchant,* 80–93; Curry, *Creating an American Institution,* 170–84, 277–78. Slightly different versions of the principles are given in Beasley and Penney. Not until 1962 did Penney stores begin offering credit nationwide.
39. Walton, *Made in America,* viii, 29, 36, 41–42, 219–33, 246–49; Trimble, *Sam Walton,* 34, 84. Walton's very first store was actually one

in Newport, Arkansas, which also did very well. However, Walton's landlord refused to renew his lease when it expired, teaching him a painful lesson and forcing him to look elsewhere for a new start.

40. Walton, *Made in America,* 43–51, 97–98, 105, 200–01, 216; Trimble, *Sam Walton,* 92–93, 208–09; Tedlow, *Giants of Enterprise,* 355.

41. Walton, *Made in America,* 52, 186–87, 206–09, 213, 253; Trimble, *Sam Walton,* 149, 194, 217; Tedlow, *Giants of Enterprise,* 345–47, 353.

42. John F. Love, *McDonald's: Behind the Arches* (New York, 1986), 2, 4, 10–19, 56, 115; Kroc, *Grinding It Out,* 193.

43. Love, *McDonald's,* 6, 119, 134–35.

44. Hughes, *Vital Few,* 150; Josephson, *Edison,* 428; Conot, *A Streak of Luck,* 470.

45. Conot, *Streak of Luck,* 327–28, 335, 397; Josephson, *Edison,* 146, 276–77, 381–83, 392–93.

46. Prout, *Westinghouse,* 9–10, 14, 24–61, 78, 80–85, 214–20. For a list of Westinghouse's companies and patents see pages 12–13, 331–67. Westinghouse and some railroad men considered the friction draft gear an even more important contribution than the air brake. And he did take out four telephone patents, the first in 1879. See page 248.

47. McDonald, *Insull,* 37; Prout, *Westinghouse,* 87, 96–157, 179, 185–87. Prout noted that "for years Niagara Falls was the only seat of the aluminum industry in America." (p. 156.)

48. William Rodgers, *Think: A Biography of the Watsons and IBM* (New York, 1969), 9, 69, 113, 179; Belden and Belden, *Lengthening Shadow,* 92–93, 125–26; Tedlow, *Giants of Enterprise,* 223, 235.

49. Rodgers, *Think,* 10, 113; Belden and Belden, *Lengthening Shadow,* 209; Watson and Petre, *Father, Son & Co.,* 112–13, 179, 186–87, 202–03. By 1945 IBM already had representation in seventy-eight countries but derived only an eighth of its profits from abroad. (Watson and Petre, p. 174.)

50. Wensberg, *Land's Polaroid,* 1, 3, 12, 53–80, 247; Livesay, *American Made,* 278; McElheny, *Insisting on the Impossible,* 126–60, 278–302.

51. Wensberg, *Land's Polaroid,* 11, 90–99, 132–85, 222, 234; Livesay, *American Made,* 279, 284–85; McElheny, *Insisting on the Impossible,* 168; *Moody's Industrial Manual* (1983), 2:J-7, 5853. Wensberg thought that Land's invention of the SX-70 "changed more of the commonly

accepted mechanics of photography than any man since Fox Talbot." (Wensberg, page 181.)

52. Leslie R. Berlin, "Robert Noyce and Fairchild Semiconductor, 1957–1968," *Business History Review* (Spring 2001); 63–101, 64, 79, 81, 99; Tedlow, *Giants of Enterprise,* 369–70, 394, 403; Wolfe, "Tinkerings of Robert Noyce," 364; *Time,* (February 20, 1978): 51. Jack Kilby of Texas Instruments devised a similar integrated circuit about six months earlier than Noyce, but it did not use silicon or the insulating process created by one of Noyce's colleagues, Jean Hoerni, and was not as practical or efficient. Wolfe, "Tinkerings of Robert Noyce," 358.
53. Wolfe, "Tinkerings of Robert Noyce," 360, 362.
54. Manes and Andrews, *Gates,* 3–4, 84, 176, 301–07, 436, 439; *Business Week,* (June 17, 2002): 66.
55. Ibid., 88, 193, 241, 403, 446; Lowe, *Gates,* 123. Manes and Andrews add that "allowing for a certain amount of Gatesian self-aggrandizement," the claims were "largely true."
56. Lowenstein, *Buffett,* xiii, 413.
57. Ibid., 49, 58, 64–66, 73–74, 285, 325, 330–32, 413.
58. Ibid., xv, 114, 194, 236, 412.

4: THE TALENTS OF THE GREAT ENTREPRENEURS

1. Lowe, *Buffett,* 65.
2. Brayer, *Eastman,* 523. Buffett and Gates are not included because they are still living. Of course, Gould and Harriman were not considered relatively young at the time in which they lived, when the life span was much shorter.
3. Chernow, *Titan,* 343; Chandler and Salsbury, *du Pont,* 584.
4. Klein, *Rainbow's End,* 277; Curry, *Creating an American Institution,* 316; McElheny, *Insisting on the Impossible,* 268. According to Curry, Penney still came to the office three times a week at age ninety-five.
5. Hughes, *Vital Few,* 165; Winkler, *Tobacco Tycoon,* 69; Winkler, *Five and Ten,* 215; Appel, *Wanamaker,* 225; Crowther, *Patterson,* 193; Lowe, *Gates,* 226; Lowe, *Buffett,* 15, 73.
6. Appel, *Wanamaker,* 226; McElheny, *Insisting on the Impossible,* 200; Walton, *Made in America,* 251; Wall, *Carnegie,* 666; Conot, *Streak of Luck,* 156; Brayer, *Eastman,* 160–61.

7. Hughes, *Vital Few,* 330; Klein, *Harriman,* 403–04; Kroc, *Grinding It Out,* 79; Wensberg, *Polaroid's Land,* 5; Lowe, *Buffett,* 73; Penney, *Fifty Years,* 60, 172.

8. Lane, *Vanderbilt,* 14; McElheny, *Insisting on the Impossible,* 38; Appel, *Wanamaker,* 337; Herbert A. Gibbons, *John Wanamaker* (New York, 1926), 2:33; Klein, *Gould,* 316; Hawke, *John D.,* 17.

9. Appel, *Wanamaker,* 232; Winkler, *Tobacco Tycoon,* 127; Livesay, *American Made,* 282; Kroc, *Grinding It Out,* 81; Walton, *Made in America,* 39.

10. Watson and Petre, *Father, Son & Co.,* 218; Penney, *Fifty Years,* 196; William T. Hutchinson, *Cyrus Hall McCormick: Harvest, 1856–1884* (New York, 1935), 754; Sobel, *Entrepreneurs,* 169; Winkler, *Tobacco Tycoon,* 71. Emphases are in the originals.

11. Beasley, *Main Street Merchant,* 43; Crowther, *Patterson,* 7, 173; Kroc, *Grinding It Out,* 75; Walton, *Made in America,* 190.

12. Klein, *Harriman,* 144.

13. Crowther, *Patterson,* 198; Penney, *Fifty Years,* 52, 84–85.

14. Conot, *Streak of Luck,* 249; Berlin, "Robert Noyce and Fairchild Semiconductor," 79; Wallace and Erickson, *Hard Drive,* 297. As Conot described it, "Edison envisioned the [West Orange] laboratory as a mill that would transform ideas into commercial products. New things would pour out in an endless stream."

15. Wall, *Carnegie,* 637; Hughes, *Vital Few,* 239; Baldwin, *Edison,* 387; Hounshell, *From the American System to Mass Production,* 271; Klein, *Gould,* 340; Lowenstein, *Buffett,* xiv. Rubinstein was a great twentieth-century pianist.

16. Kroc, *Grinding It Out,* 157.

17. Trimble, *Walton,* 142; Kroc, *Grinding It Out,* 6; McElheny, *Insisting on the Impossible,* 199; Beasley, *Main Street Merchant,* 40; Tedlow, *Giants of Enterprise,* 383.

18. Chandler and Salsbury, *du Pont,* 600; Lowenstein, *Buffett,* 60; Klein, *Harriman,* 126–28; Livesay, *American Made,* 166; Crowther, *Patterson,* 131; Manes and Andrews, *Gates,* 344, 398, 422–23, 445. Crowther called Patterson an "almost uncannily skilled adapter rather than an originator."

19. Manes and Andrews, *Gates,* 448; Klein, *Gould,* 67, 492, passim.

20. McDonald, *Insull,* 11, 106; Josephson, *Edison,* 100; Prout, *Westinghouse,* 306–307; Tedlow, *Giants of Enterprise,* 78.

21. Lowenstein, *Buffett,* 406; Wall, *Carnegie,* 306; Livesay, *American Made,* 273, 282; Winkler, *Tobacco Tycoon,* 266; Chernow, *Titan,* 285.
22. Lane, *Vanderbilt,* 109; Hughes, *Vital Few,* 231; Wall, *Carnegie,* 773; Hawke, *John D.,* 206.
23. Kluger, *Ashes to Ashes,* 25; Winkler, *Tobacco Tycoon,* 74; Tedlow, *Giants of Enterprise,* 93; Chandler and Salsbury, *du Pont,* 38; Klein, *Harriman,* 38, 317.
24. Hutchinson, *Harvest,* 749; Crowther, *Patterson,* 15; Prout, *Westinghouse,* 250; Watson and Petre, *Father, Son & Co.,* 179; Kroc, *Grinding It Out,* 107–08; Paine, *Vail,* 240, 284.
25. Penney, *Fifty Years,* 54–55; Winkler, *Five and Ten,* 215; Trimble, *Walton,* 107; Walton, *Made in America,* 8.
26. Manes and Andrews, *Gates,* 286–87, 423; Wallace and Erickson, *Hard Drive,* 211; Lowenstein, *Buffett,* 70, 312. Emphasis is in the original.
27. McDonald, *Insull,* 90.
28. Wensberg, *Land's Polaroid,* 7, 148.
29. Tedlow, *Giants of Enterprise,* 405.
30. Lowenstein, *Buffett,* 230; Francis E. Leupp, *George Westinghouse: His Life and Achievements* (Boston, 1919), 11; McElheny, *Insisting on the Impossible,* 16; Chernow, *Titan,* 140; Crowther, *Patterson,* 198. Emphasis is in the original.
31. Prout, *Westinghouse,* 262; Winkler, *Tobacco Tycoon,* 283; Beasley, *Main Street Merchant,* 61, 217; Belden and Belden, *Lengthening Shadow,* 290; Walton, *Made in America,* xiii. Emphasis is in the original.
32. McElheny, *Insisting on the Impossible,* 375; Hawke, *John D.,* 38; Winkler, *Tobacco Tycoon,* 285.
33. Hughes, *Vital Few,* 240–41; Belden and Belden, *Lengthening Shadow,* 153; Winkler, *Tobacco Tycoon,* 137; McDonald, *Insull,* 101; McElheny, *Insisting on the Impossible,* 368–69; Wallace and Erickson, *Hard Drive,* 264.
34. Walton, *Made in America,* 215–16; Penney, *Fifty Years,* 63; Winkler, *Five and Ten,* 125; Crowther, *Patterson,* 222.
35. Love, *McDonald's,* 32, 112; Hughes, *Vital Few,* 240; Livesay, *American Made,* 275; Berlin, "Noyce and Fairchild Semiconductor," 77; Trimble, *Walton,* 35, 110; Rodgers, *Think,* 10.
36. Hughes, *Vital Few,* 241; Winkler, *Tobacco Tycoon,* 287; Klein, *Harriman,* 130–31, 255.

37. Winkler, *Five and Ten*, 142, 215; Walton, *Made in America*, 215–16.

38. Crowther, *Patterson*, 103, 161, 170; Wall, *Carnegie*, 351; Brayer, *Eastman*, 63; Wensberg, *Land's Polaroid*, 211; McDonald, *Insull*, 183.

39. Appel, *Wanamaker*, 390; Sobel, *Entrepreneurs*, 76; Walton, *Made in America*, 26, 45–46, 63.

40. Hughes, *Vital Few*, 224, 315; Leupp, *Westinghouse*, 274; McDonald, *Insull*, 210.

41. Weisberger, *Dream Maker*, 234; Josephson, *Edison*, 387; Klein, *Harriman*, 125; Sobel, *Entrepreneurs*, 76; Wall, *Carnegie*, 290.

42. Paine, *Vail*, 342; Josephson, *Edison*, 178; Tedlow, *Giants of Enterprise*, 121; Klein, *Gould*, 371; Walton, *Made in America*, 219.

5: THE ENTREPRENEURS AT WORK

1. Kroc, *Grinding It Out*, 116.

2. Klein, *Harriman*, 423–24.

3. Tedlow, *Giants of Enterprise*, 189; Hughes, *Vital Few*, 212; Walton, *Made in America*, 119; Wensberg, *Polaroid's Land*, 85. Emphasis is in the original.

4. This template is taken from Maury Klein and Harvey A. Kantor, *Prisoners of Progress: American Industrial Cities, 1860–1920* (New York, 1976), 35–37.

5. Hughes, *Vital Few*, 332; Chernow, *Titan*, 148; Klein, *Harriman*, 279–80.

6. McElheny, *Insisting on the Impossible*, 7, 466; Penney, *Fifty Years*, 74–75; Trimble, *Walton*, 93; Walton, *Made in America*, 62.

7. Klein, *Gould*, 157; Klein, *Harriman*, 159.

8. Klein, *Harriman*, 254–55. For similar examples, see pages 131–33.

9. Livesay, *American Made*, 102–03, 119; Wall, *Carnegie*, 291–92, 337, 343, 345; Hughes, *Vital Few*, 241.

10. Livesay, *American Made*, 173; Chernow, *Titan*, 179–80; Winkler, *Five and Ten*, 215; Hughes, *Vital Few*, 329.

11. Brayer, *Eastman*, 44; Hounshell, *From the American System to Mass Production*, 154; Hughes, *Vital Few*, 323, 327; Livesay, *American Made*, 175.

12. Hughes, *Vital Few*, 324–25; Hounshell, *From the American System to Mass Production*, 228; Tedlow, *Giants of Enterprise*, 164. For an excellent discussion of Ford and mass production, see Hounshell, *From the American System to Mass Production*, 217–330.

13. Hounshell, *From the American System to Mass Production,* 218, 316–18; Hughes, *Vital Few,* 324; Livesay, *American Made,* 175–76. Emphasis is in the original. The murals are reproduced in Hounshell, pages 323–27.
14. Penney, *Fifty Years,* 81; Winkler, *Five and Ten,* 56, 67, 147.
15. Winkler, *Five and Ten,* 105, 121, 141–42, 147–48.
16. Ibid., 138–41, 170.
17. Ibid., 138, 215.
18. Appel, *Wanamaker,* 49, 65–72, 105–07, 384; Sobel, *Entrepreneurs,* 100.
19. Appel, *Wanamaker,* 102–08.
20. Ibid., xv–xvi, 96, 102–06.
21. Beasley, *Main Street Merchant,* 45, 94; Penney, *Fifty Years,* 56–57; Trimble, *Walton,* 35. Beasley notes that Penney "made no attempt to attract the so-called better trade."
22. Beasley, *Main Street Merchant,* 35–37, 43, 70–71; Penney, *Fifty Years,* 52–53, 70.
23. Beasley, *Main Street Merchant,* 60, 73–77, 82, 98–99; Curry, *Creating an American Institution,* 148.
24. Beasley, *Main Street Merchant,* 75; Penney, *Fifty Years,* 102–03; Curry, *Creating an American Institution,* 134, 144.
25. Trimble, *Walton,* 34; Walton, *Made in America,* 33, 78.
26. Walton, *Made in America,* 42, 79, 190; Trimble, *Walton,* 92–93. Cunningham returned the compliment. "From the time anybody first noticed Sam," he said, "it was obvious he had adopted almost all of the original Kmart ideas. I always had great admiration for the way he implemented—and later enlarged on—those ideas." (Walton, *Made in America,* 191.)
27. Trimble, *Walton,* 102, 110–13, 137–38; Walton, *Made in America,* 35, 50–51.
28. Trimble, *Walton,* 118–19, 124; Walton, *Made in America,* 109–13, 207–08.
29. Love, *Behind the Arches,* 42–55.
30. Ibid., 43, 56.
31. Ibid., 57–64, 132; Kroc, *Grinding It Out,* 79.
32. Kroc, *Grinding It Out,* 94; Love, *Behind the Arches,* 135–40.
33. Kroc, *Grinding It Out,* 95, 118; Love, *Behind the Arches,* 6–7, 121, 147–49, 207.

34. Livesay, *American Made*, 146–48; Conot, *Streak of Luck*, 258–59, 386; McDonald, *Insull*, 28.
35. Belden and Belden, *Lengthening Shadow*, 126–27; Tedlow, *Giants of Enterprise*, 237; Crowther, *Patterson*, 238.
36. Belden and Belden, *Lengthening Shadow*, 129, 132, 143, 148; Rodgers, *Think*, 100–01.
37. Belden and Belden, *Lengthening Shadow*, 16, 129–32; Rodgers, *Think*, 92–93, 98, 113–14; Watson and Petre, *Father, Son & Co.*, 48, 69.
38. Tedlow, *Giants of Enterprise*, 190; Belden and Belden, *Lengthening Shadow*, 148, 154, 162–68; Watson and Petre, *Father, Son & Co.*, 73.
39. Prout, *Westinghouse*, 90, 190, 244, 308–09; Leupp, *Westinghouse*, 156, 243–44.
40. Livesay, *American Made*, 275, 281–82; Wensberg, *Land's Polaroid*, 124, 192; McElheny, *Insisting on the Impossible*, 199–200, 224, 365.
41. Berlin, "Robert Noyce and Fairchild Semiconductor, 1957–1968," 77–78, 100; Wolfe, "Tinkerings of Robert Noyce," 356, 359, 372; Malone, *Big Score*, 81; Tedlow, *Giants of Enterprise*, 391.
42. Wolfe, "The Tinkerings of Robert Noyce," 362, 367.
43. Ibid., 367–68, 372.
44. Manes and Andrews, *Gates*, 177, 197, 446–47; Lowe, *Gates*, 143–44, 151; Wallace and Erickson, *Hard Drive*, 260.
45. Lowe, *Gates*, 55, 60, 65; Manes and Andrews, *Gates*, 58, 95, 123, 308–09; Wallace and Erickson, *Hard Drive*, 161, 265, 304, 419; Wolfe, "Tinkerings of Robert Noyce," 368.
46. Lowe, *Gates*, 91, 144; Manes and Andrews, *Gates*, 444.
47. Lowe, *Gates*, 44, 69, 72, 82, 225.

6: FOLLIES AND FOIBLES

1. Gordon Thomas and Max Morgan-Witts, *The Day the Bubble Burst* (Garden City, N.Y., 1979), 45.
2. McElheny, *Insisting on the Impossible*, 200, 415; Appel, *Wanamaker*, 232.
3. Penney, *Fifty Years*, 143–50; Curry, *Creating an American Institution*, 223, 267–69; Paine, *Vail*, 341.
4. Paine, *Vail*, 189–97.
5. Hutchinson, *Harvest*, 133–200; Hawke, *John D.*, 195; Chernow, *Titan*, 373, 624, 664, 666. "In spite of his phalanx of able advisers," wrote Chernow, "Rockefeller had a very uneven record as an investor."

6. Winkler, *Five and Ten,* 137; Klein, *Gould,* 315.

7. Weisberger, *Dream Maker,* 133, 143, 199, 225–32. Durant originally asked the directors for a $1 million loan, but they thought such a transaction was improper and might be illegal. Instead they awarded him a salary of $500,000 retroactive to 1916, which gave him the same amount.

8. Ibid., 230–74; Chandler and Salsbury, *du Pont,* 482–91. For a brief version of these events, see Klein, *Rainbow's End,* 32–41.

9. Albert P. Sloan, Jr., *My Years with General Motors* (New York, 1963), 4; Weisberger, *Dream Maker,* 293–305.

10. Weisberger, *Dream Maker,* 305–06, 331–41, 352–53.

11. McDonald, *Insull,* 91, 144–56.

12. Ibid., 158–61, 165–214; Klein, *Rainbow's End,* 153–54.

13. McDonald, *Insull,* 95, 205, 245–47; Klein, *Rainbow's End,* 153–54.

14. McDonald, *Insull,* 248–51; Klein, *Rainbow's End,* 154–55.

15. McDonald, *Insull,* 274–85; Klein, *Rainbow's End,* 155, 193.

16. McDonald, *Insull,* 282–84.

17. Ibid., 285–304.

18. Ibid., 305–33.

19. Conot, *Streak of Luck,* 273, 316, 391–93, 424; Josephson, *Edison,* 318–19, 326, 331–32, 467; Baldwin, *Edison,* 184, 318, 337, 357, 360–62.

20. Conot, *Streak of Luck,* 327–28, 331, 340; Josephson, *Edison,* 383–93, 401; Baldwin, *Edison,* 211, 220, 239–42, 339.

21. McDonald, *Insull,* 25–30; Josephson, *Edison,* 182, 207; Hughes, *Vital Few,* 176–78; Sobel and Sicilia, *The Entrepreneurs: An American Adventure,* 14–15; Conot, *Streak of Luck,* 253, 471.

22. McDonald, *Insull,* 43–45; Josephson, *Edison,* 344–50; Hughes, *Vital Few,* 194, 202; Sobel and Sicilia, *The Entrepreneurs: An American Adventure,* 15; Baldwin, *Edison,* 201–02; Harold C. Passer, *The Electrical Manufacturers* (Cambridge, Mass., 1953), 74.

23. Josephson, *Edison,* 370–75; Baldwin, *Edison,* 213–19; Conot, *Streak of Luck,* 202, 299–300. The quotation is from Conot.

24. Josephson, *Edison,* 378–89; Conot, *Streak of Luck,* 290, 303, 345–49; Baldwin, *Edison,* 276–98. The poured cement house has received relatively little attention, but Baldwin called it "one of his most quintessential inventions." Baldwin, *Edison,* (p. 298.)

25. Tedlow, *Giants of Enterprise,* 17, 136, 143; Hughes, *Vital Few,* 298, 312.

26. Tedlow, *Giants of Enterprise,* 165; Hughes, *Vital Few,* 346.
27. Hounshell, *From the American System to Mass Production,* 263–64, 276; Hughes, *Vital Few,* 335.
28. Hounshell, *From the American System to Mass Production,* 263–95; Tedlow, *Giants of Enterprise,* 168. The rise of Chevrolet under Knudsen and the technical difficulties of producing the Model A are both clearly and expertly explained by Hounshell.
29. Hughes, *Vital Few,* 301–04, 332–33; Tedlow, *Giants of Enterprise,* 163; Livesay, *American Made,* 179.
30. McElheny, *Insisting on the Impossible,* 373.
31. Ibid., 414–16.
32. Ibid., 416–25; Wensberg, *Land's Polaroid,* 237.
33. McElheney, *Insisting on the Impossible,* 426–59; Wensberg, *Land's Polaroid,* 227. The Jobs quotation is in McEleheny, page 455.
34. Watson and Petre, *Father, Son & Co.,* 189–202; Belden and Belden, *Lengthening Shadow,* 261–62.
35. Trimble, *Walton,* 194; Walton, *Made in America,* 91.
36. Walton, *Made in America,* 30–31, 177.
37. Kroc, *Grinding It Out,* 113–15; Love, *Behind the Arches,* 191–94.
38. Love, *Behind the Arches,* 413–14; Kroc, *Grinding It Out,* 171–74.
39. Appel, *Wanamaker,* 121–26.
40. Prout, *Westinghouse,* 224–31.
41. Brayer, *Eastman,* 114, 504; Wall, *Carnegie,* 589, 598; Lowe, *Gates,* 119. Wall called Mesabi "the greatest opportunity of his entire business career."
42. Details on all these episodes can be found in Klein, *Gould.*
43. Ibid., 93.
44. Lowe, *Gates,* 216; Wall, *Carnegie,* 197; Winkler, *Tobacco Tycoon,* 287.
45. Livesay, *American Made,* 148; Lowe, *Buffett,* 22.
46. Lowe, *Gates,* 54, 82.

7: ALL IN THE FAMILY

1. Lowe, *Gates,* 150.
2. Chernow, *Titan,* 529.
3. Watson and Petre, *Father, Son & Co.,* 13; Marcosson, *Wherever Men Trade,* 245; Trimble, *Walton,* 34; Walton, *Made in America,* 131; Brayer, *Eastman,* 161.

4. Beasley, *Main Street Merchant*, 77, 104; Walton, *Made in America*, 217.

5. McDonald, *Insull*, 3, 14–15; Hughes, *Vital Few*, 205, 281; Conot, *Streak of Luck*, 381–82; Wallace and Erickson, *Hard Drive*, 270.

6. Beasley, *Main Street Merchant*, 90; Penney, *Fifty Years*, 85–86, 103–06, 114; Appel, *Wanamaker*, 105, 428–29; Walton, *Made in America*, 219–33.

7. Walton, *Made in America*, 62, 127, 157–67.

8. Love, *Behind the Arches*, 92, 139–49; Kroc, *Grinding It Out*, 118.

9. Sobel, *Entrepreneurs*, 65; Hutchinson, *Seed-Time*, 353–58; Crowther, *Patterson*, 88–89, 130, 137, 152–54, 248–50; Marcosson, *Wherever Men Trade*, 37, 114–16, 134, 231.

10. Watson and Petre, *Father, Son & Co.*, 15; Rodgers, *Think*, 84, 100–01, 113–14; Belden and Belden, *Lengthening Shadow*, 132–41, 157.

11. Winkler, *Five and Ten*, 129; Penney, *Fifty Years*, 202; Appel, *Wanamaker*, 46, 56, 65–72, 79, 385, 389; Sobel, *Entrepreneurs*, 84–89.

12. Appel, *Wanamaker*, 385, 389, 402, 405–10. For Wanamaker's advertising techniques, see pages 383–99.

13. Appel, *Wanamaker*, xv–xvi, 131–32; Sobel, *Entrepreneurs*, 76.

14. Walton, *Made in America*, 57, 61.

15. Ibid., 58–62.

16. Kroc, *Grinding It Out*, 106; Love, *Behind the Arches*, 205–07.

17. Love, *Behind the Arches*, 207–11.

18. Ibid., 212–24.

19. Ibid., 224–26.

20. McElheny, *Insisting on the Impossible*, 383; Winkler, *Tobacco Tycoon*, 60–61, 197; Hutchinson, *Seed-Time*, 271–74, 331, 364.

21. Crowther, *Patterson*, 90–91, 286–87.

22. Josephson, *Edison*, 166–69; Leupp, *Westinghouse*, 175–76.

23. McElheny, *Insisting on the Impossible*, 341–49, 376–86, 412–21; Manes and Andrews, *Gates*, 130, 398; Wallace and Erickson, *Hard Drive*, 359–61.

24. Lowe, *Gates*, 42.

25. Wall, *Carnegie*, 322; Hawke, *John D.*, 52; Klein, *Harriman*, 357.

26. Penney, *Fifty Years*, 70; Appel, *Wanamaker*, 145, 366; Sobel, *Entrepreneurs*, 89; Walton, *Made in America*, 6; Trimble, *Walton*, 237–38. Trimble says the trust was set up in 1954.

27. Hutchinson, *Harvest*, 519–21, 627–40; Wall, *Carnegie*, 237–39, 418; McDonald, *Insull*, 223–28.

28. Brayer, *Eastman,* 485, 498.
29. Ibid. 517–19, 523; Tedlow, *Giants of Enterprise,* 114.
30. Hutchinson, *Harvest,* 761; Klein, *Gould,* 355, 376; Appel, *Wanamaker,* 157, 403.
31. Chernow, *Titan,* 343, 507–08, 510–12, 521, 550.
32. Baldwin, *Edison,* 348–53, 411–15; Conot, *Streak of Luck,* 421–25; Lane, *Vanderbilt,* 201; Smith, *Commodore Vanderbilt,* 139–40; Klein, *Gould,* 202–03.
33. Watson and Petre, *Father, Son & Co.,* viii–ix, 2, 212–13.
34. Ibid., 172–73, 208, 250–52, 263, 271, 292; Belden and Belden, *Lengthening Shadow,* 311–12.
35. Klein, *Harriman,* 6, 444–47; Trimble, *Walton,* 8–9.
36. Lacey, *Ford,* 253–63.
37. Ibid., 263–65, 389–98.
38. Tedlow, *Giants of Enterprise,* 172–75; McDonald, *Insull,* 228; Weisberger, *Dream Maker,* 315; Sobel, *Entrepreneurs,* 191; Winkler, *Tobacco Tycoon,* 254; Winkler, *Five and Ten,* 229–32.
39. Wall, *Carnegie,* 688, 813–19; Chandler and Salsbury, *du Pont,* 534, 561–62, 584, 587; Penney, *Fifty Years,* 105–06; Curry, *Creating an American Institution,* 99, 179–80, 199, 203–04, 220.
40. Crowther, *Patterson,* 208, 211–12, 349–50. For a brief sketch of Frederick Patterson, see *National Cyclopedia of American Biography* (New York, 1938), E:175.
41. Paine, *Vail,* 329; Love, *Behind the Arches,* 237, 254–70, 274; Kroc, *Grinding It Out,* 145–57.
42. Tedlow, *Giants of Enterprise,* 407, 411–18; Wolfe, "Tinkerings of Robert Noyce," 372. Tedlow provides a good brief account of the issues raised by the Japanese threat. The name "Sematech" was taken from the first letters of semiconductor manufacturing technology.
43. Wensberg, *Land's Polaroid,* 205–07; McElheney, *Insisting on the Impossible,* 351, 435–40, 455, 465.
44. Lowe, *Buffett,* 21, 48.
45. *Business Week* (June 17, 2002): 66–75.
46. Ibid.; Associated Press release, January 13, 2000.
47. Wall, *Carnegie,* 540–77. The quotation is on page 576.
48. Klein, *Gould,* 358–62; Robert F. Durden, *The Dukes of Durham, 1865–1929* (Durham, N.C., 1975), 38.

49. Hughes, *Vital Few,* 301, 330; Tedlow, *Giants of Enterprise,* 134, 164; Winkler, *Five and Ten,* 52, 123–24, 136.
50. Hughes, *Vital Few,* 328, 331–32.
51. Hutchinson, *Harvest,* 485; Hawke, *John D.,* 159; Chernow, *Titan,* 177, 574; Klein, *Harriman,* 268.
52. Brayer, *Eastman,* 352; Tedlow, *Giants of Enterprise,* 112.
53. Crowther, *Patterson,* 192.
54. Rodgers, *Think,* 38.
55. Marcosson, *Wherever Men Trade,* 48, 226–37; Crowther, *Patterson,* 302–05; Belden and Belden, *Lengthening Shadow,* 76–79.
56. Paine, *Vail,* 241–42, 248–50.
57. McDonald, *Insull,* 112, 192–94.
58. Prout, *Westinghouse,* 296–98; Leupp, *Westinghouse,* 247–49, 254.
59. Leupp, *Westinghouse,* 249–52.
60. Josephson, *Edison,* 339–40, 428; Conot, *Streak of Luck,* 111.
61. Belden and Belden, *Lengthening Shadow,* 150–53; Watson and Petre, *Father, Son & Co.,* 66, 73–75.
62. Belden and Belden, *Lengthening Shadow,* 82–84.
63. Crowther, *Patterson,* 76; Belden and Belden, *Lengthening Shadow,* 83.
64. Watson and Petre, *Father, Son & Co.,* 82, 151–53, 252; Rodgers, *Think,* 92.
65. Tedlow, *Giants of Enterprise,* 236–37.
66. Wensberg, *Land's Polaroid,* 155; McElheny, *Insisting on the Impossible,* 199–201.
67. McElheny, *Insisting on the Impossible,* 374; Wensberg, *Land's Polaroid,* 2.
68. Malone, *Big Score,* 73, 81–83.
69. Wallace and Erickson, *Hard Drive,* 264; Lowe, *Gates,* 37, 61, 64.
70. Walton, *Made in America,* 128–31.
71. Ibid., xii, 126, 171.
72. Beasley, *Main Street Merchant,* vii.

8: THE LAW AND THE HIGHER LAW

1. Lowe, *Gates,* 94, 99.
2. Crowther, *Patterson,* 207.
3. Redlich, *Steeped in Two Cultures,* 34; Lowe, *Buffett,* 134.
4. Trimble, *Walton,* 249, 253; Walton, *Made in America,* 179.

5. J. Willard Hurst, *Law and the Conditions of Freedom in the Nineteenth-Century United States* (Madison, Wis., 1967), 9–10.
6. Ibid., 14, 39, 53.
7. Oliver Wendell Holmes, *The Common Law* (Boston, 1881), 5; Henry Steele Commager, *The American Mind* (New Haven, Conn., 1950), 378–81.
8. For a brief summary of the legal issues involved, see Alfred H. Kelly and Winfred A. Harbison, *The American Constitution* (New York, 1963), 496–614.
9. Klein, *Harriman,* 238–42, 308–13, 408–09.
10. Chernow, *Titan,* xx. The classic work on the evolution of Standard Oil's organization is Ralph W. Hidy and Muriel E. Hidy, *Pioneering in Big Business* (New York, 1955). Chernow has more on Rockefeller's own role in these events.
11. Hidy and Hidy, *Pioneering in Big Business,* 40–49.
12. Ibid., 671–708; Chernow, *Titan,* 539–53.
13. Chernow, *Titan,* 542, 554.
14. Ibid., 554–59.
15. Chandler and Salsbury, *du Pont,* 104, 260–98; Winkler, *Tobacco Tycoon,* 213–43; Sobel, *Entrepreneurs,* 189–90; Durden, *Dukes of Durham,* 167–68.
16. Winkler, *Tobacco Tycoon,* 241; Brayer, *Eastman,* 214, 389–91.
17. Brayer, *Eastman,* 392–99.
18. Rodgers, *Think,* 40–54; Belden and Belden, *Lengthening Shadow,* 63–68. As the Beldens note, NCR was already embroiled in a restraint of trade suit in Michigan.
19. Rodgers, *Think,* 59–64; Belden and Belden, *Lengthening Shadow,* 72–87.
20. Belden and Belden, *Lengthening Shadow,* 291–93; Rodgers, *Think,* 211–12.
21. Belden and Belden, *Lengthening Shadow,* 294–99; Watson and Petre, *Father, Son & Co.,* 215–19.
22. Belden and Belden, *Lengthening Shadow,* 298–311; Watson and Petre, *Father, Son & Co.,* 220, 268–70.
23. Sobel, *Entrepreneurs,* 236–41; Paine, *Vail,* 238, 249.
24. *USA Today,* January 14, 2000, has a convenient chronology of these events.

25. *Business Week* (March 1, 1993): 82–86.
26. *New York Times,* November 3, 2001. Terms of the settlement are given in the article.
27. Lowe, *Gates,* 97, 101, 105–06; Wallace and Erickson, *Hard Drive,* 375, 380.
28. Hutchinson, *Seed-Time,* 423–52; Josephson, *Edison,* 354–58, 401–02.
29. Josephson, *Edison,* 342–50; Conot, *Streak of Luck,* 280–82.
30. Brayer, *Eastman,* 98–100, 386–89.
31. Durden, *Dukes of Durham,* 33–48.
32. Ibid., 49–55.
33. Brayer, *Eastman,* 27, 30–31; Mark D. Hirsch, *William C. Whitney: Modern Warwick* (New York, 1948), 556–58; Lacey, *Ford,* 98–100; Peter Collier and David Horowitz, *The Fords: An American Epic* (New York, 1987), 53–54. Whitney was involved in trying to manufacture an electric vehicle and was seeking protection against infringement.
34. Lacey, *Ford,* 100–01.
35. Ibid., 101; Hirsch, *Whitney,* 560–61.
36. Wensberg, *Land's Polaroid,* 236–40; McElheny, *Insisting on the Impossible,* 441–48.
37. McElheny, *Insisting on the Impossible,* 449–53.
38. Wallace and Erickson, *Hard Drive,* 352–56; Manes and Andrews, *Gates,* 357–64, 383–84, 437–38.
39. Julius Grodinsky, *Jay Gould: His Business Career, 1867–1892* (Philadelphia, 1957), 300, 450.
40. Klein, *Gould,* 114–15, 245, 254, 310–11, 330, 379.
41. Thomas Frank, *One Market Under God* (New York, 2000), xiv–xv.
42. Lowe, *Buffett,* 164. Part of this paragraph is taken from Maury Klein, "Coming Full Circle: The Study of Big Business Since 1950," *Enterprise and Society* (September 2001): 460.
43. Hutchinson, *Seed-Time,* 462.
44. Klein, *Harriman,* 348.
45. Chernow, *Titan,* 529; Hawke, *John D.,* 171.

9: THE ENTREPRENEURS OFF DUTY

1. Brayer, *Eastman,* 442.
2. McElheny, *Insisting on the Impossible,* 17, 29, 392.
3. Lowe, *Buffett,* 15, 19, 29, 31.

4. Ibid., 23, 47, 64, 66; Walton, *Made in America,* 171; Kroc, *Grinding It Out,* 178; Crowther, *Patterson,* 213.

5. Chernow, *Titan,* 403; Appel, *Wanamaker,* 333–34; Brayer, *Eastman,* 244–59; Wolfe, "Tinkerings of Robert Noyce," 371.

6. Conot, *Streak of Luck,* 87; Baldwin, *Edison,* 167, 224; Leupp, *Westinghouse,* 259–70; Winkler, *Tobacco Tycoon,* 117, 157, 276, 284–88; Kluger, *Ashes to Ashes,* 41; Durden, *Dukes of Durham,* 61, 168–69, 195–96.

7. Weisberger, *Dream Maker,* 308–11; Penney, *Fifty Years,* 119–20; Curry, *Creating an American Institution,* 199–201; Rodgers, *Think,* 102; Watson and Petre, *Father, Son & Co.,* 18, 21.

8. Wall, *Carnegie,* 689, 855; Paine, *Vail,* 213–16, 251–53.

9. Winkler, *Five and Ten,* 123–32, 209–10, 223.

10. Manes and Andrews, *Gates,* 410–15; *New York Times* (January 12, 1995): C1, 6.

11. Margaret Talbot, "Gates's Heaven," *New Republic* (October 20, 1997): 46. For an example of intellectual angst generated by the house, see *Assemblage* 35 (April 1998):62ff.

12. Hutchinson, *Harvest,* 3–4, 128, 741–42; McDonald, *Insull,* 239–45.

13. Brayer, *Eastman,* 424–26.

14. Paine, *Vail,* 270–71, 304; Lowe, *Buffett,* 15; Lowe, *Gates,* 178; Kroc, *Grinding It Out,* 184; Wall, *Carnegie,* 880.

15. Brayer, *Eastman,* 345; Wall, *Carnegie,* 828–29, 893–99.

16. Wall, *Carnegie,* 818–19; 870–83. More detail on Carnegie's philanthropies can be found on pages 797–884.

17. Chernow, *Titan,* 49–50, 237–40. One of the many strong points of Chernow's excellent biography is that it has the fullest account of Rockefeller's career as a philanthropist.

18. Ibid., 468–92; Hawke, *John D.,* 195; Wall, *Carnegie,* 832. The hookworm campaign, overseen by the Rockefeller Sanitary Commission, took place between 1910 and 1913. Rockefeller University acquired its new name in 1965.

19. Chernow, *Titan,* 491–92, 563–70.

20. Lowe, *Gates,* 178. Unless otherwise indicated, all material on Gates and his foundations is taken from Jean Strouse, "How to Give Away $21.8 Billion," *New York Times Magazine* (April 16, 2000): 56–63, 78, 88, 96,

101. The $24 billion figure is taken from *Newsweek* (February 4, 2002): 45.

21. *Newsweek* (February 4, 2002): 47; Strouse, "How to Give Away $21.8 Billion," 56, 61.

22. Strouse, "How to Give Away $21.8 Billion," 59, 61.

23. Lowenstein, *Buffett*, 342–47.

24. Strouse, "How to Give Away $21.8 Billion," 59.

25. Brayer, *Eastman*, 289, 335, 345–46, 365, 427–67. For a fuller account of Eastman's contributions to Rochester, see pages 363–85.

26. Ibid., 270–78, 340–45, 363–85, 430–31, 499–500. For some other causes that received support from Eastman, see pages 474–78.

27. Ibid., 323, 504.

28. Lane, *Vanderbilt*, 317; Durden, *Dukes of Durham*, 90, 107–21, 199, 230.

29. Winkler, *Tobacco Tycoon*, 288–90; Durden, *Dukes of Durham*, 199–246.

30. Hutchinson, *Harvest*, 5, 282–307. Emphasis is in the original.

31. Lacey, *Ford*, 137–47, 223–27, 307, 450.

32. Ibid., 451–54.

33. Penney, *Fifty Years*, 129–35, 150–51; Curry, *Creating an American Institution*, 207–17, 296; McDonald, *Insull*, 134–35.

34. Kroc, *Grinding It Out*, 184–85.

35. Ibid., 185–87; Love, *Behind the Arches*, 366.

36. Belden and Belden, *Lengthening Shadow*, 285–86; McElheny, *Insisting on the Impossible*, 317.

37. Chernow, *Titan*, 124; Lowenstein, *Buffett*, 60, 142, 335–36; Lowe, *Gates*, 178.

38. *Esquire* (December 1983): 374.

39. Hughes, *Vital Few*, 198–99; Conot, *Streak of Luck*, 196, 263, 355–57, 403; Baldwin, *Inventing the Century*, 247. The quotation is from Baldwin.

40. Lane, *Vanderbilt*, 81; Smith, *Commodore Vanderbilt*, 79–81; Appel, *Wanamaker*, 333; Crowther, *Patterson*, 212; Penney, *Fifty Years*, 138.

41. Wall, *Carnegie*, 688; Winkler, *Tobacco Tycoon*, 254–55, 275, 307; Kroc, *Grinding It Out*, 27, 69, 185.

42. McDonald, *Insull*, 80; Paine, *Vail*, 217, 219; Tedlow, *Giants of Enterprise*, 146.

43. Lacey, *Ford,* 52, 151–52, 159, 260–61, 366, 394–95, 401–03.

44. McElheny, *Insisting on the Impossible,* 215. For Harriman's expeditions, see Klein, *Harriman,* 181–200, 285–91; Weisberger, *Dream Maker,* 314–16.

45. Hutchinson, *Harvest,* 759–62.

46. Rodgers, *Think,* 102; Watson and Petre, *Father, Son & Co.,* 4–5, 20.

47. Walton, *Made in America,* 68, 71–73; Trimble, *Walton,* 8–9, 85; Lowe, *Gates,* 188.

48. Conot, *Streak of Luck,* 352, 400.

49. Kroc, *Grinding It Out,* 5, 69; Winkler, *Five and Ten,* 219, 229; Klein, *Gould,* 423; Watson and Petre, *Father, Son & Co.,* 21.

50. Brayer, *Eastman,* 17, 403.

51. Lowenstein, *Buffett,* 226–30.

EPILOGUE: PROFILING THE GREAT ENTREPRENEUR

1. Lowe, *Gates,* 73.

2. *Sports Illustrated* (July 8, 2002): 69.

3. Chernow, *Titan,* 367; Lane, *Vanderbilt,* 231; Hughes, *Vital Few,* 162.

4. Lowe, *Buffett,* 28.

5. Ibid., 19; Lowe, *Gates,* 39.

6. Kroc, *Grinding It Out,* 57; McElheny, *Insisting on the Impossible,* 240.

7. McDonald, *Insull,* 3; Paine, *Vail,* 341.

8. Walton, *Made in America,* xii.

| Bibliography |

GENERAL

Allen, Frederick Lewis. *The Lords of Creation.* New York: 1935.

Hounshell, David A. *From the American System to Mass Production: The Development of Manufacturing Technology in the United States.* Baltimore: 1984.

Josephson, Matthew. *The Money Lords.* New York: 1972.

————. *The Robber Barons.* New York: 1934.

Malone, Michael S. *The Big Score: The Billion-Dollar Story of Silicon Valley.* Garden City, N.Y.: 1985.

Myers, Gustavus. *History of the Great American Fortunes.* New York: 1910.

Noble, David. *America by Design.* New York: 1977.

Passer, Harold C. *The Electrical Manufacturers, 1875–1900.* Cambridge, Mass.: 1953.

BIOGRAPHY AND AUTOBIOGRAPHY

Appel, Joseph H. *The Business Biography of John Wanamaker: Founder and Builder.* New York: 1930.

Baldwin, Neil. *Edison: Inventing the Century.* New York: 1995.

Beasley, Norman. *Main Street Merchant: The Story of the J. C. Penney Company.* New York: 1948.

Belden, Thomas and Marva. *The Lengthening Shadow: The Life of Thomas J. Watson.* Boston: 1962.

Berlin, Leslie R. "Robert Noyce and Fairchild Semiconductor, 1957–1968." *Business History Review* (Spring 2001): 63–101.

Brayer, Elizabeth. *George Eastman: A Biography.* Baltimore: 1996.

Chandler, Alfred D. Jr. and Stephen Salsbury. *Pierre S. du Pont and the Making of the Modern Corporation.* New York: 1971.

Chernow, Ron. *Titan.* New York: 1998.

Conot, Robert. *A Streak of Luck.* New York: 1979.

Crowther, Samuel. *John H. Patterson: Pioneer in Industrial Welfare.* Garden City, N. Y.: 1926.

Curry, Mary Elizabeth. *Creating an American Institution: The Merchandising Genius of J. C. Penney.* New York: 1993.

Durden, Robert F. *The Dukes of Durham, 1865–1929.* Durham, N.C.: 1975.

Gibbons, Herbert A. *John Wanamaker,* 2 vols. New York: 1926.

Hawke, David Freeman. *John D.: The Founding Father of the Rockefellers.* New York: 1980.

Hutchinson, William T. *Cyrus Hall McCormick: Seed-Time, 1809–1856.* New York: 1930.

———. *Cyrus Hall McCormick: Harvest, 1856–1884.* New York: 1935.

Josephson, Matthew. *Edison: A Biography.* New York: 1959.

Klein, Maury. *The Life and Legend of Jay Gould.* Baltimore: 1986.

———. *The Life and Legend of E. H. Harriman.* Chapel Hill, N.C.: 2000.

———. "The First Tycoon." *Forbes* (October 22, 1990): 44–52.

Kroc, Ray (with Robert Anderson). *Grinding It Out: The Making of McDonald's.* Chicago: 1977.

Lacey, Robert. *Ford: The Men and the Machine.* Boston: 1986.

Lane, Wheaton J. *Commodore Vanderbilt: An Epic of the Steam Age.* New York: 1942.

Leupp, Francis E. *George Westinghouse: His Life and Achievements.* Boston: 1919.

Lewis, David L. *The Public Image of Henry Ford.* Detroit: 1976.

Lewis, Michael. "The Temptation of St. Warren." *New Republic* (February 17, 1982): 22–25.

Love, John F. *McDonald's: Behind the Arches.* New York: 1986.

Lowe, Janet. *Bill Gates Speaks.* New York: 1998.

Lowenstein, Roger. *Buffett: The Making of an American Capitalist.* New York: 1995.

Manes, Stephen, and Paul Andrews. *Gates: How Microsoft's Mogul Reinvented an Industry—and Made Himself the Richest Man in America.* New York: 1993.

Marcosson, Isaac F. *Wherever Men Trade: The Romance of the Cash Register.* New York: 1945.

McDonald, Forrest. *Insull.* Chicago: 1962.

McElheny, Victor K. *Insisting on the Impossible: The Life of Edwin Land.* Reading, Mass.: 1998.

Nevins, Allan, and Frank Ernest Hill. *Ford: Expansion and Challenge, 1915–1933.* New York: 1957.

———. *Ford: Decline and Rebirth, 1933–1962.* New York: 1962.

———. *Ford: The Times, the Man, the Company.* New York: 1954.

Paine, Albert Bigelow. *Theodore M. Vail: A Biography.* New York: 1929.

Penney, J. C. *Fifty Years with the Golden Rule.* New York: 1950.

Prout, Henry G. *A Life of George Westinghouse.* New York: 1921.

Rodgers, William. *Think: A Biography of the Watsons and IBM.* New York: 1969.

Smith, Arthur D. Howden. *Commodore Vanderbilt: An Epic of American Achievement.* New York: 1927.

Sward, Keith. *The Legend of Henry Ford.* New York: 1972.

Trimble, Vance H. *Sam Walton: The Inside Story of America's Richest Man.* New York: 1990.

Wall, Joseph Frazier. *Andrew Carnegie.* New York: 1970.

Wallace, James, and Jim Erickson. *Hard Drive: Bill Gates and the Making of the Microsoft Empire.* New York: 1992.

Walton, Sam (John Huey). *Made in America: My Story.* New York: 1992.

Watson, Thomas J. Jr. and Peter Petre. *Father, Son & Co.: My Life at IBM and Beyond.* New York: 1990.

Weisberger, Bernard A. *The Dream Maker: William C. Durant, Founder of General Motors.* Boston: 1979.

Wensberg, Peter C. *Land's Polaroid.* Boston: 1987.

Winkler, John K. *Five and Ten: The Fabulous Life of F. W. Woolworth.* Freeport, N.Y.: 1970.

———. *Tobacco Tycoon: The Story of James Buchanan Duke.* New York: 1942.

Wolfe, Tom. "The Tinkerings of Robert Noyce." *Esquire* (December 1983): 346–48, 353–74.

———. "Robert Noyce and His Congregation." *Forbes ASAP* (August 25, 1997): 103–6.

CREATIVITY

Arieti, Silvano. *Creativity: The Magic Synthesis.* New York: 1976.

Austin, James H. *Chase, Chance, and Creativity.* New York: 1969.

Barron, Frank. *Creative Person and Creative Process.* New York: 1969.

Fange, Eugene K. von. *Professional Creativity.* Englewood Cliffs, N.J.: 1959.

Getzels, Jacob W. and Mihaly Csikszentmihalyi. *The Creative Vision.* New York: 1976.

Grudin, Robert. *The Grace of Great Things.* Boston: 1990.

Koestler, Arthur. *The Act of Creation.* London: 1964.

Kuhn, Thomas. *The Structure of Scientific Revolutions.* Chicago: 1962.

May, Rollo. *The Courage to Create.* New York: 1975.

Perkins, D. N. *The Mind's Best Work.* Cambridge, Mass.: 1981.

Rothenberg, Albert. *The Emerging Goddess: The Creative Process in Art, Science, and Other Fields.* Chicago: 1979.

Storr, A. *The Dynamics of Creation.* London: 1972.

Wertheimer, Max. *Productive Thinking.* New York: 1945.

Westcott, M. R. *Toward a Contemporary Psychology of Intuition.* New York: 1968.

ENTREPRENEURSHIP

Cochran, Thomas C. "Entrepreneurship." In *International Encyclopedia of the Social Sciences,* 5: 87–91. New York: 1968.

Drucker, Peter F. *Innovation and Entrepreneurship.* New York: 1985.

Gilder, George. *The Spirit of Enterprise.* New York: 1984.

Gunderson, Gerald. *The Wealth Creators: An Entrepreneurial History of the United States.* New York: 1990.

Hughes, Jonathan R. T. *The Vital Few: The Entrepreneur and America Economic Progress.* New York: 1986.

Kanter, Rosabeth M. *The Change Masters.* New York: 1983.

Livesay, Harold C. *American Made: The Men Who Shaped the American Economy.* Boston: 1979.

Miller, William, ed. *Men in Business: Essays in the History of Entrepreneurship.* Cambridge, Mass.: 1952.

Novak, Michael. *Business as a Calling.* New York: 1996.

Redlich, Fritz. *Steeped in Two Cultures.* New York: 1971.

Schumpeter, Joseph A. *The Theory of Economic Development.* New York: 1969.

———. *Capitalism, Socialism, and Democracy.* New York: 1950.

———. "The Creative Response in Economic History." *Journal of Economic History.* (November 1947): 149–59.

Shook, Robert L. *The Entrepreneurs.* New York: 1980.

Silver, A. David. *The Entrepreneurial Life: How to Go for It and Get It.* New York: 1983.

Sobel, Robert. *The Entrepreneurs: Explorations Within the American Business Tradition.* New York: 1974.

Sobel, Robert, and David B. Sicilia. *The Entrepreneurs: An American Adventure.* Boston: 1986.

Tedlow, Richard S. *Giants of Enterprise: Seven Business Innovators and the Empires They Built.* New York: 2001.

| Acknowledgments |

Special thanks are due Dan Freedberg, whose inquiry and subsequent conversations gave birth to this project. I hope he likes the final product. Gratitude is also extended to a host of librarians at the University of Rhode Island and other institutions and public libraries for their cheerful help in locating and obtaining source materials. Judith Swift read the first chapter and offered her usual shrewd insights and suggestions. I am grateful to my editor, Robin Dennis, who was unfailingly supportive and helpful in shaping the manuscript. As in past projects, Marian Young, my agent, was steadfast in her support and efforts to bring this book into being.

| Index |

About the Author

A professor at the University of Rhode Island, MAURY KLEIN is an acclaimed historian of business in the United States. He is the author of twelve books, including *Rainbow's End* and *The Life and Legend of Jay Gould*, a finalist for the Pulitzer Prize. He lives in East Greenwich, Rhode Island.